Lines of Red & Blue

Lines of Red & Blue
The Battles of the British Army against the Armies of Napoleonic France, 1801-15

Robert M. Blackwood

Lines of Red & Blue
The Battles of the British Army against the Armies of Napoleonic France, 1801-15
by Robert M. Blackwood

FIRST EDITION

Leonaur is an imprint of Oakpast Ltd
Copyright in this form © 2017 Oakpast Ltd

ISBN: 978-1-78282-672-9 (hardcover)
ISBN: 978-1-78282-673-6 (softcover)

http://www.leonaur.com

Publisher's Notes

The views expressed in this book are not necessarily those of the publisher.

Contents

The Battle of Alexandria, 1801	7
The Battle of Assaye, 1803	24
Capture of the Cape of Good Hope, 1806	35
The Battle of Maida, 1806	43
The Battle of Rolica, 1808	50
The Battle of Vimiero, 1808	59
The Battle of Corunna, 1809	67
The Battle of Talavera, 1809	85
The Battle of Busaco, 1810	102
The Battle of Barrosa, 1811	113
The Battle of Fuentes d'Onoro, 1811	123
The Battle of Albuera, 1811	131
The Siege of Ciudad Rodrigo, 1812	143
The Siege of Badajoz, 1812	151
The Battle of Salamanca, 1812	163
The Siege of Burgos, 1812	178
The Battle of Vitoria, 1813	187
The Battles of the Pyrenees: Part First, 1813	201
The Siege of San Sebastian, 1813	211

The Battles of the Pyrenees: Part Second, 1813	218
The Battles of the Pyrenees: Part Third, 1813	224
The Battles of the Pyrenees: Part Fourth, 1814	234
The Battle of Toulouse, 1814	242
The Battle of Quatre Bras, 1815	249
The Battle of Waterloo, 1815	263
The Battle of Waterloo (continued), 1815	270
The Battle of Waterloo (continued), 1815	284

CHAPTER 1

The Battle of Alexandria, 1801

In 1800, an attempt on Cadiz was planned and abandoned; and an army, the *corps élite* of Britain, was kept idly afloat in transports at an enormous expense, suffering from tempestuous weather, and losing their energies arid discipline, while one scheme was proposed after another, only to be considered and rejected. By turns Italy and South America were named as countries where they might be successfully employed—but to both designs, on mature deliberation, strong objections were found; and on the 25th of October final orders were received from England, directing the fleet and army forthwith to rendezvous at Malta, and thence proceed to Egypt.

The troops on reaching the island were partially disembarked while the ships were refitting; and the fresh provisions and salubrious air of Valetta soon restored many who had suffered from long confinement and salt rations. Five hundred Maltese were enlisted to serve as pioneers. Water-casks were replenished, stores laid in, the troops reembarked; and on the 20th of December, the first division got under weigh, followed by the second on the succeeding day.

Instead of sailing direct for their destination, the fleet proceeded to the Bay of Macri. Finding that roadstead too open, the admiral shaped his course for the coast of Caramania. There he was overtaken by a gale of wind—and though close to the magnificent harbour of Marmorrice, its existence appears to have been known, out of a fleet of two hundred vessels, only to the captain of a brig of war. As the fleet were caught in a heavy gale on a lee shore, the result might have been most disastrous to the transports, who could not carry sufficient canvas to work off the land. Fortunately, Marmorrice proved a haven of refuge; and the surprise and pleasure of the soldiers can scarcely be described, when they found themselves in smooth water, and surrounded by the

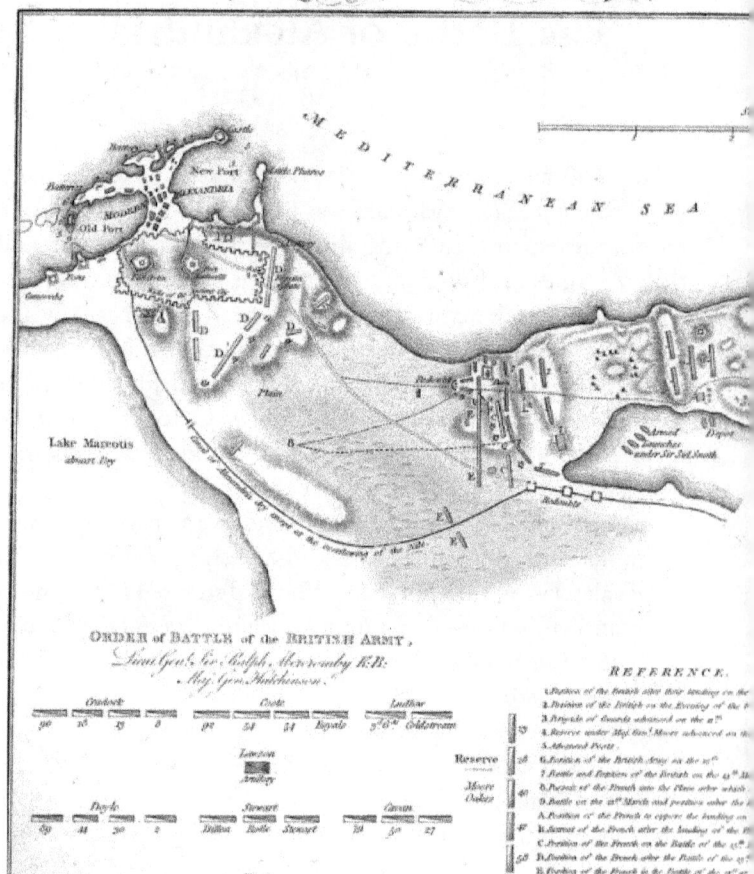

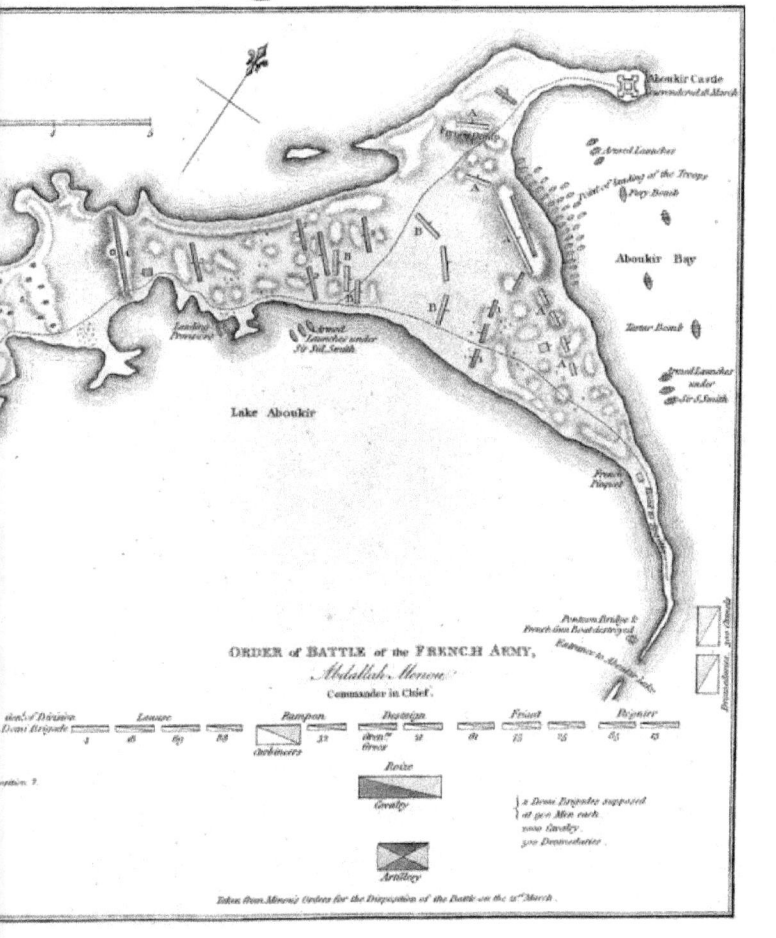

grandest scenery imaginable, "though, the instant before, the fleet was labouring in a heavy gale, and rolling in a tremendous sea."

Another landing of the troops took place, and no advantages resulted from it to compensate the loss of time which allowed the French to obtain strong reinforcements. Goat's flesh was abundant, and poultry plentiful; but the Turks had probably been apprised beforehand of the munificence of the British, as every article was advanced on the arrival of the fleet four hundred *per cent*, in price.

The remount of the cavalry formed an ostensible, almost an only reason, for the expedition visiting Asia Minor, and consuming time that might have been so successfully employed. The horses arrived, but from their wretched quality and condition they proved a sorry equivalent for the expense and trouble their acquisition cost.

While the expedition was in the harbour of Marmorrice, an awful tempest came suddenly on, and raged with unintermitting fury for two days. It thundered violently—hailstones fell as large as walnuts—deluges of water rushed from the mountains, sweeping everything away. The horses broke loose—the ships drove from their anchors—the *Swiftsure*, a seventy-four, was struck with lightning—and many others lost masts, spars, and were otherwise disabled. Amid this elemental war, signal-guns fired from vessels in distress, and the howling of wolves and other wild animals in the woods, added to the uproar.

After a protracted delay in waiting for the Turkish armament, which was expected to have been in perfect readiness, the expedition left the harbour without it on the 23rd of February. The sight, when the fleet got under weigh, was most imposing; the men-of-war, transports, and store-ships amounting to one hundred and seventy-five sail.

The British Army was composed of the whole or portions of twenty-seven regiments, exclusive of artillery and pioneers.

★★★★★★

Effective Strength of the Egyptian Army:

Guards—Major-General Ludlow.

1st, or Royals, 2nd battalions 54th and 92nd—Major-General Coote.

8th, 18th, 90th—Major-General Craddock.

2nd, or Queen's, 50th, 79th—Major-General Lord Craven.

18th, 30th, 44th, 89th—Brigadier-General Doyle.

Minorca, De Rolde's, Dillon's—Major-General Stuart.

Reserve:

40th, Flank Company, 23rd, 28th, 42nd, 58th, Corsican Rang-

ers—Major-General Moore,
Detachment 11th Dragoons, 12th Dragoons, 26th Dragoons—
Brigadier-General Finch
Artillery and Prince's—Brigadier-General Lawson.

******

Its total strength in rank and file, including one thousand sick and five hundred Maltese, was fifteen thousand three hundred and thirty men. In this number, all the *attachés* of the army were reckoned—and consequently the entire force that could have been combatant in the field would not exceed twelve thousand bayonets and sabres. This was certainly a small army with which to attack an enemy in possession of the country, holding fortified posts, with a powerful artillery, a numerous cavalry, and having a perfect acquaintance with the only places on the coast where it was practicable to disembark in safety.

On the 1st of March the Arab's tower was in sight, and next morning the whole fleet entered Aboukir Bay. (The men-of-war brought up exactly in the place where the Battle of the Nile was fought, the *Foudroyant* chafing her cables on the wreck of the French admiral's ship. The anchor of the *L'Orient* was crept for and recovered). On the following morning, a French frigate was seen running into Alexandria, having entered the bay in company with the British fleet.

The weather was unfavourable for attempting a landing of the troops. This was a serious disappointment, and an accidental occurrence added to the inconvenience it would have otherwise caused. Two engineer officers, engaged in reconnoitring the coast, advanced too far into the bay through an over-zealous anxiety to mark out a landing-place. They were seen and overtaken by a French gunboat, who fired into the cutter, killing one of the engineers and making the other prisoner. The survivor was brought ashore, and forwarded to Cairo to General Menou; and thus, had the British descent been before doubtful, this unfortunate discovery would have confirmed the certainty of an intended landing, and allowed ample time for preparations being made to oppose it.

The weather moderated in the morning of the 7th, and the signal was made by the flag-ship "to prepare for landing." But the sea was still so much up that the attempt was postponed, and with the exception of an affair between the boats of the *Fondroyant* and a party of the enemy, whom they drove from a block-house, that day passed quietly over.

The 8th was more moderate—the swell had abated—and prepara-

ALEXANDRIA. LANDING OF THE BRITISH ARMY IN ABOUKIR BAY

tions for the landing commenced. At two o'clock the first division were in the boats, amounting to five thousand five hundred men, under General Coote; while the ships, on board of which the remainder of the army still remained, were anchored as near the shore as possible, to allow the landing brigades their immediate support. The right and left flanks of the boats were protected by launches and gun-brigs; three sloops of war, with springs from their cables, had laid their broadsides towards the beach; and the Fury and Tartarus had taken a position to cover the troops with the fire of their mortars.

The French were drawn up on a ridge of sandhills, with an elevated hillock in their centre, and twelve pieces of artillery in position along their line. The moment was one of absorbing interest—and many a heart beat fast as, in half-companies, the soldiers stood under arms in the launches, impatiently waiting for the signal to advance.

A gun was fired; off sprang the boats, while the men-of-war opened their batteries, and the bomb-vessels commenced throwing shells. The cannonade from the shipping was promptly returned by the French lines and castle of Aboukir; while on swept the regiments towards the beach, under a furious discharge of shot and shells, and a torrent of grape and musketry, that ploughed the surface of the water, or carried death into the dense masses of men crowded in the launches. But nothing could exceed the glorious rivalry displayed by both services in advancing; while shot was hailing on the water, the sailors as the spray flashed from their oar-blades, nobly emulated each other in trying who should first beach his boat.

Each cheered the other forward, while the soldiers caught the enthusiastic spirit and answered them with loud huzzas. The beach was gained, the 23rd and 40th jumped into the surf, reached the shore, formed as they cleared the water, and rushed boldly up the sandhills, never attempting to draw a trigger, but leaving all to be decided by the bayonet. The French regiments that confronted them were driven from the heights; while pressing on, the Nole hills in the rear, with three pieces of artillery, were captured.

The 42nd were equally successful; they formed with beautiful regularity in the face of a French battalion protected by two guns, and after defeating a charge of two hundred cavalry, stormed and occupied the heights.

While these brilliant attacks had been in progress, the Guards were charged by the French dragoons in the very act of landing, and a temporary disorder ensued. The 58th had formed on the right, and, by a well-directed fire, repulsed the cavalry with loss. The Guards corrected their line, and instantly showed front, while the French, unable to shake the formation of the British, retired behind the sandhills.

The transport boats had been outstripped by those of the men-of-war—and consequently, the Royals and 54th only touched the shore as the dragoons rode off. Their landing was, however, admirably timed; for a French column, under cover of the sandhills, was advancing with fixed bayonets on the left flank of the Guards. On perceiving these newly-landed regiments, its courage failed; it halted, delivered a volley, and then hastily retreated.

The British had now possession of the heights; the brigade of Guards was formed and advancing, and the boats returning to the ships for the remainder of the army. Observing this, the enemy abandoned their position on the ridge, and, retiring behind the sandhills in the rear, for some time kept up a scattered fire. But on the British moving forward they deserted the ground entirely, leaving three hundred killed and wounded, eight pieces of cannon, and a number of horses to the victors. The remainder of the brigades were safely disembarked, Sir Ralph Abercrombie landed, and a position taken up, the right upon the sea, and the left on Lake Maadie.

A landing in the face of an enemy, prepared and in position like the French, under a heavy cannonade, and effected on a dangerous beach, would naturally occasion a severe loss of life; and several promising officers, and nearly five hundred men, were killed, wounded, and missing. The only surprise is, that the casualties were not greater. The mode in which an army is debarked exposes it unavoidably to fire, and troops, packed by fifties in a launch, afford a striking mark for an artillerist. Guns, already in position on the shore, enable those who work them to obtain the range of an approaching object with great precision; and the effect of a well-directed shot upon a boat crowded with troops is necessarily most destructive.

After the army had been united, it advanced by slow marches, some trifling skirmishing daily occurring between the advanced posts. The British bivouac was at the town of Mandora, and Sir Ralph moved forward to attack the enemy, who were posted on a ridge of heights.

The French, reinforced by two half brigades of infantry, a regiment of cavalry from Cairo, and a corps from Rosetta, mustered about five thousand five hundred of that arm, with five hundred horse, and five-and-twenty pieces of artillery. Their position was well chosen, as it stood on a bold eminence having an extensive glacis in its front, which would allow full sweep for the fire of its numerous and well-appointed artillery. The British attack was directed against the right wing, and in two lines the brigades advanced in columns of regiments, the reserve covering the movements, and marching parallel with the first.

Immediately on debouching from a date-wood, the enemy descended from the heights, and the 92nd—the leading regiment on the left—was attacked by a furious discharge of grape and musketry; while the French cavalry charged down the hill, and threw themselves upon the 90th, which led the right column. Though the charge was most gallantly made, Latour Maubourg leading the dragoons at a gallop, a close and shattering volley from the 90th obliged them to turn along the front of the regiment, and retreat with a heavy loss.

A few of the leading files, however, had actually reached the line, and were bayoneted in a desperate effort to break it. The attempt failed, and in executing his duty gloriously, their gallant leader was desperately wounded. The British pushed the reserve into action on the right; the Guards, in the rear, to support the centre, and Doyle's brigade, in column, behind the left. The French were on every point forced from their position—but, covered by the fire of their numerous guns and the fusillade of their *voltigeurs*, they retreated across the plain, and occupied their own lines on the heights of Alexandria.

Dillon's regiment during this movement made a brilliant bayonet charge, captured two guns, and turned them instantly on the enemy. Wishing to follow up this success, Sir Ralph attempted to carry the position by a *coup de main*; and advancing across the plain, he directed the brigades of Moore and Hutchinson to assault the flanks of the French position simultaneously. To attempt dislodging a force posted as the enemy were, could only end in certain discomfiture. The troops could make no way—a murderous fire of artillery mowed them down; "the French, no longer in danger, had only to load and fire: aim was unnecessary, the bullets could not but do their office and plunge into the lines." For several hours, the British remained, suffering this exterminating fire patiently; and at sunset, the order being given to fall back, the army retired and took up a position for the night.

The British loss, its strength considered, was immense. Eleven hundred men were killed and wounded; while that of the enemy amounted barely to a third, with four field-pieces, which they were obliged to abandon.

A strong position was now taken by Sir Ralph; the right reached the sea, resting on the ruins of a Roman palace, and projecting a quarter of a mile over heights in front. This promontory of sandhills and ruins was some three hundred yards across, sloping gradually to a valley, which divided it from the hills which formed the rest of the lines. The extreme left *appuied* on two batteries, and Lake Maadie protected the rear—and the whole, from sea to lake, extended about a mile. In front of the right, the ground was uneven; but that before the centre would admit cavalry to act. The whole space had once been a Roman colony—and, on its ruined site, a hard-fought day was now about to be decided.

The French position was still stronger than the British lines, as it stretched along a ridge of lofty hills, extending from the sea on one side to the canal of Alexandria on the other. A tongue of land in the advance of their right, ran nearly for a mile parallel with the canal, and had obliged the British posts to be thrown considerably back, and thus obliqued their line.

In a classic and military view, nothing could be more imposing than the ground on which Menou's army were encamped. In the centre stood Fort Cretin; on the left, Fort Caffarelli; Pompey's Pillar showed boldly on the right; Cleopatra's Needle on the left; while Alexandria appeared in the background, with its walls extending to the sea; and at the extremity of a long low neck of land, the ancient Pharos was visible. Wherever the eye ranged, objects of no common interest met it; some of the "wonders of the world" were contiguous; and "the very ruins under foot were sacred from their antiquity."

The British Army had little leisure, and probably as little inclination, to indulge in classic recollections. The men were busily engaged in fortifying the position, bringing up guns for the batteries, and collecting ammunition and stores. The magazines were inconveniently situated; and to roll weighty spirit-casks through the deep sands was a most laborious task, and it principally devolved upon the seamen. The fuel was particularly bad, the billets being obtained from the date-tree, which it is almost impossible to ignite, and whose smoke, when kindling, pains, by its pungency, the eyes of all within its influence. Water was abundant, but of indifferent quality; and as Menou, with a most unjustifiable severity, inflicted death upon the Arabs who should be found bringing sheep to the camp, the price of fresh provisions was high, and the supply precarious.

On the 10th, an affair took place between an enemy's patrol and a detachment of British cavalry, under Colonel Archdale. It was a very gallant, but very imprudent, encounter—a third of the men, and half the officers, being killed or taken. Another casualty occurred also, to the great regret of all. Colonel Brice, of the Guards, in going his rounds, was deceived by a mirage; and coming unexpectedly on an enemy's post, received a wound of which he died the third day, a prisoner.

Menou was reported to be advancing; and an Arab chief apprised Sir Sydney Smith, that the French intended an attack upon the British camp next morning. The information was discredited; but the result proved that it was authentic.

On the 21st of March, the army, at three o'clock, as usual, stood to their arms, and for half an hour all was undisturbed. Suddenly, a solitary musket was fired, a cannon-shot succeeded it, and a spattering fusillade, broken momentarily with the heavier booming of a gun, announced that an attack was being made. The feebleness of the fire rendered it doubtful against what point the real effort of the French would be directed. All looked impatiently for daybreak, which, though faintly visible in the east, seemed to break more tardily the more its assistance was desired.

On the right, a noise was heard; all listened in breathless expectation; shouts and a discharge of musketry succeeded; the roar increased; momentarily it became louder—there indeed the enemy were in force—and there the British line was seriously assailed.

Favoured by broken ground, and covered by the haze of morning, the French had partially surprised the videts, attacked the pickets, and following them quickly, drove them back upon the line. One column advanced upon the ruin held by the 58th, their drums beating the *pas de charge*, and the officers cheering the men forward. Colonel Houston, who commanded the regiment, fearing lest his own pickets might have been retiring in front of the enemy's column, reserved his fire until the glazed hats of the French were distinguishable in the doubtful light.

The 58th lined a wall partly dilapidated, but which in some places afforded them an excellent breastwork; and the twilight allowed the French column to be only distinctly seen when within thirty yards of the post. As the regiment occupied detached portions of the wall, where its greater ruin exposed it to attack, an irregular but well-sustained fusillade was kept up, until the enemy's column, unable to bear the quick and well-directed musketry of the British, retired into a hollow for shelter. There they reformed, and wheeling to the right endeavoured to turn the left of the redoubt, while another column

FRENCH CAMEL CORPS

marched against the battery occupied by the 28th.

On the front attack the regiment opened a heavy fire, but part of the enemy had gained the rear, and another body penetrated through the ruined wall. Thus, assailed on every side, the 58th wheeled back two companies, who, after delivering three effective volleys, rushed forward with the bayonet. The 23rd now came to support the 58th, while the 42nd moved round the exterior of the ruins, cutting off the French retreat; and of the enemy, all who entered the redoubt were killed or taken.

The situation of the 28th and 58th was, for a time, as extraordinary as it was dangerous, for at the same moment they were actually repelling three separate attacks, and were assailed simultaneously on their front, flanks, and rear.

The 42nd, in relieving the 28th, was exposed to a serious charge of French cavalry. Nearly unperceived, the dragoons wheeled suddenly round the left of the redoubt, and though the ground was full of holes, rode furiously over tents and baggage, and, charging *en masse,* completely overthrew the Highlanders. In this desperate emergency, the 42nd, with broken ranks, and in that unavoidable confusion which, when it occurs, renders cavalry so irresistible, fought furiously hand to hand, and opposed their bayonets fearlessly to the sabres of the French. The flank companies of the 40th, immediately beside them, dared not, for a time, deliver their fire, the combatants were so intermingled in the *mêlée.* At this moment, General Stuart brought up the foreign brigade in beautiful order, and their heavy and well-sustained fusillade decided the fate of the day. "Nothing could withstand it, and the enemy fled or perished."

During this charge of cavalry, Sir Ralph Abercrombie, who had ridden to the right on finding it seriously engaged, advanced to the ruins where the contest was raging, after having despatched his *aide-de-camp,* (see note below), with orders to the more distant brigades. He was quite alone, and some French dragoons having penetrated to the spot, one, remarking that he was a superior officer, charged and overthrew the veteran commander. In an attempt to cut him down, the old man, nerved with a momentary strength, seized the uplifted sword, and wrested it from his assailant, while a Highland soldier transfixed the Frenchman with his bayonet. Unconscious that he was wounded in the thigh, Sir Ralph complained only of a pain in his breast, occasioned, as he supposed, by a blow from the pommel of the sword during his recent struggle with the dragoon. The first officer that came up was Sir Sydney Smith, who, having broken the blade of his sabre, received from Sir Ralph the weapon of which he had despoiled the French hussar.

******

Note:—A curious incident occurred immediately afterwards. An *aide-de-camp* of General Craddock. in carrying orders, had his horse killed, and begged permission of Sir Sydney Smith to mount a horse belonging to his orderly dragoon. As Sir Sydney was turning round to give the order to dismount, a cannon-shot took off the poor fellow's head. "This," said the admiral, "settles the question; Major, the horse is at your service."

******

The cavalry being completely repulsed, Sir Ralph walked firmly to the redoubt on the right of the Guards, from which a commanding view of the entire battlefield could be obtained. The French, though driven from the camp, still maintained the battle on the right, and charging with their reserve cavalry, attacked the foreign brigade. Here, too, they were resolutely repulsed; and their infantry finding their efforts everywhere unsuccessful, changed their formation and acted *en tirailleur* with the exception of one battalion, which still held a fleche in front of the redoubt, on either flank of which the Republican colours were planted.

At this time the ammunition of the British was totally exhausted: some regiments, particularly the reserve, had not a single cartridge; and in the battery the supply for the guns was reduced to a single round. In consequence, the British fire on the right had nearly ceased, but in the centre the engagement still continued.

There the attack had commenced at daybreak: a column of grenadiers, supported by a heavy line of infantry, furiously assailing the Guards, and driving in the flankers which had been thrown out to check their advance. Observing the echelon formation of the British, the French general instantly attempted to turn their left; but the officer commanding on that flank as promptly prevented it, by throwing some companies sharply back, while Coote's brigade having come up, and opening its musketry, obliged the enemy to give way and retire. Finding the attack in column fail, the French broke into extended order and opened a scattered fusillade, while every gun that could be brought to bear by their artillery was turned on the British position. But all was vain; though suffering heavily from this murderous fire, the formation of the Guards was coolly corrected when disturbed by the cannonade, while the fine and imposing attitude of these regiments removed all hope that they could be shaken, and prevented any renewal of attack.

The British left had never been seriously attempted, consequently its casualties were very few, and occasioned by a distant fire from the French guns, and a trifling interchange of musketry.

While the British right was, from want of ammunition, nearly *hors de combat*, the French approached the redoubt once more. They, too, had expended their cartridges, and both the assailants and assailed actually pelted the other with stones, of which missiles there was a very abundant supply upon the ground. A sergeant of the 28th had his skull beaten in by a blow, and died upon the spot. The grenadiers of the 40th, however, not relishing this novel mode of attack and defence, moved out to end the business with the bayonet. Instantly the assailants ran, the sharpshooters abandoned the hollows, and the battalion, following their example, evacuated the fleche, leaving the battle ground in front unoccupied by any save the dead and dying.

Menou's attempts had all been signally defeated. He perceived that the British lines had sustained no impression that would justify a continuation of the attack, and he determined to retreat. His brigades accordingly moved off under the heights of their position in excellent order; and though, for a considerable distance, they were forced to retire within an easy range of cannon shot, the total want of ammunition obliged the British batteries to remain silent, and permit the French march to be effected with trifling molestation.

The cannon on the British left, and the guns of some men-of-war cutters, which had anchored close in with the land upon the right, kept up a galling fire, their shots plunging frequently into the French ranks, and particularly into those of a corps of cavalry posted on a bridge over the canal of Alexandria to observe any movement the British left might threaten.

At ten o'clock the action had ended. Sir Ralph Abercrombie previously refused to quit the field, and remained exposed to the heavy cannonade directed on the battery where he stood, until perfectly assured that the French defeat had been decisive. From what proved a fatal wound he appeared at first to feel but little inconvenience, complaining only of the contusion on his breast. When, however, the day was won, and exertion no longer necessary, nature yielded, and in an exhausted state he was carried in a hammock off the field, accompanied by the tears and blessings of the soldiery. In the evening, he was removed, for better care, on board the flag-ship, where he continued until his death.

Immediate attention was bestowed upon the wounded, who, from the confined nature of the ground on which the grand struggles of the day had occurred, were lying in fearful numbers all around. Many of the sufferers had been wounded by grapeshot, others mangled by the sabres, or trodden down by the horses of the cavalry. Death had been busily employed. Of the British, two hundred and forty were dead, including six officers; eleven hundred and ninety men and sixty officers wounded; and thirty privates and three officers missing. Other casualties had occurred. The tents had been shred to pieces by the French guns, and many of the wounded and sick, who were lying there, were killed. No wonder could be expressed that the loss of life had been so terrible, for thousands of brass cannon-balls were lying loosely about, and glistening on the sands.

The French loss had been most severe. One thousand and fifty bodies were buried on the field of battle, and nearly seven hundred wounded were found mingled with the dead. The total loss sustained by Menou's army could not have been much under four thousand; and in this the greater portion of his principal officers must be included. General Roiz was found dead in the rear of the redoubt, and the French order of battle discovered in his pocket. Near the same place two guns had been abandoned, and these, with a stand of colours, fell, as trophies of their victory, to the conquerors.

No army could have behaved more gallantly than the British. Surrounded, partially broken, and even without a cartridge left, the contest was continued and a victory won. That the French fought bravely, that their attacks were vigorously made, and, after discomfiture, as boldly repeated, must be admitted; and that, in becoming the assailant, Menou conferred an immense advantage on the British, ii equally true. There Menou betrayed want of judgment; for had he but waited forty-eight hours the British must have attacked him.

Indeed, the assault was already planned; and, as it was to have been made in the night, considering the strength of their position, and the fine *matériel* of the Republican troops, a more precarious trial could never have been hazarded. But the case was desperate; the successes of the 8th and 13th—and dearly bought, though gloriously achieved, they were—must have been rendered nugatory, unless forward operations could have been continued. In short, Menou fought Abercrombie's battle, and he who must have been assailed, became himself the assailant.

Military criticism, like political disquisitions, comes not within the design of a work merely intended to describe the action of the battle, or the immediate events that preceded or resulted; but, if the truth were told, during these brief operations, from the landing to the evening of the 21st, mistakes were made on both sides. The military character of Britain had been sadly lowered by mismanagement at home, and still more ridiculously undervalued abroad, and it remained for future fields and a future conqueror to re-establish for Britain a reputation in arms, and prove that the island-spirit wanted only a field for its display.

After lingering a few days, the French Generals Lannuse and Bodet died of their wounds; and on the evening of the 28th March the British Army had to lament the decease of their gallant and beloved commander. An attempt to extract the ball, attended with great pain, was unsuccessful. Mortification ensued, Sir Ralph sank rapidly, and while his country and his army engrossed his every thought, he expired, full of years and honour, universally and most justly lamented.

The eulogy of his successor in command thus concludes:

> Were it permitted for a soldier to regret any one who has fallen in the service of his country, I might be excused for lamenting him more than any other person; but it is some consolation to those who tenderly loved him, that as his life was honourable so was his death glorious. His memory will be recorded in the annals of his country, will be sacred to every British soldier, and embalmed in the recollection of a grateful posterity.

Chapter 2

The Battle of Assaye, 1803

The death of Tippoo Saib, and the fall of Seringapatam, were astounding tidings for the native chiefs. Their delusory notions regarding their individual importance were ended, and a striking proof had been given of what little reliance could be placed on Indian mercenaries and places of strength, when Britain went forth in wrath and sent her armies to the field.

As the fear of Britain became confirmed, so did the hatred of the native princes to everything connected with her name. A power that had proved herself so formidable was to be dreaded, fixed as she was in the very heart of India; and, as the difficulty increased, so did the desire of freeing themselves from that thrall, which daily appeared to press upon them more heavily.

Affairs again began to assume a threatening look. The Mahratta chiefs exhibited an unfriendly attitude; and to cement an alliance with the Peishwah, and thus tranquillise the country, a portion of Tippoo's territory was offered and rejected. Scindia, with his army, was at Poona, and his influence directed every act of that dependent court.

A misunderstanding between Scindia and Holkar brought on a war between those chiefs. Holkar advanced on Poona, compelling Scindia to accept battle, in which he was defeated, the Peishwah deserting his ally in the hour of need, and concluding a treaty with the British. To effectuate this, Wellesley, now a major-general, took the field, with orders to drive Holkar from Poona., and secure the Peishwah's return to his capital; and learning that the Mahrattas intended to plunder Poona, the general saved it by an extraordinary forced march, accomplishing sixty miles in thirty hours—a marvellous exertion indeed to be made under an Indian sun.

All for a short time was quiet; but those restless chiefs again assumed a hostile position. Scindia and the Rajah of Berar moved towards the Nizam's frontier; while the former was negotiating with Holkar, his late enemy, to arrange their differences, and make common cause against the British.

To prepare for the threatened attack, the Marquis Wellesley invested the officers commanding the armies of Hindoostan and the Deccan with full powers; and to General Wellesley a special authority was given to make peace, or commence hostilities, as his own judgment should determine. In accordance with this power, a demand was made on Scindia that he should separate from the Rajah of Berar, and re-cross the Nerbuddah. To this demand an evasive reply was returned, and Eastern cunning was employed to obtain such delay as should permit the chieftains' plans to be matured, and enable them to take the field in force. This shuffling policy was, however, quite apparent; and on the first information that his political agent had quitted Scindia's camp, Wellesley suddenly broke up his cantonments, and marched directly on Ahmednuggur.

This ancient town was defended in the Eastern fashion with a high wall, flanked at its bends and angles by a tower, and garrisoned by some of Scindia's infantry and an auxiliary force of Arabs, while a body of the chieftain's cavalry occupied the space between the *Pettah* and the fort. Wellesley, without delay, assaulted the town, and carried it by escalade. On the 10th September, the British cannon opened on the fort, the *keeladar* in command proposed terms, and the British general expressed a readiness to listen to his propositions, but the guns continued working. Indian diplomacy has no chance when batteries are open; and, on the 12th, a garrison of fourteen hundred marched out, and the place was delivered up. This fortress, from its locality, was valuable; it secured the communications with Poona, made a safe depot for military stores, and was centrically placed in a district whose revenue was above 600,000 *rupees*.

With a short delay, Wellesley moved on Aurungabad, and entered that splendid city on the 29th. The enemy moved in a south-easterly direction, threatening Hyderabad, while the British, marching by the left bank of the Godaverey, secured their convoys from Moodgul, and obliged Scindia to retire northwards. As yet the Mahratta chiefs were moving a cavalry force north, with but a few matchlock men; but they were joined now by their whole artillery and sixteen battalions of infantry, officered chiefly by Frenchmen.

On the 21st September, at a conference at Budnapoor, General

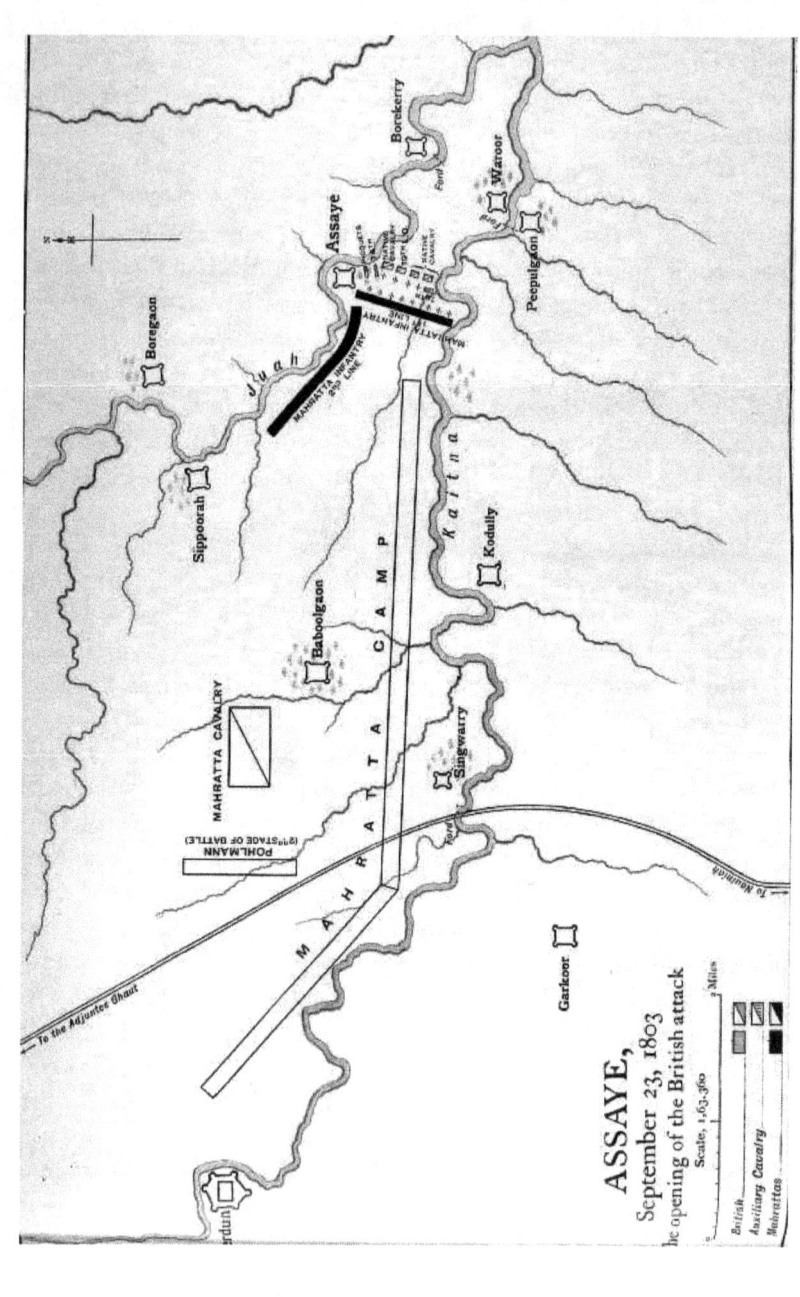

Wellesley and Colonel Stevenson arranged a combined attack for the 24th. They were to move east and west, pass the defiles on the same day, and thus prevent any movement of the enemy southward. A mistake, in distance, brought General Wellesley much sooner to his halting-place than had been calculated; and learning that the Mahratta Army were already breaking up to retire, he sent orders to Colonel Stevenson to advance; and announcing his immediate march on Scindia, begged his colleague to hurry forward to his assistance.

The cavalry consisted of the 19th Light Dragoons, and three native regiments, under the command of Colonel Maxwell, a bold and skilful officer. General Wellesley accompanied the horse, the infantry following in light marching order. After passing a league and half of ground, the advance reached an eminence; and on the right, and covering an immense extent of country, the Mahratta Army appeared.

In brilliant sunshine, nothing could be more picturesque than Scindia's encampment. The varied colours of the tents, each disposed around its own chieftain's banner without order or regularity, with "streets crossing and winding in every direction, displayed a variety of merchandise, as in a great fair. Jewellers, smiths, and mechanics were all attending as minutely to their occupations, and all as busily employed, as if they were at Poona and in peace."

In this enormous camp, fifty thousand men were collected—the River Kaitna running in their front, the Suah in their rear. These rivers united their waters at some distance beyond the left of the camp, forming a flat peninsula of considerable extent. The native infantry and all the guns were in position on the left, retired upon the Suah, and *appuied* on the village of Assaye—the cavalry were entirely on the right. The position was naturally strong; for the banks of the Kaitna are steep and broken, and the front very difficult to attack.

As the British cavalry formed line on the heights, it presented a strange but glorious contrast to the countless multitude of Mahratta horsemen, who were seen in endless array below. The British brigade, scarcely numbering three thousand sabres, took its position with all the boldness of a body having an equal force opposed. In number Scindia's cavalry were fully ten to one; as it was ascertained that, with his allies, the horsemen actually on the field exceeded thirty thousand. Having made a careful reconnaissance, General Wellesley determined to attack, and when the infantry came up it was instantly executed.

While examining the position, immense masses of Scindia's cavalry moved forward, and threw out skirmishers, which were directly driven in. Wellesley having discovered a neglected ford, decided on crossing over, and, by attacking the infantry and guns, embarrass the immense cavalry force of Scindia, and oblige it to manoeuvre to disadvantage, and act on the confined space the ill-selected ground afforded.

The infantry had now come up, and, in column, they were directed on the river. A fire from the Mahratta guns immediately opened, but the range was far too distant to permit the cannonade to be effective, or check the forward movement of the columns. The whole were now across the river; the infantry formed into two brigades, and the cavalry in reserve behind them, ready to rush on any part of the battle-ground where advantage could be gained, or support should be required. The Mysore horse and the contingent of the Peishwah were merely left in observation of the enemy's right.

This flank attack obliged Scindia to change his front. He did so with less confusion than was expected; and by his new disposition rested his right upon the Kaitna, and his left upon the Suah and Assaye. His whole front bristled with cannon, and the ground immediately around the village seemed, from the number of guns, like one great battery.

The fire from this powerful artillery was of course destructive, and the British guns were completely overpowered, and in a very few minutes silenced entirely. This was the crisis; and on the determination of a moment hung the fortune of a very doubtful day. Without hesitation Wellesley abandoned his guns, and advanced with the bayonet. The charge was gallantly made, the enemy's right forced back, and his guns captured.

While this movement was being executed, the 74th and light infantry pickets in front of Assaye, were severely cut up by the fire from that place. Perceiving the murderous effect of the fusillade, a strong body of the Mahratta horse moved swiftly round the village, and made a furious onset on the 74th. Maxwell had watched the progress of the battle, and now was his moment of action. The word was given, the British cavalry charged home, down went the Mahrattas in hundreds beneath the fiery assault of the brave 19th, and their gallant supporters the *sepoys*, while, unchecked by a tremendous storm of grape and musketry, Maxwell pressed his advantage, and cut through Scindia's left. The 74th and the light infantry reformed, and, pushing boldly on, completed the disorder of the enemy, preventing any effective attempt to renew a battle, the doubtful result of which was thus in a few minutes decided by the promptitude of the general.

Remanning the guns at Assaye

Some of Scindia's troops fought bravely, and the desperate obstinacy with which his gunners stood to the cannon, was almost incredible. They remained to the last—and were bayoneted around the guns, which they refused, even in certain defeat, to abandon.

The British charge was, indeed, resistless; but in the enthusiasm of success, at times there is a lack of prudence. The *sepoys* rushed wildly on—their elated ardour was uncontrollable; while a mass of the Mahratta horse arrayed upon the hill were ready to rush upon ranks disordered by their own success.

But Wellesley foresaw, and guarded against the evil consequences that a too excited courage might produce. The 78th were kept in hand; and cool, steady, and with a perfect formation, they offered an imposing front, that the Mahratta cavalry perceived was unassailable.

A strong column of the enemy, however, that had been only partially engaged, now rallied and renewed the battle, joined by a number of Scindia's gunners and infantry, who had flung themselves as dead upon the ground, and thus escaped the sabres of the British cavalry. Maxwell's brigade, who had re-formed their ranks and breathed their horses, dashed into the still disordered ranks of these half-rallied troops—a desperate slaughter ensued, and the Mahrattas were totally routed; but the British lost their chivalrous leader, and in the moment of victory, Maxwell died in front of the battle, "and, fighting foremost, fell."

The last effort of the day was made by a part of the artillery who were in position near the village of Assaye—and in person Wellesley led on the 78th Highlanders and the 7th Native Cavalry. In the attack the general's horse was killed under him; but the enemy declined the charge, broke, fled, and left a field cumbered with their dead, and crowded with cannon, bullocks, caissons, and all the *matériel* of an Eastern Army, to the conquerors.

The evening had fallen before the last struggle at Assaye was over, but the British victory was complete. Twelve hundred of Scindia's dead were found upon the field; while, of his wounded, scarcely an estimate could be hazarded, for all the villages and adjacent country were crowded with his disabled soldiery. The British loss was of necessity severe, and it might be estimated that one-third of the entire army was *hors de combat*.

In comparison with Assaye, all fighting that had hitherto taken place in India was child's play. To call it a brilliant victory is only using a term simply descriptive of what it was. It was a magnificent

THE 74TH HIGHLANDERS
ATTACKED BY THE MAHRATTA CAVALRY

display of skill, moral courage, and perfect discipline, against native bravery and an immense numerical superiority. But it was not a mass of men, rudely collected, ignorant of military tactics, and unused to combinations, that Wellesley overthrew. Scindia's army was respectable in every arm, his cavalry excellent of their kind, and his artillery well served. His infantry were for a long time under the training of French officers; and the ease and precision with which he changed his front when the British crossed the Kaitna to assail his flank, showed that the lessons of the French disciplinarians had not been given in vain.

The total *déroute* of Assaye was followed by a tide of conquest. Fortress after fortress was reduced, and Scindia sought and obtained a truce. The British arms were next turned against the Rajah of Berar—General Wellesley marched against him—for the truce was ended suddenly, and Scindia joined his colleague with all his disposable force.

On the plains of Argaum, Wellesley found the confederated chiefs drawn up in order of battle. Scindia's immense cavalry formed the right, on the left were the Berar infantry and guns, flanked by the Rajah's cavalry, while a cloud of Pindaries were observed on the extreme right of the whole array.

The British moved down and formed line, the infantry in front, and the cavalry in reserve. The battle was short and decisive. The Berar's Persian infantry attacked the 74th and 78th regiments, and were literally annihilated; while Scindia's cavalry charge failed totally, the 26th Native regiment repulsing it most gloriously. The British now rushed forward, and the Mahrattas broke and fled in every direction, abandoning their entire park of over one hundred pieces of artillery, and thirty-eight were captured at Argaum; while the cavalry pursued by moonlight the scattered host, and captured an immense number of elephants and beasts of burden, the entire baggage, and stores and arms of every description.

The fall of some places of strength, and the total defeat of their armies in the field, humbled Scindia and his ally, the *rajah*, and obliged them to sue and obtain a peace. The brilliant career of General Wellesley had gained him a name in arms which future victories were to immortalise. To commemorate the Battle of Assaye, a monument was erected in Calcutta, a sword presented to the victor by the citizens, and a gold vase by the officers he commanded. He was also made a Knight Companion of the Bath, and honoured by the thanks of Parliament. Even from the inhabitants of Seringapatam he received an address, remarkable for its simplicity and affection, committing him to

The 19th Light Dragoons drive the Mahrattas across the River Assaye

the care of "the God of all castes," and invoking for him "health, glory, and happiness." In 1805 he returned to his native land, "with war's red honours on his crest," bearing with him from the scene of glory the high estimation and affectionate wishes of every caste and colour.

Chapter 3

Capture of the Cape of Good Hope, 1806

In 1805, the British Government, having ascertained that the Cape of Good Hope had only a force under two thousand regular troops for its protection, and that the militia and inhabitants were well inclined to assist a British Army, in case a landing should be made, determined to attempt the reduction of that colony, by the employment of a body of troops cantoned in the neighbourhood of Cork, assisted by some regiments already on board the India ships at Falmouth.

The expedition was to be a secret one, and the troops embarked at Cork were ostensibly intended for service in the Mediterranean. It was supposed that this report would prevent suspicion, particularly as the Company's fleet sailed alone, as if its destination was really Madras direct. Sealed orders were, however, given to the commanders to be opened in a certain latitude, and in these they were ordered to rendezvous at Madeira.

The troops composing the expedition were placed under the command of General Baird. They comprised the 24th, 38th, 59th, 71st, 72nd, 83rd, and 98th, part of the 20th Light Dragoons, with artillery, artificers, and recruits, making a total force of six thousand six hundred and fifty rank and file.

It was at first suspected that some troops which had left Rochfort in two line-of-battle ships and escaped the vigilance of our cruisers, might have been intended to reinforce the garrison at the Cape, and General Baird conceived the corps intrusted to him not sufficiently strong to achieve the objects of the expedition. He asked, under this impression, for an additional force, and stated the grounds on which the request was made; but, in the meantime, it was ascertained that the

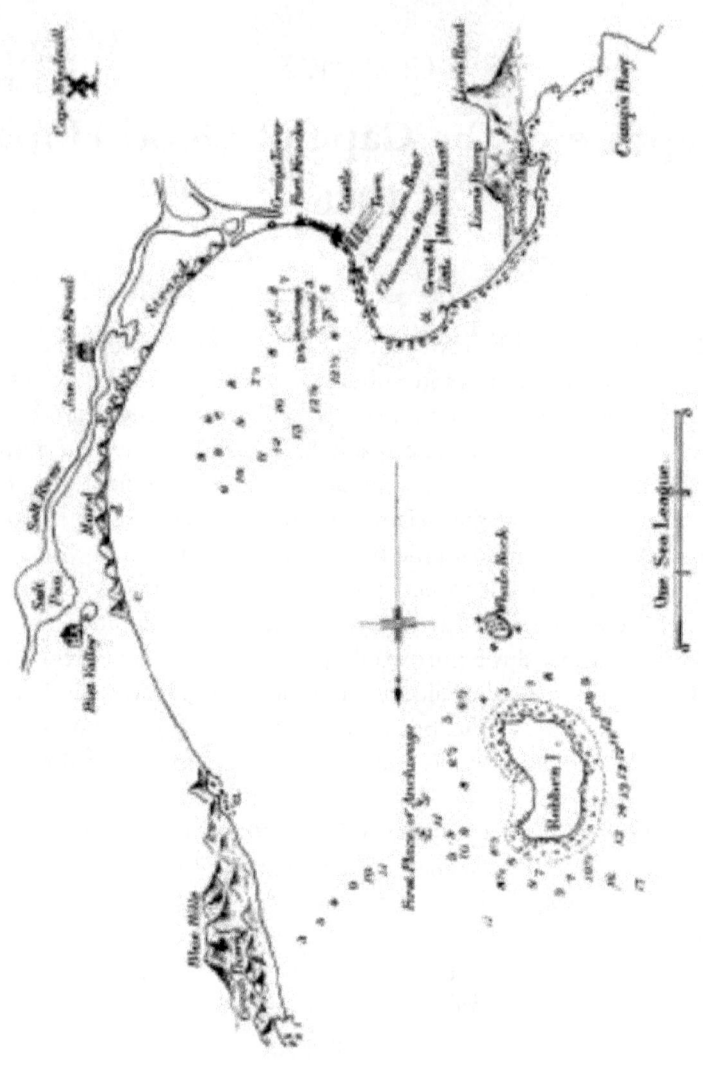

French troops had proceeded to the West Indies: and that, therefore, the Cape of Good Hope had received no increase to its military establishment.

After another application to obtain an increase to the corps already under his orders, by having the 8th regiment added to the force, the expedition sailed, stopping at Madeira and St. Salvador to obtain water and provisions. Nothing of moment occurred in the voyage to South America; the passage was tedious, and an Indiaman and transport ran on a low sandy island, called the Roccas, and were totally lost. Fortunately, the men on board and twelve chests of dollars were saved from the wreck. Only three individuals perished; of these, General Yorke, in command of the artillery, was one, and Major Spicer, the next in seniority, succeeded him. While staying at St. Salvador, the regiments were landed and inspected, a remount of fifty horses obtained for the cavalry, and, all arrangements being completed, the expedition sailed for its final destination on the 28th of November, and made the African coast, a little to the northward of the Cape, on the 4th of January, 1806.

Table Bay, on the shore, and almost in the centre of which Cape Town stands, receives its name from that extraordinary eminence called Table Mountain, which rises about three thousand six hundred and eighty-seven feet above the level of the sea, and which terminates in a perfectly flat surface at that height, where the face of the rock on the side of Cape Town descends almost perpendicularly. To the eastward of the mountain, separated from it by a chasm, is Charles's Mount, more generally called the Devil's Tower; and on the westward, a round hill rises on the right hand of the bay, called the Lion's Head, from which a ridge of high land, terminating in another smaller hill, called the Lion's Rump, stretches towards the sea.

The town itself is handsome and extensive; and the streets, intersecting each other at right angles, are broad and airy, generally built with stone, and with terraces in front. The Company's gardens, walks, parade, and castle, all add to the beauty of the place, and render it superior to any colonial city in the possession of Great Britain.

The coast is everywhere dangerous—landing, excepting in the bays, and that, too, in favourable weather, almost impracticable—and hence, a very inferior force on shore, if the surf were at all up, might successfully resist any attempt at the disembarkation of an army.

The troops in garrison consisted of a detachment of Batavian artillery, the 22nd Dutch regiment of the line, a German regiment of

Waldecks, and a native corps, which acted as light infantry. To these, an auxiliary battalion, formed from the seamen and marines of a frigate and corvette which had been wrecked upon the coast, were added; while a number of irregulars, mounted and dismounted, comprised of the boors, and armed with guns of enormous length of barrel, completed the force of General Janssens, who was then commandant at the Cape.

The governor had a high reputation, both as a soldier and a civilian, and from the excellence of his measures since his arrival at the Cape, was held most deservedly in great estimation by the colonists. On the appearance of the British fleet, although his numerical superiority was greater than that of his enemy, he wisely considered that the *matériel* of the invaders was far more efficient than his own; and leaving a garrison in Cape Town, he determined to fall back on the interior with the remainder of his troops, and carry on a desultory war, until the arrival of a French or Dutch fleet from Europe should enable him to resort to active measures and save the colony. This plan, though ruinous to the inhabitants, if carried out, would have rendered the subjugation of the Cape a very difficult and tedious undertaking for the British, and in this posture of affairs the expedition made the coast, and came to anchor just out of range of the batteries in Table Bay.

The weather was fortunately calm, but the day was too far advanced to admit a landing of the troops, but all was prepared for effecting it on the morrow. The coast was sounded, the approaches to the town reconnoitred, and a small inlet, sixteen miles north-east of the town, called Leopard's Bay, was selected as the point on which the troops should be disembarked. The transports accordingly weighed and took their stations, while the men-of-war got into a position to cover the landing, in case of opposition, with their guns.

During the night, the surf had risen so prodigiously, that at daylight it was declared unsafe for boats to attempt the beach, and a landing at Saldana Bay was proposed. There it could be easily effected, but it would carry the army a distance from the town, separate it on its march from the fleet, oblige it to depend for its supplies on what provisions it could carry, or any which by accidental circumstances it could obtain on its route; it would also entail a harassing march of seventy miles on soldiers so long cooped up on shipboard; and that, too, in the hot season of the year, over a heavy sand, where water was not procurable. Still, the uncertainty of the weather, and the necessity of an immediate attack, overcame all other objections; and on the evening of the 5th, General Beresford, with the 38th regiment and the 20th Light Dragoons, sailed for Saldana, with an understanding that the remainder of the army should proceed thither on the following morning.

But daylight on the 6th January broke with happier promise; the surf had gone down considerably; and it was at once decided that the troops should be landed without farther loss of time. The Highland brigade was instantly transferred from the transports to the boats, and the 71st, 72nd, and 93rd, effected a landing with but a single casualty, and that arising from the swamping of a launch, by which five-and-thirty Highlanders were drowned.

No other loss attended the operation—the light company of the 93rd cleared the brushwood of a few skirmishers that had been thrown out by the enemy, and the remainder of the troops debarked without any opposition.

The artillery, consisting of four six-pounders and a couple of howitzers, were landed on the 7th; and the whole of the force being now safely on shore, the British general commenced his march direct on Cape Town, the guns being dragged through the sands by fatigue parties furnished from the fleet.

The advance was unopposed until the British Army had approached a line of heights, some four miles distant from the landing place. The Blawberg, as one of these eminences is called, was occupied by *burgher* cavalry, and the videts announced that General Janssens was in position on the other side of the high grounds, and his whole disposable force drawn up in order of battle. The march was steadily continued, and when the Blawberg was crowned by the advance guard, the Batavian Army, formed in two lines, with twenty-five pieces of artillery and a large corps of irregular cavalry, was discovered.

General Baird formed his corps into two columns of brigades; the right, comprising the 24th, 59th, and 83rd, under Lieutenant-Colonel Baird, commanding in the absence of General Beresford; and the left, consisting of the Highland regiments, under General Fergusson. While deploying into line, the Batavian guns opened, and their cavalry, by a left extension, threatened the right of the British. Baird's brigade refused its right, checking the *burgher* horse with its musketry; and the Highland regiments on the left made a rapid movement under a heavy cannonade, and advanced to the charge. The right wing of the Batavian Army broke without waiting an assault, the left followed the example, and the field was totally abandoned by the enemy, with a

THE HIGHLANDERS ADVANCE

considerable loss in killed and wounded.

Without cavalry, it was impossible to complete the *déroute*. The guns were, therefore, carried off; and quitting the road to Cape Town, Janssens, in pursuance of his previous plan, marched eastward, and moved towards Hottentot Holland, with a hope of protracting a war in the interior. Of course, the capital was the object of the conqueror. The fleet was in an exposed anchorage, and to equip his army for ulterior operations, and secure hi a communication with the sea, it was necessary to possess Cape Town.

The advance was very distressing, and the troops suffered much. The badness of the roads, the heat of the weather, and worse still, the scarcity of water, was severely felt before the brigades, at a late hour, reached their bivouacs in Reit Valley, a farming establishment belonging to the Dutch Government. Here some salt provisions, which had been floated through the surf, were brought up by the marines and partitioned among the soldiers; while the few and scanty springs attached to the farm afforded them an indifferent supply of water. An immediate movement on the capital was imperative; and the next day the British reached a position beside the Salt River—an inlet some short distance from the strong lines which cover Cape Town.

These defences are formed of a chain of redoubts, with a connecting parapet, furnished with banquettes and a dry ditch. They extend about eight hundred yards, and unite the Devil's Berg with the sea. These lines were very formidable, as they had been considerably strengthened by the British during their possession of the colony. One hundred and fifty guns and howitzers were mounted on the works; and several batteries had been erected on the escarp of the mountain, that would have exposed assailing troops to a flanking fire, and, in storming the lines, occasioned a severe loss of life.

One battery and blockhouse were placed on a shoulder of the hill, thirteen hundred feet above the level of the plain. But this was probably the least effective of the defences; as, in modern warfare, a plunging fire is not regarded much. A mile behind the lines the castle of Good Hope is situated at the entrance of the town. It is a pentagon, with outworks strong enough to require a regular approach; and that side of the city which overlooks the bay is secured alike by the fire of the castle, and a number of batteries mounted with guns of heavy calibre.

To carry works so extensive, and so formidable in their defences, with a small corps like Baird's, unprovided with any artillery but the light field-pieces they had brought through the sands, was not to be attempted; and it was determined to obtain some heavy guns, and a reinforcement of seamen and marines from the fleet. But these were not required; the enemy sent out a flag of truce, and an armistice was agreed upon, which terminated ultimately in a capitulation. The town and its defences were given up to the British Army, and without a shot, works were surrendered to a force of not four thousand men, on which were mounted four hundred and fifty-six guns and mortars, most of them of the heaviest calibre.

Janssens, after his defeat, retired towards the interior; and having disbanded the militia and burgher cavalry, which had accompanied him, he took a position at Kloof, with twelve hundred regular troops, and some five-and-twenty guns. General Baird, anxious to effect the tranquillity of the colony and terminate hostilities at once, despatched General Beresford to make overtures to the Dutch governor, and induce him to capitulate. A long and doubtful negotiation took place between the British and Batavian commanders, which eventually ended in the whole of the colony of the Cape of Good Hope and its dependencies, with all the rights and privileges held and exercised by the Dutch Government, being formally transferred to His Britannic Majesty.

Although the capture of the Cape was effected with trifling loss, and the opposition given to the British troops was far less formidable than might have been anticipated, still the operations which were so deservedly crowned with success, were boldly planned and bravely executed. Janssens exhibited no military talent, and in a country abounding in strong positions, to offer battle in an open plain, and oppose an irregular force to a well-disciplined army, was a strange decision of the Batavian commander, and could only terminate in defeat. In an engagement in which the Dutch Army was so easily routed, and the ulterior operations which followed, there was nothing of that brilliancy which marked other victories achieved by British bravery, but no conquest was attended with more advantages and permanent results. A noble colony was obtained for Great Britain with little loss of life, and the only portion of Africa worth her occupation was secured to the "Mistress of the Seas."

CHAPTER 4

The Battle of Maida, 1806

It has been remarked with great justice, that until the Peninsular war had been for some time in progress, the military enterprises of Great Britain invariably failed from the blind policy of those who planned them. Instead of condensing the power of the empire into one grand and sustained effort, its strength was frittered away in paltry and unprofitable expeditions. An army, imposing in its full integrity, if subdivided into corps, and employed on detached services, and in different countries, can achieve nothing beyond a partial success, for soon after its divided brigades are landed on their scenes of action, their weakness produces their discomfiture, and they retire necessarily before a superior force. In the first moment of disembarkation it may create a temporary alarm; but beyond this no object can be gained, and the result ends in an idle demonstration.

Political details are generally unconnected with the actual occurrences on the battlefield; and it will be enough to remark, that Sicily should have at this period commanded more attention from Britain than she did. Naturally defensible, with a well affected population of nearly a million and a half, she had been taught to place but little reliance on her allies. One British corps held Messina, but a French force was moving to the extremity of Calabria, avowedly to drive it from the island. Though well-affected, the Sicilians were distrustful; they feared that they should be abandoned to the vengeance of those troops who had already overrun Naples, and they believed that the British regiment waited only until the French army should make its descent, when they would embark for Malta, and leave the Sicilians to their fate.

At this time, Sir John Stuart succeeded Sir James Craig, a man best described by terming him an "old-school commander." Under

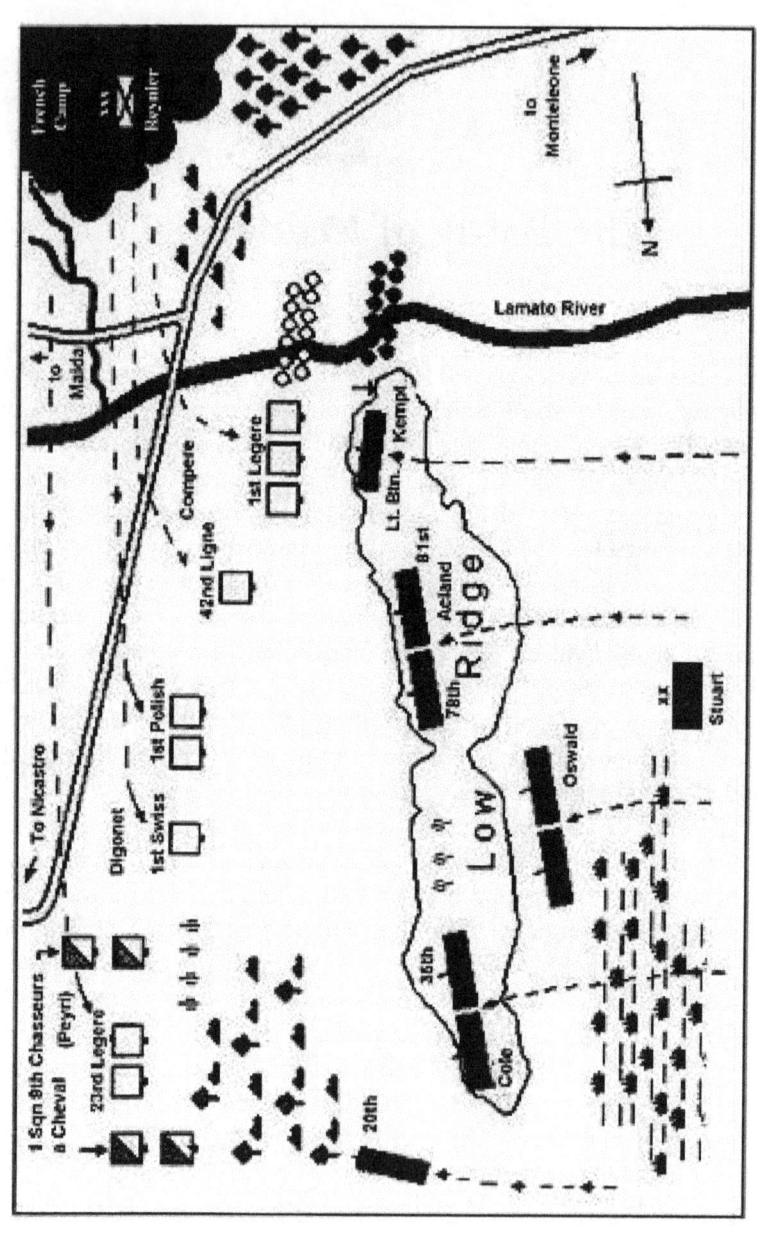

him the army had been totally inactive; and eight thousand excellent troops were permitted to occupy their quarters idly, when so much depended upon a bold, even though not a very fortunate, display of energy in the British. Stuart at once perceived the mischievous consequences this indolence of his predecessor had occasioned; and he determined by active operations to redeem the British Army from the apathetic character it had too justly obtained among the Sicilian people.

The British corps, amounting to eight thousand men, was concentrated at Messina. In Calabria, the French were considerably detached; and though numerically stronger, with three thousand in the South, four thousand in Upper Calabria, and the remainder occupying numerous posts, it was quite practicable to take them in detail, effect a landing between the two corps, engage them separately, and clear the country from St. Euphemia to the Castle of Scylla. To insure success, despatch and secrecy were required. The first rested with Stuart, and every arrangement necessary on his part was effected; the latter depended on the Sicilian court, and by it the secrecy of the intended expedition was undoubtedly betrayed.

On the 28th of June, at Melazao, the embarkation of five thousand men was quietly accomplished, and on the third morning they landed on the beach of St. Euphemia. During the 2nd and 3rd stores and supplies were disembarked; and moving forward, on that evening the pickets of the rival armies confronted each other. The enemy's force was at first supposed to be merely the division of Upper Calabria; but that of the South had formed a junction; and Reynier had now seven thousand infantry, and a few troops of cavalry amounting to three hundred and fifty sabres.

The British in numbers were greatly inferior. Five thousand infantry, six six-pounders and eight mountain guns formed their whole strength. Reynier was also in position—his army being posted on some heights which overlooked the march of the British as they moved through a low country, at first partially wooded, but opening into a spacious plain, and of course permitting their numbers and dispositions to be correctly ascertained by their enemy during the advance.

This, as the result proved, was an unfortunate advantage for the French general. Whether reckoning too much on his opponent's inferiority of force, or undervaluing the character of his soldiers, Reynier, supposing that Stuart, having advanced in error, would retire on dis-

The 1st Light breaks at Maida

covering his mistake, abandoned the heights, passed a, river in his front, and offered battle on the plain. As his columns approached, General Stuart at once perceived, from the ground they covered, that Reynier's force was much larger than he had expected, and that he had united his detached brigades; but, with the just confidence of a British leader he trusted to the bravery of his troops; and in that safe reliance boldly stood "the hazard of the die."

The battle commenced (6th July) about nine o'clock, and there was no manoeuvring on either side. The ground was level, and both armies, under cover of their light troops, advanced steadily and deployed into line. The enemy's left was composed of *voltigeurs*, and the right of the British that opposed them (Kempt's brigade) was formed of a light infantry battalion and the Corsican Rangers.

After an interchange of three volleys, the French were ordered to advance; at the same time the British lowered their bayonets, and both pressed boldly forward. The front ranks were now within six paces of each other—the French advancing, cheered by the "*En avant, mes enfans!*" of their officers. The British needed no encouragement; on they came, with that imposing steadiness which told what the result must be, when bayonets crossed, and "steel met steel." The *voltigeurs* had not firmness to abide the shock; they broke and turned, but too late for flight to save them. Their front rank was bayonetted and trodden down, while the rear endeavoured to escape by a disorderly rush from the field, exposed to severe loss from the British artillery.

Kempt's gallant and successful charge was ably seconded by Ackland's brigade, which held the right centre. They advanced against the demi-brigade opposed to them, forced it back across the Amato, and never allowed the routed wing one moment to rally. The pursuit was so ardently continued that for a mile the French were followed by the victors, suffering heavily in killed and wounded, and losing a number of prisoners.

This success, though brilliant, was far from being decisive. The ardour of the right wing had carried it away, leaving the left totally unsupported, and open to Reynier's undivided efforts. From the superiority of his force, he showed a larger front, and availing himself of this advantage, endeavoured to turn the British left, and in this attempt his cavalry had nearly succeeded. After a feint upon the centre, they wheeled sharply to the right, making a flank movement, while their infantry threatened the British line with a charge. This wag the crisis of the action. The French advanced, Stuart refusing his flank, and obliquing his line from the centre. Reynier's cavalry were about to charge, when, fortunately, the 20th regiment, under Colonel Ross, which had landed after the march of the army, came up.

The attack was already made, the cavalry advancing, when Ross, under cover of some underwood, deployed in double-quick. Within a short distance, a close and murderous volley was thrown in, and the cavalry completely broken. The British line cheered and moved forward, the French gave way, and a complete *déroute* succeeded. No victory, considering the numbers opposed, could have been more decisive. Seven hundred killed, a thousand prisoners, and a large proportion of wounded, were the estimated loss of the enemy, while this was achieved by an amount of casualties greatly disproportioned, the victors having but one officer and forty-four men killed, and eleven officers and two hundred and seventy-one men wounded.

For that night, the British Army bivouacked on the battleground, and having received supplies from the shipping, advanced on the 6th to overtake the enemy's rear; while a brigade under Colonel Oswald marched on the French depot at Montelione, of which it took possession, making six hundred prisoners. The whole of the commissariat stores, with the entire baggage, and the military chest, were captured; and the remnant of the French army was saved only by abandoning arms and accoutrements, and retiring with all the confusion attendant upon a signal defeat.

Nothing could exceed the enthusiasm with which the victors were received. The defended places along the coast, turned on the land side by the army, of course surrendered unconditionally. The whole of the Peninsula was rapidly crossed, and on the 11th of July, the leading British brigade invested the Castle of Scylla.

This place, so deeply associated with ancient recollections, stands on a sheer rook, commanding the eastern point of the entrance of the Straits of Messina. The difficulties experienced by navigators occasionally in this confined channel, almost realise the old-world legends of its dangers. Once caught in the currents, when passing Cape Pelorus with light or contrary winds, a vessel must run for the anchorage, which lies directly beneath the batteries of the castle; and hence the possession of the place, especially to a maritime nation, was an object of paramount importance.

For some days, the efforts of the English were confined to firing on the castle with the field guns. Of course, artillery of a light calibre could effect nothing but annoyance; until, on the 19th, when some heavy cannon were obtained from Messina. On the 21st they were placed in battery and opened with great effect; and on the same evening, as the guns were breaching rapidly, the commandant accepted terms, and surrendered the castle to the besiegers.

Although military achievements, on a minor scale, have been eclipsed by the more brilliant conquests obtained by British armies in subsequent campaigns, still Maida was not only a glorious, but, in its results, a most important victory. Independently of humbling a presumptuous enemy, raising the depressed reputation of the British Army, and converting the distrusting population of Sicily into grateful admirers, the positive results of Sir John Stuart's expedition were the destruction of all the military and naval resources of Calabria, and the occupation of a post which for eighteen months secured the navigation of the Straits of Messina, and, in a great degree, occasioned the meditated descent on Sicily to fail.

Chapter 5

The Battle of Rolica, 1808

Spain and Portugal having been overrun by the French armies, Britain determined to make an effort in the cause of freedom, and come to the assistance of the oppressed.

The force destined for the relief of Portugal was sent partly from Ireland, and partly from Gibraltar. Nine thousand men, from Cork, under Sir Arthur Wellesley, landed in Mondego Bay on the 6th of August, and these were joined, two days afterwards, by Spencer's division of five thousand, making thus a total force of about fourteen thousand, in which two hundred of the 20th Light Dragoons and eighteen pieces of artillery were included.

A combined movement with a Portuguese corps under Bernardine Friere having been arranged, it was determined to move at once upon the capital; and on the morning of the 9th the British advanced guard, consisting of a part of the 60th and 95th Rifles, commenced the march, supported by the brigades of Generals Hill and Ferguson. On the next day, the remainder of the army followed—the men provided with sixty rounds of cartridges, provisions for three days, and attended by a number of mules, loaded with stores of various descriptions.

> No troops ever took the field in higher spirits, or in a state of more perfect discipline. Confident in their leader likewise, and no less confident in themselves, they desired nothing more ardently than to behold their enemy.

On the 12th, Friere's corps joined at Leiria, but, under different pretexts, the Portuguese commander declined co-operating as he had promised, and limited his assistance to one weak brigade of infantry and two hundred and fifty horse. Undaunted by this early disclosure of imbecility and bad faith. Sir Arthur determined to push on, and

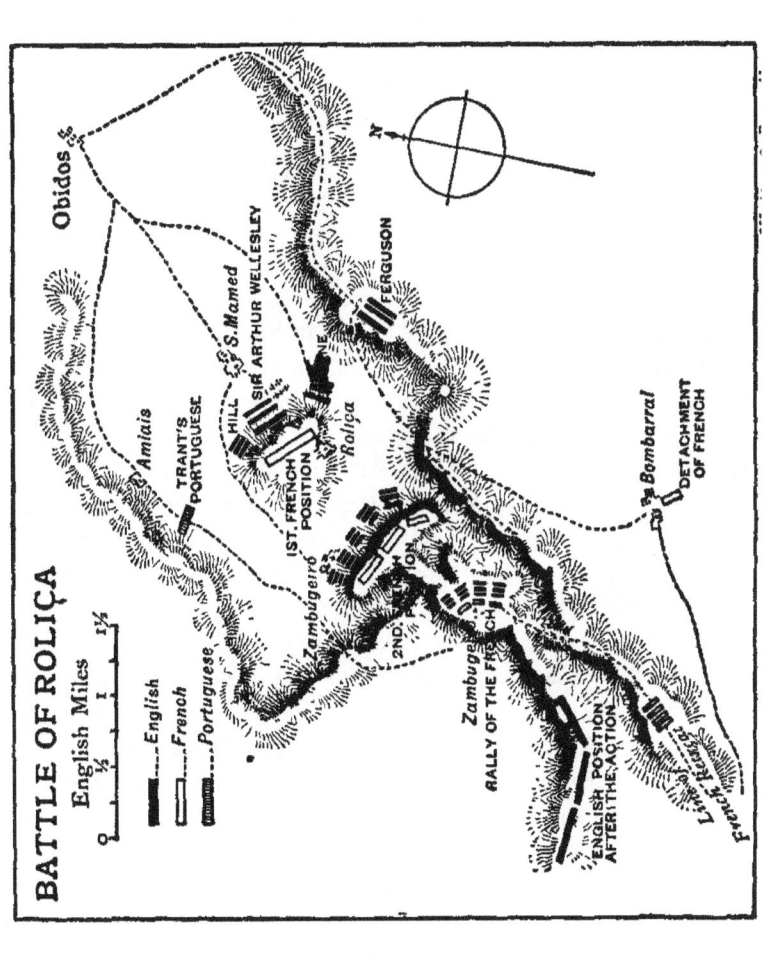

endeavour to engage the Duke of Abrantes before he could unite himself with Loison.

On receiving intelligence of the descent of the British, Junot, adding the brigade of Thomières to that of Delaborde, despatched the latter towards Mondego, to observe the enemy closely, and use every means to retard their advance. Delaborde, accordingly moving to the coast, found himself on the eve of an affair with the British, and he fell back leisurely as they advanced. His rear-guard quitted Caldas the evening before Sir Arthur entered it; and on the following morning, and for the first time on the Peninsula, the rival armies of France and Britain found themselves in each other's presence.

On the 15th, a trifling affair of outposts produced a few casualties, and on the 16th, Delaborde's position was reconnoitred and dispositions made to attack it.

This, in a European command, was to be Wellington's maiden field. In the numbers engaged, Rolica bore no proportion to the masses combatant in future battles, but it' was a well-contested and sanguinary encounter, and worthy to be the name first engraven on the long scroll of victories of which it gave such glorious promise.

The French position, in natural strength and romantic beauty, was unequalled; and when Delaborde had made up his mind to risk a battle, he displayed consummate judgment in selecting the ground on which the trial of strength should be decided.

The villages of Rolica and Caldas stand at either extremity of an extensive valley, opening to the west. In the centre, Obidos, with its ruined castle and splendid aqueduct, recalls the days of Moorish glory. The village of Rolica stands on a bold height, surrounded by vineyards and olive groves, and a sandy plain extends in front, thickly studded with shrubs and dwarf wood. The eminence on which the village is placed, and where the French general formed his line of battle, had one flank resting on a rugged height, and the other on a mountain impassable to any but a goatherd. Behind, lay a number of passes through the ridges in his rear, affording Delaborde a means of retreat; or, if he chose to contest them, a formidable succession of mountain posts.

All the arrangements for attack having been completed on the preceding evening, at dawn the British got under arms. A sweeter morning never broke—the mountain mists dispersed, the sun shone gloriously out, a thousand birds were singing, and myriads of wild flowers shed their fragrance around. Nature seemed everywhere in quiet and repose, presenting a strange contrast to the roar of battle which im-

BATTLE OF ROLICA

mediately succeeded, and the booming of artillery, as, repeated by a thousand echoes, it reverberated among the lately peaceful hills.

In three columns, the allied brigades left their bivouacs. The right (Portuguese), consisting of twelve hundred infantry and fifty dragoons, were directed to make a considerable detour, turn the enemy's left flank, and bear down upon his rear. The left, two brigades of infantry, three companies of rifles, a brigade of light artillery, and forty horse, were to ascend the hills of Obidos, drive in Delaborde's posts, and turn his right at Rolica. Ferguson, who commanded, was also to watch lest Loison should move from Rio Mayor, and, if he came up, engage him, and prevent a junction with Delaborde. The centre, composed of four brigades—those of Hill, Crawford, Nightingale, and Fane—two brigades of guns, the remainder of the cavalry, and four hundred Portuguese light infantry, were directed to advance up the heights and attack the enemy in front.

To traverse the distance between the British bivouac and French outposts (three leagues), consumed a good portion of the morning; and the march to the battleground, whether viewed with relevance to the beauty of its scenery, or the order of its execution, was most imposing.

When sudden irregularities of the surface disturbed the order of a column, it halted until the distances were corrected, and then marched silently on with the coolness of a review. Presently the light troops became engaged, the centre broke into columns of regiments, while the left pressed forward rapidly, and the rifles, on the right, bore down on the tirailleurs. Delaborde's position was now critical, for Ferguson, topping the heights, threatened his rear. But the French general acted promptly—he abandoned the plain, and falling back upon the passes of the Sierra, took up a new position less assailable than the former one; and, from the difficult nature of the mountain surface, requiring, on Sir Arthur's part, a new disposition of attack.

Five separate columns were now formed, and to each a different pass was allotted. The openings in the heights were so narrow and difficult, that only a portion of the columns could come into fire. The pass on the extreme right was attacked by the Portuguese; the light troops of Hill's brigade and the 5th regiment advanced against the second; the centre was to be carried by the 9th and 29th, the fourth by the 45th, and the fifth by the 82nd.

Unfortunately, the front attack was made either too soon, or difficulties had delayed the flanking corps—and, in consequence, the passes were all stormed, before Delaborde had been even aware that he was endangered on his flank and rear. Regardless of the ground, than which nothing could be more formidable, the assailants mounted the ravines. Serious obstacles met them at every step rocks and groves overhung the gorges in the hills—and where the ground was tolerably open for a space from rocks, it was covered thickly with brushwood and wild myrtle. the order of the column was deranged; while a broken surface concealed the enemy, and suffered the French to keep up a withering fusillade on troops who had not leisure to return it.

The centre pass, on which the 29th and 9th were directed to advance, was particularly difficult. The 29th led, and the 9th supported it. Entering the gorge undauntedly, the leading companies were permitted to approach a ravine, with precipitous rocks on one side and a thick myrtle wood on the other. From both a tremendous fire was unexpectedly opened. In front and on the flanks, the men fell by dozens; and, as the leading company was annihilated, the column, cumbered by its own dead and wounded, was completely arrested in its movement. But the check was only momentary.

Colonel Lake, who led the regiment on horseback, waved his hat and called on the men to follow. A wild cheer was returned, and a rush made up the pass. Notwithstanding the sustained fusillade on every side, the forward movement was successful—and after overcoming every attempt to repel their daring charge, with diminished numbers the 29th crowned the plateau.

But the enemy were not to be easily beaten. Before the 9th could clear the pass, or the 29th form their line, a French battalion advanced and charged. They were most gallantly received; a severe contest ensued; and, after a mutual slaughter, the enemy were repulsed. With increased numbers, again and again the charges were repeated and repelled. At last the 9th got into action; and the head of the 5th regiment began to show itself as it topped the summit of the second pass. On every point the attacks had been successful, and to save himself from being cut off, Delaborde retired in perfect order; and from the difficulty of the ground and his superiority in cavalry, although pressed by the light troops, effected his retreat with little molestation.

This brilliant affair, from the strength of their position, and the obstinacy with which the French contested every inch of ground, cost the British a heavy loss. Even, when forced from the heights, Delaborde attempted to take a new position, and hold the village of Zambugeira. But he was driven back with the loss of three guns—and

8°
4°
C. Ortega
Corunna
Ferrol
C. Penas
Santander
Oviedo
Lugo
Minho
Leon
Espinosa
Villafranca
Astorga
R. Esla
Saldana
Vigo
R. Sil
Carrion
Benevente
Valdaras
Villapando
Valladolid
Medina
Oporto
R. Douro
Tordessilas
Salamanca
Villacastian
Almeida
Ciudad Rodrigo
Busaco
Fuentes de Onoro
Guadarama
40°
Coimbra
Aranjuez
Talavera
Abrantes
Toledo
Vimieiro
Tagus R.
Santarem
Torres Vedras
Badajos
LISBON
Medellin
Albuera
Guadiana R.
Sierra
Baylen
Cordova
Guadalquivir R.
PORTUGAL
Seville
C. St. Vincent
Malaga
Cadiz
Barrosa
36°
C. Trafalgar
Gibraltar
8°
4°

retreating through the pass of Runa, by a long night march, he gained Montecheque next day.

The French casualties in killed, wounded, and prisoners amounted to a thousand men, and the British to about half that; number. Delaborde was among the wounded, and Colonel Lake in the return of the killed.

Delaborde's defeat having left the road to Torres Vedras open, Sir Arthur pursued the French to Villa, Verde, where the British halted for the night, and, cheered by his opening success, the British leader seemed determined to improve it. Orders were accordingly issued to prepare for a rapid march next day, and "it seemed as if no check would be given to the ardour of the troops till they should have won a second victory." But despatches were received that night, announcing the arrival of General Anstruther with a reinforcement of troops and stores. The fleet were reported to be at anchor off Peniche; and, to cover the disembarkation, and unite himself with the corps on board the transports, Sir Arthur's march was directed on Lourinho. There the British bivouacked that night, and on the next morning took a position beside the village of Vimiero.

CHAPTER 6

The Battle of Vimiero, 1808

Vimiero stands at the bottom of a valley, and at the eastern extremity of a ridge of hills extending westward towards the sea. The River Maceira flows through it, and on the opposite side, heights rise eastward, over which winds the mountain road of Lourinho. In front of the village a plateau of some extent is slightly elevated above the surrounding surface; but it, in turn, is completely overlooked by the heights on either side. The British, never anticipating an attack, had merely taken up ground for the night, and with more attention to convenience than security. Six brigades occupied the high ground westward of Vimiero—one battalion, the 50th, with some rifle companies, were bivouacked on the plateau, having a half brigade of nines, and a half brigade of six pounders. The eastern heights were occupied by pickets only, as water could not be procured in the vicinity—and in the valley, the cavalry and reserve artillery had taken their ground for the night.

The communication immediately made by Sir Arthur Wellesley to his senior officer, Sir Harry Burrard, both of the past and the intended operations, had been unfavourably received—and Sir Harry declined the daring but judicious step of an immediate advance on Mafra, by which the position taken by the French on the heights of Torres Vedras must have been necessarily turned. In fact, to every suggestion of Sir Arthur he raised continuous objections, and seemed totally opposed to any forward movement. He pleaded, in apology for inaction, that the cavalry was weak, the artillery badly horsed; that a march, which should remove the British from their shipping, would interrupt their supplies and endanger the army; and the best of the bad reasons which he gave was the expected arrival of Sir John Moore with a strong reinforcement.

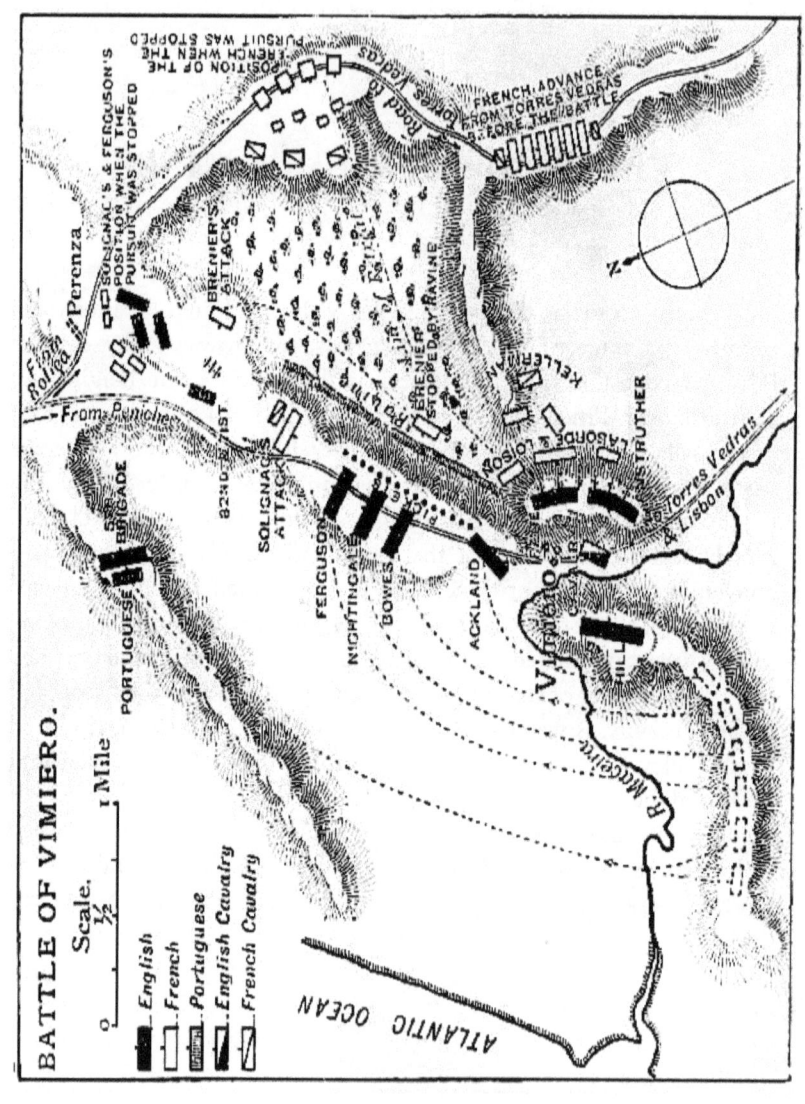

It was useless in Sir Arthur Wellesley to point out, as he did, the advantages of an advance, with an assurance, which proved true, that if they did not, the French would become assailants. Sir Harry appeared to have formed a stubborn resolution of remaining quiet that no argument or remonstrance could disturb, and Sir Arthur Wellesley returned to his camp, convinced that the military incapacity of his superior officer would, when it paralysed early success as it did that of Rolica, entail upon the expedition ulterior disaster and disgrace. It was otherwise decreed, and the decision of an enemy wreathed the laurel on Wellesley's brow, of which the timidity of a feebleminded colleague would have robbed him.

Delaborde had executed his orders to check the advance of the British with a zeal and ability that added greatly to his military reputation. Junot, in the interim, was actively engaged in concentrating his brigades, and drawing every disposable man from his garrisons, to enable him to bring a force to bear against the British, that, from its superior formation, must ensure success. His whole corps was formed into two divisions; Delaborde commanding one, and Loison the other, while the reserve, composed entirely of grenadiers, was entrusted to Kellerman. All his dispositions having been completed, the Duke of Abrantes advanced to Vimiero, where he had ascertained that his enemy was halted.

Sir Arthur was awakened at midnight by a German officer in charge of the outlying picket, with the intelligence of Junot's movements, and an assurance that an attack was certain, as the French advance was not above a league distant. Patrols were immediately sent out; and while every care was taken against surprise, the line was not alarmed, nor the men permitted to be disturbed.

Junot quitted his position on the evening of the 20th, and marched all night by roads bad in themselves, and interrupted by numerous defiles; consequently, great delay occurred, and it was seven o'clock next morning, when he arrived within four miles of the British outposts. The formation of his columns was effected unseen, as the broken ground behind which he made his dispositions, entirely concealed his movements. The first intimation of a serious attack was only given when a mass of Junot's cavalry deployed in front of the picket that was observing the Lourinho road. Perceiving instantly the point on which the French were about to direct their column, Sir Arthur crossed the ravine with the brigades of Ferguson, Nightingale, Aucland, and Bowes, thus securing his weakest point—the left—before Junot had made a demonstration against it.

Presently the enemy's columns came on; the right by the Lourinho road, and left marching on the plateau, occupied by the 50th and Rifles. The onset of both divisions was made with the usual impetuosity of Frenchmen, and in both the British skirmishers were driven in.

The British right was furiously attacked. Unchecked by the light troops covering the line, the French came boldly forward, until it found itself directly in front of the 36th, 40th, and 71st It deployed instantly, and several volleys of musketry were mutually returned, and at a distance so close as to render the effect murderous. But the fusillade was ended quickly; the 82nd and 29th pushed forward, and joined their comrades when pressed by an enormous superiority. "Charge!" was the order; and a cheer, "loud, regular, and appalling," announced that Britain was coming on.

The French stood manfully; but though they waited the onset, they could not withstand it. They were driven from the field—a vain attempt to rally, when the 71st and 82nd had flung themselves on the ground to recover breath, failed—and six guns were taken. The front rank of the French division was literally annihilated; it lay as it had fallen, and told with what determination it had stood, and the desperation with which it had been assaulted.

On the left, the French column having pushed the rifles before it, advanced upon the 50th formed in line. The regiment was strong, numbering about nine hundred bayonets, and supported by a half brigade of guns; and though the French had seven pieces with their column, it suffered heavily from the British cannonade. The enemy's advance was made in close order of half battalions. Sheltered from the fire of the artillery, the French halted behind a broken hillock, closed up their ranks, and advanced to the attack. The 50th remained until this moment with "ordered arms."

With excellent judgment, the colonel, leaving the left wing of his regiment in line, throw his right into echelons of companies, and ordered it to form line upon the left. But there was not time to complete the formation, as the enemy came on, opening a hot but inefficient fire from its flanks. Part of the right wing of the 50th bore directly on the angle of the advancing column—and when within twenty paces, the order was given to fire, and that to "Charge!" succeeded. Broken totally by the close discharge, the angle of the column forced itself on the centre; all was instantly disorganised, and the artillery cutting their traces, added to the confusion. The British pressed on, the French got

Battle of Vimiero

mobbed, and assisted by part of the 20th light dragoons, a column five times numerically superior were for two miles fairly driven from their ground by one regiment, until they were relieved by the French cavalry reserve, which came up in a force not to be resisted.

While these more important operations were repulsed, the town of Vimiero was attacked by a lesser column (Kellerman's reserve), that had flanked the larger, and the 43rd regiment was furiously assailed. One company occupied the churchyard, another held some houses that covered the road by which the French attack was made; and the fire of both was so destructive, that the column was repelled with immense slaughter. On the extreme left, the 97th and 52nd repulsed Delaborde with considerable loss; on every point the attack failed, and the field was won.

No troops fought better than the French, and no battle could have been more determinately contested. The enemy's reserve "performed prodigies of valour, advancing under a cross fire of musketry and cannon, and never giving way until the bayonets of the British troops drove them down the descent." But they were routed on every side; and, with relation to the numbers engaged, the slaughter was terrific. Upwards of three thousand Frenchmen were killed and wounded, and a number of prisoners made, while the British loss was computed, in killed, wounded, and missing, at seven hundred and eighty-three.

One casualty was sincerely deplored. In leading a squadron of the 20th, Lieutenant-Colonel Taylor was killed. He had charged the broken infantry of Kellerman, and committed sad havoc among the *élite* of the reserve, when, surrounded by a whole brigade of French cavalry, he fell in the *mêlée*, shot through the heart.

Sir Harry Burrard landed after the battle commenced, but very prudently left the termination of the contest in his hands by whom the first disposition had been made. Sir Harry was not in time to assist in the victory—but he had ample leisure to mar its results. Wellesley urged that this was the moment to advance, push on to Torres Vedras, place Junot between two fires, and oblige him to begin a retreat of immense difficulty by Alenquer and Villa Franca. All was admirably prepared for the movement. The supply of ammunition was sufficient, provisions were abundant, and the troops in high courage and superb discipline. The French, on the contrary, were depressed by an unexpected defeat; and, greatly disorganised and wearied by long marches, were certain of being materially inconvenienced by an immediate advance of the British.

71st Highlanders turn the guns on Brennier's division

But Sir Harry was immovable. He had made his mind up to await the arrival of Sir John Moore before he should advance a step from Vimiero. A victory had been gained—a complete and brilliant victory. But what was that to him? He said:

"The cavalry, were certainly not strengthened, nor the artillery horses improved, by the exertions they had undergone."

Stop he would and Junot was permitted to return without annoyance; and the British, who should have never halted until they had reached Lisbon, rested on the ground they won.

Is it not inconceivable, that Britain should have consigned her armies to the leading of antiquated tacticians, bigoted in old-world notions, and who would scarcely venture beyond a second bridge without spending half the day in reconnoitring? But such things were—and the energies of the first military people in the world were paralysed for half a century, by commands being entrusted to men, who, in cases of ordinary embarrassment, would have been found incompetent to extricate a regiment from a difficulty. But such things were!

CHAPTER 7

The Battle of Corunna, 1809

A period of inaction succeeded the victory at Vimiero. Burrard was superseded in his command by Sir Hew Dalrymple, and the convention of Cintra perfected, by which an army was restored to France, that, had Sir Arthur Wellesley's advice been attended to, must have been eventually destroyed or driven into such extremity as should have produced an unconditional surrender. Other articles in this disgraceful treaty recognised a full exercise of rights of conquest to the French, secured to them the enormous plunder their rapacity had accumulated, and granted an amnesty to every traitor who had abandoned his country, and aided the invaders in effecting its subjugation. No wonder that this precious convention occasioned in Britain a universal feeling of disgust. No wonder that blood spilled in vain, and treasure uselessly wasted, roused popular indignation to a pitch of excitement which no occurrence in modern history can parallel.

Within twelve months from the commencement of the war Britain had sent over to the Spanish armies (besides 2,000,000) 150 pieces of field artillery, 42 thousand rounds of ammunition, 200 thousand muskets, 61 thousand swords, 79 thousand pikes, 23 million ball cartridges, 6 million leaden balls, 15 thousand barrels of gunpowder, 92 thousand suits of clothing, 356 thousand sets of accoutrements and pouches, 310 thousand pairs of shoes, 37 thousand pairs of boots, 40 thousand tents, 250 thousand yards of cloth, 10 thousand sets of camp equipage, 118 thousand yards of linen, 50 thousand great coats, 50 thousand canteens, 54 thousand haversacks, with a variety of other stores, far too numerous to be recapitulated.

The particulars of the treaty of Cintra, immediately on being known in Britain, occasioned the recall of Sir Hew Dalrymple; while under the plea of ill health, his colleague, Sir Harry Burrard, resigned and returned home. What a different result the Portuguese campaign would have exhibited had these two old gentlemen been left in a district command, and not been allowed to check a career of victory which opened with such glorious promise!

Sir Arthur Wellesley had already returned to Britain, and many officers of all ranks followed his example. The command of the army devolved on Sir John Moore, a man most deservedly respected by the country, and popular with his soldiers.

Meanwhile, the general indication of national resistance to French oppression on the part of the Spaniards, encouraged hopes that if assisted by Britain, the independence of the Peninsula might be restored. This was a consideration worthy of a statesman's serious regard in both France and Britain—for the thraldom or independence of Spain was an object of vital importance. As to what might be expected from the Spaniards themselves in any attempt made for their own liberation, their invaders and their allies seemed to have formed an erroneous estimate—the British over-rating the importance of their exertions in the field, as much as the French undervalued that patriotic impulse, which had wakened up the slumbering spirit of the people.

The British cabinet, however, determined to foster this national feeling, and by munificent supplies and the presence of a British Army, stimulate the Spanish people to assert their lost liberty, and fling off a yoke no longer tolerable. For this purpose, a force of twenty thousand men was directed to be assembled at Valladolid, and a reinforcement of thirteen thousand, under Sir David Baird, was despatched from Britain to join them; the whole were to be placed under the orders of Sir John Moore.

Although Sir David's corps was landed by the middle of October, the army of Lisbon was not in a condition to move until the end of the month; and then, under a false belief that the direct route to Salamanca was impracticable for the passage of artillery, the batteries and cavalry, with a protecting brigade of three thousand infantry, were moved by Badajoz and the Escurial, entailing on them an additional march of upwards of one hundred and fifty miles. Worse still, a delay in commencing operations was unavoidable, and that was attended with the worst results.

The whole of Sir John Hope's corps having been at last collected, and the cavalry assembled at Villa Vicosa, the order to move forward was given.

On the 5th of November, Sir John Moore was at Atalia, on the 8th he reached Almeida, and on the 11th his advanced guard crossed the rivulet that divides Spain from Portugal, and entered Cuidad Rodrigo. At San Martin, he slept in the house of the *curé*, and occupied the same bed that had the former year been assigned to Junot and Loison on their respective marches, and on the 13th he entered Salamanca.

There, disastrous news awaited him—for one of his supporting armies was already *hors de combat*. Count Belvidere, having made an absurd movement on Burgos, was attacked by a superior force, and his raw levies completely routed; while previously, Blake's army had been utterly dispersed, and the magazines at Reynosa taken. To add to this mass of evil tidings, intelligence arrived that the fall of Madrid might be confidently expected, while, instead of his advance into Spain being covered with an army of seventy thousand men, Moore found himself in an open town without a gun, without a Spanish picket, with only three infantry brigades, and the French outposts but three marches distant.

Madrid fell—the news could not be credited—and it was asserted that, though the Retiro was taken, the town held obstinately out. The inaction of the British was generally censured; the envoy had remonstrated on the subject; and the army did not conceal their impatience. Influenced by these considerations, Moore determined to make a diversion on the capital, and attack Soult, who was at Saldanha, on the Carion. A forward movement followed—Baird was directed to march from Astorga, and Romana was informed of the intended operation, and requested to assist.

The decision of attacking Soult was known to the army and gave general satisfaction. On the 16th, headquarters were at Toro, and passing Villapondo and Valderosa, on the 20th Sir John reached Majorga, and was joined by Baird's division, making an united force of twenty-three thousand five hundred infantry, two thousand four hundred cavalry, and, including a brigade of three-pounders—from its small calibre perfectly useless—an artillery of nearly fifty guns. Soult's corps amounted to sixteen thousand infantry and twelve hundred dragoons. The great portion of the former were at Saldanha, and Debelle's cavalry at Sahagun.

While thus advancing, the brilliant affair between Lord Paget and the French cavalry shed a passing glory on a series of operations, whose results were generally so calamitous. We shall give the affair in the words of the noble colonel of the 10th Hussars, than whom, on that occasion, no one "by daring deed" more effectually contributed

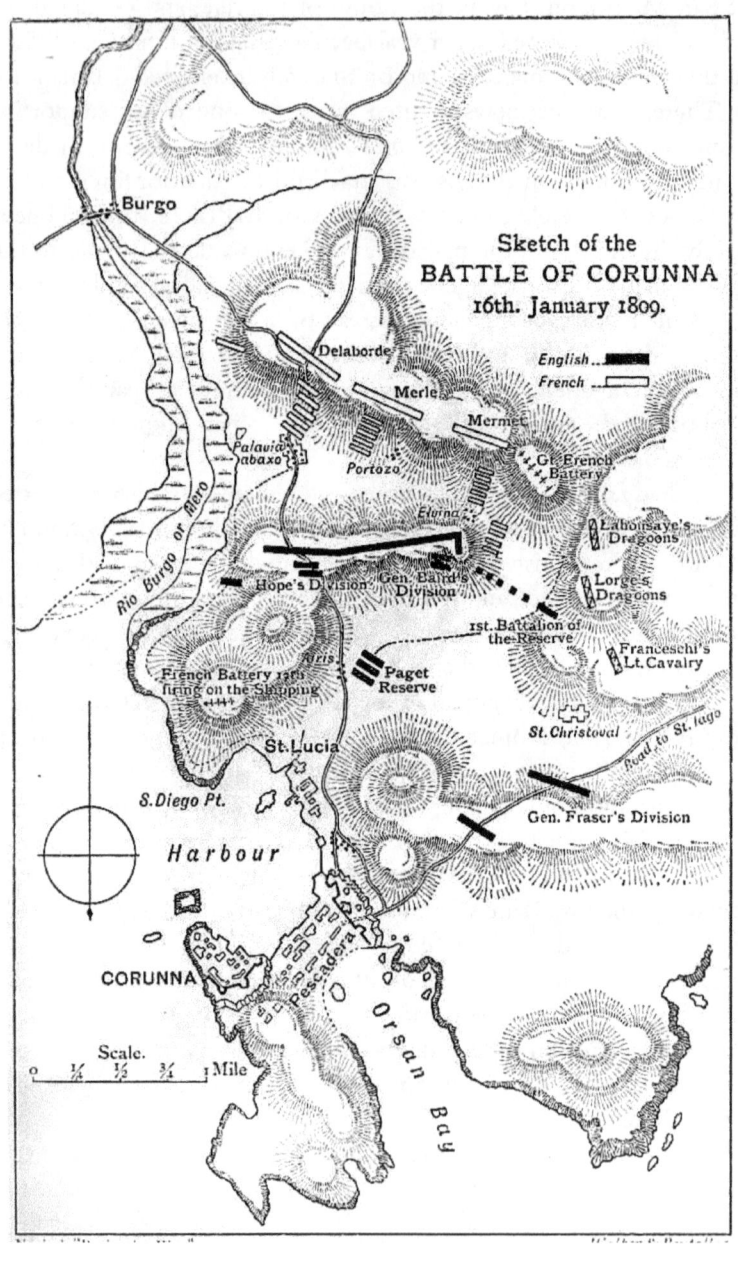

to victory.

The Monastero Melgar Abaxo is distant about three leagues from Sahagun, in which place a corps of seven hundred French cavalry were reported to be lodged. As they were at some distance from the main body of the French Army, it was deemed practicable to cut them off, and Lord Paget determined, at all events, to make the attempt. He accordingly put himself at the head of the 10th and 15th Hussars, and in the middle of a cold wintry night, when the direct route to Salamanca was impracticable, for the ground was covered with snow, set off for that purpose.

When they had ridden about two-thirds of the way, Lord Paget divided his force, and desiring General Slade, with the 10th, to pursue the course of the Cea, and to enter the town by that side, he himself, followed by the 15th, wheeled off to approach it by a different route. It was not long before his lordship's party fell in with a picket of the enemy; and all, except one man, were either cut down or made prisoners. But the escape of one was as injurious, under existing circumstances, as the escape of the whole; for the alarm was given, and before the 15th could reach the place the enemy were ready to receive them.

It was now broad daylight, and as our troops drew near, the French were soon formed in what appeared to be an open plain, at no great distance from the town. The 15th were wheeled into line in a moment, and as there was no time to be lost, they followed their leader at a brisk trot, with the intention of charging; but when they were yet fifty yards from the enemy, they found that a wide ditch divided them, and that the French had availed themselves of other inequalities in the ground, of which, when some way off, they had not been aware.

A pause was now necessarily made, but one instant served to put the whole again in motion. The regiment, wheeling to its left, soon found a convenient place for crossing; and though the enemy manoeuvred actively to hinder the formation, they were again in line, and advancing to the charge, within five minutes from the commencement of the check. A few changes of ground now took place, as each corps strove to gain the flank of the other, but they were only a few. The British cavalry effected its object, and then coming down at full speed upon their opponents, who stood to receive the shock, they overthrew them in an instant. Many were killed upon the spot, many more unhorsed, and one hundred and fifty-seven were made prisoners, including two lieutenant-colonels. On this occasion the British cavalry amounted only to four hundred men, whilst that of the French fell not short of seven hundred.

The weather continued bad; the troops were a good deal knocked up by forced marching, and Sir John halted on the 22nd and 23rd for supplies, intending by a night march to reach the Carion, and attack Soult on the morrow. Every account made the British numerically greater than the enemy, and though the French had been reinforced, still Moore's army was stronger by fully five thousand men.

All dispositions were made for the intended attack. At eight at night, the army were to move in two columns, and the right, which was to force the bridge and penetrate to Saldanha, was actually getting under arms, when couriers arrived "loaded with heavy tidings." The French were moving in all directions to cut the British off; the corps which had been marching south, was suddenly halted at Talavera; two strong divisions were moving from Placentia; the Badajoz Army was in full march on Salamanca—and Napoleon himself in the field, determined, as it was reported, to "sweep the British before him to the ocean."

This was, in truth, disastrous intelligence-. The orders to advance were countermanded instantly, the troops, who had already been mustering, were retired to their quarters, and the object of the expedition seemed virtually ended. The campaign was indeed a tissue of mistakes—operating with feeble allies, acting on fake information, advancing today, retiring tomorrow, with everything to harass and nothing to excite the soldier, until at last, the ill-fated and ill-planned expedition terminated in a ruinous retreat.

In making preparations for a rapid march before an enemy, that from report was overwhelming if not avoided, the 23rd of December was consumed, and the general plan for regressive operations was arranged by instantly retreating on Galicia.

All arrangements being completed, Moore commenced retreating on the 24th. Hope's division fell back on Castro Gonzalo, and Baird's on Valencia; while cavalry patrols were pushed forward on the Carion, with orders to retire at nightfall of the 25th, giving the reserve and light infantry, which formed the rear-guard, a start of some three or four hours in advance. All was admirably executed—and the columns, unmolested, reached their respective destinations.

The retreat continued, marked by some occasional affairs between the cavalry of the advanced and rear guard, which terminated invariably in favour of the latter. The hussar regiments behaved most nobly, and on every occasion, regardless of numbers, or the more discouraging movements of a retreat, they sought the combat, and always came off the conquerors.

The infantry already began to experience the annoyance of long marches, severe weather, and a very indifferent commissariat. To march over cut-up roads, and through an exhausted country, where no friendly place of strength protects, no well-supplied magazine refreshes, soon harasses the overloaded soldier. But that, when accomplished in the dead of winter—in cold and darkness, sleet and rain—was enough to have subdued the spirit of any army but a British one, retiring under every privation, and with seventy thousand veteran troops marching on their flanks and rear.

The army reached Benevente on the 27th—and the crossing of the Esla, though exceedingly troublesome, was effected with inconsiderable loss. The roads were wretched, the weather bad, and the French pursuit marked by the fiery character of their emperor. He crossed the Carpenteras, regardless of obstacles that would have discouraged the boldest—and, in a hurricane of sleet and hail, passed his army over the Guadarama, by a route declared impracticable even to a mountain peasant.

This bold operation, worthy of the conqueror of Italy, was followed up by an immediate advance. On the 26th the main body of the British continued retreating on Astorga the bridge across the Esla was destroyed—and the night of the 27th passed over in tolerable quiet. In the morning, however, the French were seen actively employed. Five hundred cavalry of the guard tried for the ford above the ruined bridge, found it, and passed over. The pickets forming the rear-guard at once confronted them, and, led on by Colonel Otway, charged repeatedly, and checked the leading squadron.

General Stuart put himself at the head of the pickets, while Lord Anglesea rode back to bring up the 10th. Charges were made on both sides; the pickets gave ground, the French advanced, but the 10th were speedily at hand, and came forward. The pickets rallied, they cheered and cut boldly in at speed, the French were overthrown and driven across the river, with the loss of their colonel (Le Fevre), and seventy officers and men.

This brilliant encounter had the results that boldness wins. The French kept a respectful distance, and thus, the column was enabled to gain Astorga without further molestation.

But the danger was momentarily increasing. From prisoners taken in the cavalry affair on the Esla, it was ascertained that, on the preceding evening, the headquarters of Napoleon's own corps were but sixteen miles from the bivouacs of the British, and to reach Villa Franca before the French was imperatively necessary. On that event how much depended—for on the possession of that road, in a great degree, would rest the safety or destruction of the British, as it opens through a defile into a country that for miles renders cavalry movements impracticable, and entirely protects the flanks of a retiring army.

It is astonishing how quickly a retreat in bad weather destroys the morale of the best army. The British divisions had marched from Sabugal on the 24th in the highest order; on the 30th, on reaching Astorga, their disorganisation had commenced; they seemed a mob flying from a victorious enemy, and General Moore himself exhibited a despondency that was apparent to all around him.

That he was an officer of great distinction everyone acknowledged during his life, and posterity will never deny it; but it was too manifest that a fear of responsibility, a dread of doing that which was wrong, of running himself and his troops into difficulties from which they might not be able to extricate themselves, were a great deal too active to permit either his talents or his judgment properly to exert their influence.

Sir John Moore had earned the highest reputation as a general of division; he was aware of this, and perhaps felt no inclination to risk it; at all events he was clearly incapable of despising partial obstacles in the pursuit of some great ultimate advantage; in one word, he was not a Wellington. Of this no more convincing proof need be given than the fact that, even at the moment when the preparations for the brief advance were going on, his whole heart and soul seemed turned towards the Portuguese frontier.

Romana had unfortunately given up the Leon route, and marching on Astorga, encumbering the roads with the ruins of his baggage, and worse still, filling the villages he passed through with crowds of ragged followers unable to get on—some from absolute decrepitude and want, and more from being attacked by fever of the worst type.

The retreat was renewed next morning, and the marching continued with such constancy that, by abandoning the sick and wounded, wasting the ammunition, and destroying the stores, the British outstripped pursuit, and on the 3rd of January found themselves in comparative safety. The cavalry, as usual, distinguished themselves; and at Cacabelos, where the rear-guard was overtaken, behaving with their customary *esprit*, they repelled the advance of the French hussars, and prevented the light troops from being surrounded and cut off. Indeed, the escape of the rifles was wonderful. They were retreating through the town, and part of the rear-guard had already crossed the bridge, when the French cavalry came suddenly on in overwhelming force, and galloping into the rear companies of the 95th, succeeded in making some prisoners.

The Rifles instantly broke into skirmishing order, and commenced retiring up the hill, when a body of *voltigeurs* rushed to the support of the cavalry, and the affair became serious. The 95th, however, had now thrown themselves into the vineyards behind the town, and kept up a rapid and well-directed fire. The French attempted to get in their rear, and charged boldly up the road, led on by General Colbert. But the fusillade from the vineyard was maintained with such precision that the French were driven back, leaving a number of dead on the field, among whom their brave and daring leader was included.

Sir John was also threatened with attack at Villa Franca. A strong column of infantry appeared on the heights, in full march on that division which was in position on the opposite hill. The artillery opened, and an engagement appeared inevitable. But checked by the cannonade, the forward movement of the French was arrested; and Sir John, anxious to reach the better position of Lugo, continued his retreat, and prudently avoided coming to a general action, where the ground had no military advantage to induce him to risk a combat. The main body marched to Herrieras, the reserve to Villa Franca, and the rear-guard moved at ten o'clock, and reached its bivouac at midnight.

The cavalry, no longer serviceable in a country rough, hilly, and wooded, with numerous enclosures around vineyards and plantations of mulberry trees, were sent on to Lugo; the infantry and artillery marching for the same place. During the whole day and night that distressing movement was executed, and forty miles were passed over roads on every side broken up, and in places, knee-deep. The men dropped down by whole sections on the wayside and died—some with curses, some with the voice of prayer in their mouths—while women and children, of whom an immense number had injudiciously been allowed to accompany the army, shared a similar fate.

Horrible scenes momentarily occurred—children frozen in their mothers' arms, women taken in labour, and, of course, perishing with their ill-fated progeny. Some were trying by the madness of intoxication to stimulate their worn-out frames to fresh exertion—or, when totally exhausted, to stupefy the agonies of the slow but certain death that cold and hunger must inevitably produce before another sun dawned. It was awful to observe the different modes, when abandoned to die, in which the miserable wretches met their fate. Some lay down in sullen composure—others vented their despair in oaths, and groans, and curses and not a few in heart-rending prayers to heaven that the duration of their sufferings might be abridged.

From an early period of the retreat, the discipline of the troops was shaken by rapid movements and an absence of regular supplies. Hence, the men were obliged to shift as they best could, and this laxity in discipline gradually increasing, ended in frequent scenes of drunkenness, rioting, and robbery. Every town and village was sacked in search of food, the wine stores plundered, and the casks, in mere wantonness, broken and spilled. Nothing could check the licentious spirit of the troops; and when a man was hanged at Benivedre, even that sad example had not the least effect, for many of the marauders were detected in the act of plundering within sight of the fatal tree.

During this distressing movement, the French had pressed the British rear-guard closely, and a constant scene of skirmishing ensued. Though invariably checked by the light troops, still the army was hourly becoming less effective, every league reducing it both in numbers and resources. Quantities of arms and necessaries were abandoned or destroyed, and two bullock carts loaded with dollars were thrown over a precipice into the bed of a mountain torrent. All these things proved how desperately reduced that once fine and well-appointed army had become. Indeed, its appearance was rather that of a procession of maimed invalids with a caravan of sick soldiers, than an army operating in front of a determined enemy, and expecting momentarily to come to action.

It was a matter of surprise to all, that the French leader did not force on an engagement; but, on the contrary, Soult followed this half-ruined army with a caution that appeared unaccountable and unnecessary. Still the moment of attack could not be distant; and it was certain that the marshal only waited for some embarrassment in the march, to throw his leading divisions on the retreating brigades of Britain, and force on a decisive battle.

This event was particularly to be dreaded while passing the bridge and village of Constantino. A long and difficult mountain road leads to the summit of a bold height, down which it winds again by a gradual descent till it meets the bridge. The occupation of this height, before the columns had passed the river, would expose them to a heavy fire. Sir John Moore determined to check the French pursuit, and hold the hill, until the rear of the main division had cleared the bridge and village. His dispositions were quickly made; the 28th regiment with the Rifle corps were drawn up beside the river, and the 20th, 52nd, and 91st on a hill immediately in their rear, flanked by the horse artillery.

The French attacked with their usual spirit. The cavalry and tirailleurs advanced against the bridge; but the fire from the British riflemen, assisted by the guns on the height, drove them back with loss. A second and a third attack, made with equal boldness, ended in a similar result, and darkness put a stop to the fighting. The French withdrew their light troops, the British continued their retreat, and before morning broke the rear-guard joined the army, now bivouacked in position, or cantoned in and around the town of Lugo.

The concentration of so many troops at this wretched place produced a scene of hurry and confusion with which the distant cannonade at the bridge of Constantino seemed in perfect keeping.

On one side was to be seen the soldier of every rank who had secured a habitation to shelter him, but whom duty or inclination occasioned to wander through the crowds of people, and deeply mudded streets of the town; on the other, the disconsolate person that made his appearance after the *alcalde's* ingenuity had been stretched to the uttermost in procuring quarters for the troops already arrived, and whose *personal friends* had been subjected to the unusual order for admitting strangers. The pitiableness of his case was either to be discovered by a resigned and woeful visage, or by certain ebullitions of temper, destined to waste themselves in the desert air.

Next were to be seen the conductors of baggage, toiling through the streets, their laden mules almost sinking under the weight of ill-arranged burdens swinging from side to side, while the persons in whose charge they had followed the divisions appeared undecided which to execrate most, the roads, the mules, the Spaniards, or the weather. These were succeeded by the dull, heavy sound of the passing artillery; then came the Spanish fugitives from the desolating line of the armies. Detachments with sick or lamed horses scrambled through the mud, while, at intervals, the report of a horse-pistol knelled the termination to the sufferings of an animal that a few days previously, full of life and high in blood, had borne its rider not against, but over, the ranks of Gallic chivalry.

The effect of this scene was rendered more striking by the distant report of cannon and musketry, and more gloomy by torrents of rain, and a degree of cold worthy of a Polish winter.

Preparations were made for a battle, and Sir John Moore seemed determined to retreat no further. Notwithstanding the British were suffering from cold, and wet, and hunger, they fell into their position with alacrity. The Minho protected their right, and a ravine separated them from the French, who, already in force, occupied the heights, and were evidently preparing for an immediate effort.

On the 6th January, the French deployed upon the heights, and the British stood to their arms. Some hours passed; each line looked at the other, as if waiting for its opening movement. The day passed, and at night the hostile armies occupied the same bivouacs on which their brigades had rested the preceding evening.

The 7th came; with the first dawn, as if to make up for its previous inactivity, the French guns opened. Their battery was but weak, and the fire of the British artillery silenced it. A pause ensued, the day wore on, the evening was closing, when a column of considerable strength, covered by a cloud of tirailleurs, steadily mounted the hill, driving in the pickets and a wing of the 76th. The 51st was instantly moved to its assistance, musketry was interchanged, a bayonet rush succeeded, the French were driven down the hill, and operations terminated.

Darkness came on, a wild and stormy night, a lonely hill, no fire, no food—such was the bivouac of Lugo; such the wretched and cheerless situation of the harassed but unconquerable islanders.

As the morning of the 8th dawned, the British formed line, and prepared coolly for the expected encounter; but it passed over, and the enemy made no hostile movement. The troops had been ordered to bivouac as they best could, and in a short time a number of rude huts were erected to defend them from the inclemency of the coming night. But it was not intended to remain longer before Lugo. When darkness hid their retreat, the British filed off silently by the rear. Through a frightful storm of hail and wind, their march was bravely executed; and leaving Lugo and Valmela behind them, they halted at Betanzos on the 10th.

Here the exhausted soldiery were halted from sheer necessity. They were literally marched to a standstill, and, although the rain fell in torrents, they lay down upon the soaked earth, and in that comfortless situation remained until at evening the ranks were again formed, and the retreat continued on Corunna, where Sir John had now decided on embarking the ruins of his army.

Fortunately for the wearied troops, the French, deceived by the fires left burning when the British commenced their night march

The 42nd retaking Elvina

from Lugo, did not discover the movement until daylight, and thus twelve hours were gained on the pursuers. This lost time could not be recovered; and although the whole of the 10th January was passed in Betanzos, to allow stragglers to rejoin their regiments, no serious attempt was made to embarrass the remainder of the march, and the leading division reached Corunna at noon of the 11th, while the reserve occupied the adjoining villages, and the remaining brigades took up their quarters in the suburbs.

Corunna afforded a very indifferent position to offer battle on. There was one, but its extent made it untenable by an army so weak in number as the British. After a close examination, the rising ground above the village of Elvina, a mile in front of the town, was the place selected by the general; the position was accordingly marked out, and the brigades moved to their allotted posts.

A ridge commanded the Betanzos road and formed the left of the line, and on this General Hope's division was placed. Sir David Baird's was next in station, and occupied a succession of knolls that swept inwards, and inclined to a valley beyond the Vigo road. Over the low grounds the rifle corps were extended, *appuied* upon Frazer's division, which, placed in echelon, covered the principal approach to Corunna. Paget's division was in reserve behind Hope's, and occupied a village half a mile in the rear.

The enemy appeared beyond the Mero while these dispositions were being made; but, with the exception of a partial cannonade, no hostile demonstration occurred. On the 14th, the artillery had ceased on both sides, an unusual quiet ensued, and nothing seemed likely to produce any immediate excitement, when the explosion of four thousand barrels of gunpowder burst upon the astonished ear. It is impossible to describe the effect. The unexpected and tremendous crash seemed for the moment to have deprived every person of reason and recollection:

> The soldiers flew to their arms, nor was it until a tremendous column of smoke, ascending from the heights in front, marked from whence the astounding shock proceeded, that reason resumed its sway. It is impossible ever to forget the sublime appearance of the dark dense cloud of smoke that ascended, shooting up gradually like a gigantic tower into the clear blue sky. It appeared fettered in one enormous mass; nor did a particle of dust or vapour, obscuring its form, seem to escape as it

rolled upwards in majestic circles.

On the 15th the fleet hove in sight, and immediate preparations were made to effect an embarkation of the army. The women and children, with the sick and wounded, were directly carried on board; a large portion of the artillery and stores was sent afterwards; and the cavalry, after destroying the few horses that still remained, were embarked. None but the infantry, and of these such only as were effective, were now left; and the belief was general, that they too, would be permitted to retire from their position unmolested.

Everything on the 16th continued quiet. The boats pulled from the shipping to the beach, and orders were issued for the divisions to move down, and prepare for immediate embarkation; Sir John Moore was on horseback to visit the outposts, for the last time, before they should be withdrawn, when an officer came up hastily, and announced that the French were under arms. The intelligence was correct; for an instant fusillade commenced between their *tirailleurs* and the British pickets, as their light troops pushed forward, covering the advance of four compact columns. Two directed their march upon the right, one moved upon the centre, while the fourth threatened the left of the British line.

The right, consisting of the 4th, 42nd, and 50th, supported by the guards, were fiercely attacked, and the reserve ordered to sustain it. The French threw out a cloud of skirmishers, supported by the fire of eleven pieces of artillery, and, driving the advanced posts before them, came forward with their customary boldness. On deploying partially, their line extended considerably beyond the extreme right of the British, but this was disregarded, and instead of waiting the attack, the regiments gallantly advanced to meet it. The 4th suddenly refusing its right wing, showed a double front, and unawed by a superior enemy, undaunted by a heavy and well-directed cannonade, the manoeuvre of this splendid regiment was executed with all the coolness and precision of a parade.

For a time the irregularity of ground intersected by numerous enclosures, kept the combatants apart; but these were speedily surmounted, and the French assault was made and repelled, and the village of Elvina, which had for a few minutes been in possession of the enemy, was recovered by the 50th with the bayonet.

The action was now general along the line. The 42nd, and a battalion of the Guards, by a brilliant charge, drove back the French; and,

Sir John Moore, mortally wounded

failing to force, Soult endeavoured to turn the British right, and accordingly marched a column in its rear. That the reserve attacked, and repulsed it with heavy loss. In every point, Soult's attacks failed—and, altering his dispositions, he took ground considerably to the right.

While the 42nd were lowering their bayonets, and Sir John Moore was encouraging the charge, a round shot knocked him from his horse, shattering his left arm at the shoulder—while immediately before, Sir David Baird had been wounded and removed. But the fall of their generals produced no serious results. Corunna was not a battle of manoeuvre, but a field of determined resistance. The officers commanding the different battalions fought their regiments gallantly; the dispositions for the engagement were simple and understood; the attempts upon the left and centre were repulsed; and the French, beaten on every point, fell back as night came on.

Thus, ended the conflict of Corunna; and when every disadvantage is taken into consideration under which the British fought, its results were glorious, and the courage and coolness displayed throughout most honourable to the troops employed. The numbers engaged were certainly in favour of the French. Without its light brigade, which had retreated and embarked at Vigo, the British divisions scarcely reached to fifteen thousand; while Soult was reinforced in the morning, and mustered from eighteen to twenty thousand men. The loss on both sides was severe; that of the British amounting to eight hundred killed and wounded, while the French admitted theirs to be at least double that number.

Yet it was but a melancholy triumph. The sad reverses of the retreat, the abandonment of the country, and the death of a brave and beloved commander, clouded the hour of conquest, and threw a depressing gloom around, that seemed fitter to mark a defeat than attend a well-won victory. No further attempt was made by the enemy; the brigades were removed after dark, the embarkation continued, and on the afternoon of the 17th, the whole fleet was under weigh, steering for Britain with a leading wind.

The severity of a wound like Sir John Moore's precluded, from the first moment it was received, all hope of his surviving beyond an hour or two. The arm was torn nearly from the shoulder, and the collar-bone partially carried away; but notwithstanding the desperate haemorrhage that ensued, the sufferer preserved his recollection, and remained in mental possession to the last.

He was carried from the field in a blanket by six soldiers, who evinced their sympathy by tears; and when a spring waggon came up, and it was proposed that Sir John should be transferred to it, the poor fellows respectfully objected, "as they would keep step, and carry him more easily." Their wishes were attended to, and the dying general was conveyed slowly to his quarters in the town, occasionally stopping the bearers to look back upon the field, whenever an increasing fire arrested his attention.

All hope was over; he lingered for a little, talking feebly, but collectedly, to those around, and dividing his last thoughts apparently, between his country and his kindred. The kindliness of his disposition was in death remarkable. Turning to an *aide-de-camp*, he desired to be remembered to his sister, and, feebly pressing Colonel Anderson's hand, his head dropped back, and he died without a struggle.

As a wish had been expressed by the departed, that he should be laid in the field on which he fell, the rampart of the citadel was happily chosen for his "resting place." A working party of the 9th turned up the earth—and at midnight, wrapped in a cloak and blanket, his uncoffined remains were interred by the officers of his staff; the burial-service was read by torch-light, earth fell on kindred clay, the grave was filled, and, in the poet's words, "*They left him alone with his glory.*"

In every private relation, Sir John Moore's character was perfect, and his professional career had always been distinguished. Of no man had higher hopes been formed, and hence, probably, more was expected by his country than either his means or his talents could effect. By one party he was unjustly censured, by another injudiciously praised; and in this ferment of opinion it is difficult to say whether his military reputation was most endangered by the obloquy of his enemies or the over-praise of his friends.

CHAPTER 8

The Battle of Talavera, 1809

The immediate consequence of the embarkation, was the surrender of Corunna on the second day from that on which the once proud army of Britain quitted the coast of Spain, Ferrol soon followed the example, and in both these places an immense supply of stores and ammunition was obtained. All effective resistance was apparently at an end, and French dominion seemed established in Gallicia more strongly than it had ever been before.

In every part of Spain, the cause of freedom appeared hopeless. One campaign was closed, and never did one end more hopelessly; an unvarying sense of misfortune from the commencement, it seemed to have withered every national feeling that might have existed in Spanish breasts. Fortresses that should have held out, provisioned, garrisoned, and open to receive supplies from Britain, surrendered to a weak army, who could not command "a battering gun or siege store within four hundred miles."

In fact, Spanish resistance seemed a mockery. Their military force was now the ruins of Romana's army, and some half-starved fugitives who occasionally appeared in Estremadura and La Mancha, while the French had nearly two hundred thousand veteran troops covering the whole country, and these too in masses, that set any hostile demonstration at defiance.

Portugal, in its military footing, was nearly on a par with Spain. A British corps, under Sir John Craddock, garrisoned Lisbon, and, that place excepted, there were no troops in the kingdom on which the slightest dependence could be placed. The appointment of Marshal Beresford to a chief command produced in time a wonderful reformation. The British system of drill was successfully introduced, and, before the war ended, the Portuguese, when brigaded with the

British, were always respectable in the field, and sometimes absolutely brilliant. At this period, there was but one national force in the least degree formidable to the invaders, and that was the Spanish Guerillas.

The Spanish armies in the course of the Peninsular campaign had met so many and discouraging defeats, that their military reputation sunk below the standard of mediocrity. They were despised by their enemies, and distrusted by their allies, and whether from the imbecility of the government, the ignorance of their leaders, or some national peculiarity, their inefficiency became so notorious, that no important operation could be entrusted to them with any certainty of its being successful. As an organised force, the Spanish Army was contemptible; while, in desultory warfare, the peasantry were invaluable. With few, exceptions, the history of Spanish service would be a mere detail of presumption and defeat; while their neighbours, the Portuguese, merited the perfect approbation of their officers, and proved worthy of standing in the battlefield by the side of British soldiers.

Under such unpromising circumstances as we have described, intelligence was received that three French armies were about to move on Portugal; Soult from Gallicia, Lapisse from Salamanca, and Victor from the Tagus. In fact, Portugal would have been soon at the mercy of the enemy, and Spain could have offered but a feeble resistance, when Sir Arthur Wellesley arrived to take the chief command.

He instantly proceeded to adopt measures that should enable him to take the field, and the army was concentrated, with the exception of Mackenzie's brigade, at Coimbra, and reviewed. The entire numbered twenty-six thousand men, of which six thousand formed the separate corps under Marshal Beresford. With the Germans, the British brigades mustered about seventeen thousand; the detached corps under Mackenzie, amounting to nearly three thousand, of which one-half was cavalry; and a farther augmentation was effected by brigading one Portuguese, with every two of the British battalions.

In the meantime, Soult's position became extremely dangerous. A British Army in his front, bands of guerillas in his rear; one flank hemmed in by Silviera at Amarante; and the ocean on the other. But that able marshal perceived the difficulties of his situation, and deciding at once to secure an open road in his rear, he despatched Delaborde and Loison to recover Amarante. The task was a tedious and doubtful operation; and for twelve days the place was assaulted and maintained. At last, Soult in person came forward in strength, and Silviera was driven from the bridge over the Tamaga, with the loss of his cannon, and the French retreat was for the present secured.

From the moment Sir Arthur Wellesley landed in Portugal, the character of the war had changed; and, notwithstanding the numerous and discouraging drawbacks upon a bold career which the obstinacy of the Spaniards and the deficiency of his own means were continually presenting, before the masterly decision of the British general, all obstacles ultimately gave way; and victory, which had hovered doubtfully over many a hard-contested field, at last rested on his banners, and wreathed her laurels round his brows.

The crossing of the Douro was, in military estimation, as bold and well-arranged an operation as any that marked Wellesley's Peninsular career. The passage of a river in the face of an enemy with every assistance from pontoons and ferryage, is considered a hazardous undertaking; but, circumstanced as the British commander was, the thing was generally set down as impracticable, and Soult was unprepared for the attempt.

When the news was brought that the enemy was crossing at Villa Nova, the marshal ridiculed the notion, and remained in his quarters until two in the afternoon. He was then obliged precipitately to quit the city; and so suddenly were Wellesley's measures executed, that the dinner prepared for the duke of Dalmatia, was served up to the British general and his staff. War is, *certes*, a game of chances; and little did the French marshal suppose, when at noon he regulated the *carte* presented by his *maître d'hotel*, that he was then civilly arranging an excellent repast for his opponent. Yet such was the case. Wellesley succeeded Soult—and within, a few hours the same roof covered the victor and the vanquished.

Nothing could exceed the irregularity of the French retreat. Before they could be persuaded that the passage of the Douro was seriously designed, the British were charging through the suburbs; and instead of retiring with an orderly formation on the advance of the enemy, the French rear-guard got mobbed together on the road, and allowed an opportunity to the cavalry of their pursuers to act with an audacity and success that the weakness of their squadrons could never ha.ve warranted, had not a considerable panic been previously occasioned, by the precipitation with which Soult's divisions were hurried from the city.

Night came most opportunely, and ended the pursuit, enabling the French marshal to unite himself with Loison, from whom he received the unwelcome intelligence that the bridge of Amarante was destroyed.

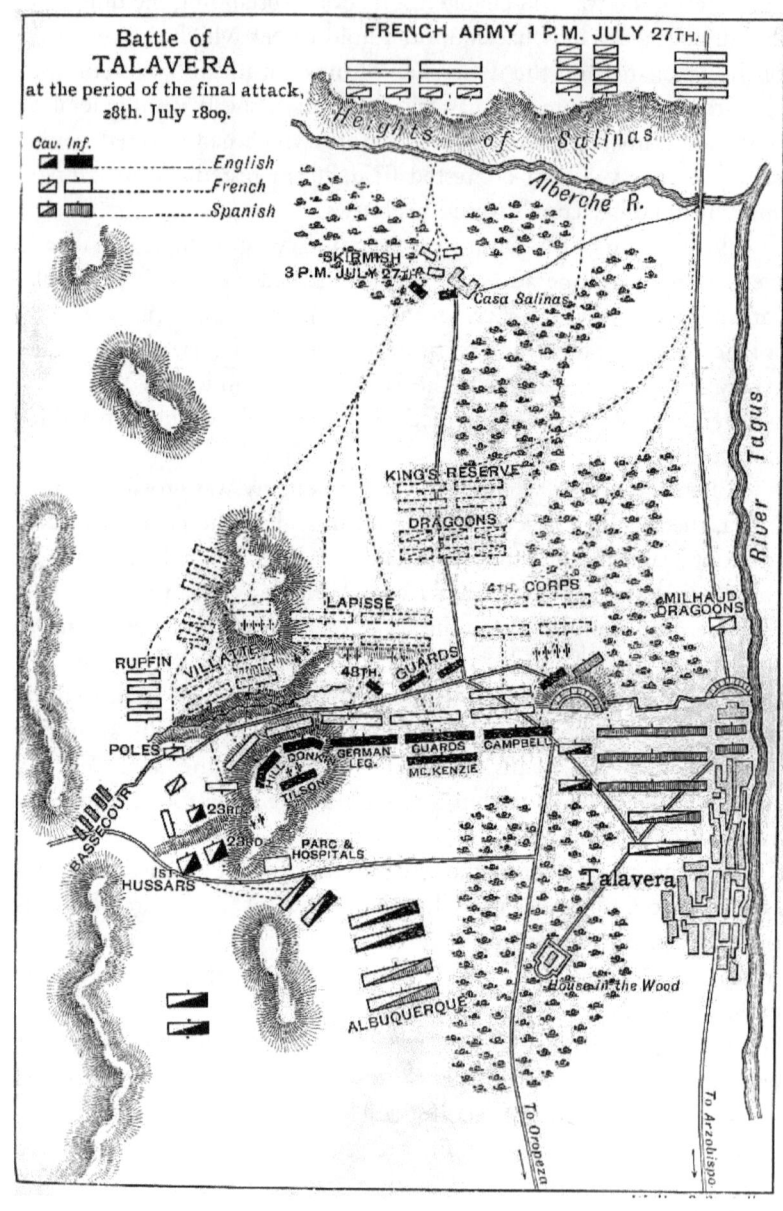

Soult's situation was almost desperate; his only line of retreat was by a mountain track; and, by taking it, he was obliged to cross the pass of Ruivans, a long narrow bridge, without a parapet on either side, spanning a frightful precipice. Should this be occupied, and no doubt Beresford was marching thither, nothing could save his army. With excellent judgment, he abandoned his artillery and baggage, pushed rapidly forward, and, having forced the Portuguese pickets which here and there occupied the mountain passes, he out-marched Silviera by several hours, and halted his rear-guard at Salamonde, to cover the bridges of Saltador and Porto Nova, while his columns were defiling.

Here, however, he was overtaken and brought to action, on the 16th June, by Sir Arthur. Although the position was strong, and the brigade of Guards were the only infantry come up, the British general instantly made his dispositions for attack. The left was turned by the rifle corps, the Guards advancing boldly in front. After delivering a volley at the head of the column when it showed itself, the French precipitately fled—and, hurrying through the village in their rear, succeeded, under cover of darkness, in escaping. Some delay in clearing a defile allowed the horse artillery to come up, and their rapid fire did considerable execution before the crowd of fugitives could get beyond its range.

The next morning's dawn renewed the pursuit; and every turn of the road, cumbered with broken vehicles and deserted baggage, showed how severely the French Army had been pressed. The bridge was nearly impassable from dead men and slain horses laid there in heaps by the grape and canister of the British guns. Arms, accoutrements, ham-strung mules, guns, tumbrils, knapsacks filled with silver plate, tapestry, and other valuable plunder were strewn indiscriminately along the line. To add to this scene of waste and suffering, the villages the advancing army entered were either in a blaze, or already reduced to ashes; for between the French troops and peasantry a deadly war of extermination was being carried on, and on both sides deeds of cruelty were every day perpetrated that can hardly be credited or described.

Indeed, the French retreat through the Gallician mountains was only paralleled by the British on Corunna; with this exception, that many a straggler from the British columns was saved by the humanity of the Spaniards, while the unhappy Frenchman who lagged but a few hundred yards behind the rear-guard, was butchered by the infuriated peasantry, bent on the work of slaughter and burning for vengeance on an enemy, who, in his day of conquest, and dominion, had taught the lesson of cruelty now practised so unrelentingly on himself.

Soult turning from Montalegre towards Orense, and a French corps from Estremadura having moved on Alcantara, induced Sir Arthur Wellesley to discontinue the pursuit. The French marshal crossed the frontier on the 18th with barely nineteen thousand men, his guns, stores, and baggage abandoned to the conquerors. Ten weeks, perfect in every arm, that army had passed through Orense on its march to Oporto, mustering twenty-six thousand veteran soldiers. A short period had wrought a fearful change, and even the debris of that once splendid corps was only extricated from total destruction by the admirable tact and unbending *hardiesse* of their brave and gifted leader.

On reaching Abrantes on the 7th July, it was correctly ascertained that, instead of retiring on Madrid, Victor was concentrating at Merida, intending, probably, to cross the Guadiana, and attack Cuesta before the British could come to his assistance. Propositions therefore for a combined movement were made by Sir Arthur Wellesley to the "Spanish general," and willingly acceded to, and the British moved forward to the Teitar, to unite, as it was believed, in an operation upon Madrid.

A most able plan for marching at once for the recovery of the capital was arranged at a conference between the allied commanders. The British and Spanish armies, taking the right bank of the Tagus, were to advance directly forward. Venegas, with fourteen thousand Spaniards, was to threaten Aranjuez, and, if possible, take possession of Toledo; while two other Spanish divisions should hold the passes of Banos and Perales; and five thousand Portuguese, under Sir Robert Wilson, were to act independently, and annoy the French flanks and rear as they best could.

The British consequently moved by Salvatiera and Placentia, effecting a junction with Cuesta at Oropesa on the 20th of July. On the 22nd Victor had retired and taken a position on the Alberche. The opportunity was at once given for attacking him, but Cuesta obstinately declined; and Victor, hearing that Wilson was already in his rear at Escalona, made a night march on Torrijos.

Cuesta was a singular medley of opposite qualities. He was exceedingly brave, had some daring, overweening pride, and a most asinine obstinacy. Finding it desirable for the prosperity of the common cause to submit to the old man's folly, Sir Arthur Wellesley acted with singular forbearance. It had been arranged that Victor should be attacked on the 23rd, and when the British general reached his confederate's quarters to arrange the necessary details on the evening of the 22nd, Cuesta was asleep, and no one dared to waken him.

At dawn, the British divisions were under arms, but Cuesta could not be disturbed till seven! At last an interview did take place, and then the weak old man positively declined to fight, because the day was *Sunday*. Victor had but twenty thousand men with him at the moment. The Alberche was fordable—the right and centre assailable; Cuesta's army numbered forty-seven thousand, and Wellesley's about twenty-one. Was ever such an opportunity lost? and all, too, through the stupid bigotry of a sleepy-headed Spaniard.

While Sir Arthur halted at Talavera, having two divisions across the river at Casa Leguas, Cuesta followed the French, who as he persuaded himself were retreating, but Sebastiani had marched from Toledo and joined Victor, while Joseph Buonaparte, having united his corps to Jourdan's, was hastening to a common centre. The whole united at Torrijos, forming a *corps d'armée* of nearly fifty thousand men.

Cuesta, with all his Spanish obstinacy, would still insist that the French were not concentrating, but retreating, but the delusion was short. Victor suddenly attacked him, and as his retreat was most disorderly, nothing but prompt assistance from Sherbrooke's division could have saved the stupid old man from destruction. When this was effected, the Guards crossed the river, leaving Mackenzie's division in possession of the wood and convent on the right bank of the Alberche.

A recent deliverance seemed to have had no effect upon Spanish obstinacy. Though certain of being attacked, Cuesta lay loosely on the Alberche, into which, had his army been defeated, it must have been driven pell-mell. Happily, Sir Arthur, in reconnoitring the ground in the neighbourhood, discovered an extensive line on which both armies might be placed to their mutual disadvantage. He took his measures with such promptitude, and issued his orders with such coolness and perspicuity, that every battalion, Spanish as well as British, stepped into the very spot which his admirable foresight had marked out for it.

The position was about two miles in length, extending perpendicularly from the Tagus, on which the right rested in the town of Talavera. It was partially retrenched, having an intersected and most difficult country in its front. The centre was more open; but the left terminated favourably on a bold and commanding height, overlooking a considerable valley, which separated the left of the position from a range of rocky mountains. To the Spaniards the right was allotted, it being considered nearly unattackable, while the British defended the more accessible ground upon the left.

Talavera stands on the northern bank of the Tagus, the houses reaching down to the water's edge. The two armies were drawn up in line; the British on the left, extending from the town nearly to the Sierra de Gata, its extreme flank occupying a bold height near Alatuza de Segusella, and having in its front a difficult ravine, and on its flank a deep valley. To the Spaniards the right was assigned. Their battalions were stationed among olive groves, with walls and fences interspersed, and an embankment running along the road, that formed an excellent breastwork, and rendered their position nearly unassailable.

It was necessary to secure the point of junction where the British right touched Cuesta's left, and to effect this, ten guns were placed in battery on the summit of a bold knoll, with a British division to protect them, and a strong cavalry corps in reserve. In the general disposition of the troops Campbell's division was on the right of the British, Sherbrooke's division adjoining; Mackenzie occupied the next portion of the battleground, while the height upon the left, the key of the position, was intrusted to General Hill.

During the morning of the 27th July, the troops had been marching on the different points marked for their occupation, and had taken ground hitherto unmolested by the enemy; but at noon Mackenzie's division was suddenly and furiously assailed by two heavy columns, which attacked the wood and convent. Partially surprised, the 87th and 88th regiments were thrown into a momentary confusion; and the French penetrated between the two brigades which formed the division. Immediately, by the exertions of their officers, the 31st, 45th, and 60th Rifles were brought forward, and these regiments covered their companions, while they retired from the wood into the plain, retreating in beautiful order along the heights on the left of the position which they were directed to occupy.

The enemy continued their attack, and it had now extended partially along the whole line, growing more animated as the evening began to fall. The left, where the British stood, at once appeared the grand object of the marshals. They directed a strong force against it, forming their infantry into columns of battalions, which advanced in double quick, supported by a furious cannonade.

Mackenzie's division having retired a little, and, at the moment, forming a second line, the brunt of the assault fell upon a smaller brigade under General Donkin, then in possession of the height. The

The flight of General Cuesta and the Spanish

French, though they came on with imposing bravery, were checked in front; but from the weakness of his brigade, Donkin's flank was turned on the left, and the hill behind crowned by the enemy.

But that success was momentary. Hill instantly led up the 48th, 29th, and 1st battalion of detachments. A close and murderous volley from the British was followed by a charge. The French were forced from the position with great loss; and the ridge was again carried by a wing of the 29th with the bayonet.

There was a brief space of quiet; but determined to win the key of the position, though darkness had now set in, the French in great force once more rushed forward to wrest the height from its defenders, and in the gloom the assailants and the assailed nearly touched each other. The red flash of a well-delivered volley disclosed to the British the dark array that threatened them. The order was given to advance, and again the British bayonet drove the columns down the hill.

No fighting could have been more desperate than that which marked this night attack. A feint had been made by Lapisse upon the Germans in the centre, while, with the *élite* of their infantry, Ruffin and Vilatte ascended the heights, which, at every loss, they seemed more resolute in winning. A terrific slaughter ensued. Could it be otherwise? So desperately was this night fighting maintained, and the regiments were so closely engaged, that in the *mêlée*, some of the men fought with clubbed muskets.

These signal repulses of a powerful and gallant enemy could not but cost a heavy expenditure of blood. Many brave officers had fallen, and at this period of the conflict the killed and wounded amounted to upwards of eight hundred men.

The troops rested upon their arms, and each battalion on the ground it had occupied the preceding day. The cavalry were stretched beside their horses; all were ready for an attack; but the night passed with some slight alarms, and no serious disturbance.

The morning was ushered in by a tremendous cannonade, while the grenadiers of Lapisse's division, in two columns, advanced again to attack the height upon the left. They were bravely led forward by their officers, and made many desperate but unavailing efforts to win the summit of the hill, but nothing could shake the firmness of the British. They allowed the columns to mount the rugged ascent, until they had nearly touched the ridge, then a close volley, a loud huzza, followed by a rapid charge, broke the formation of the French, and sent them precipitously down the hill. Again, and again the attempt was made with equal ill fortune; until, totally disheartened by repeated repulses and leaving the ground heaped with dead, the enemy abandoned all hope of carrying this well-defended position, and retreated out of fire.

It was now half-past eight, and the fighting had never intermitted from five that morning. The loss on both sides was frightful; the French infinitely greater than the British. Their repeated attacks on the height occasioned immense loss; and their troops, dispirited by want of success, and wearied by constant but unavailing exertion, showed little inclination to renew the battle.

The heat of the sun had become intolerable, and the movements, on the French part, were stayed. Indeed, the firing had ceased over the field, and the work of slaughter, by a sort of mutual consent, was for a time suspended. The French commenced cooking their dinners, and the British and their allies produced their scantier rations. During this temporary cessation of hostilities, it was a matter of some deliberation with the British commander, whether in turn he should become the assailant, or remain quietly and await the result of the enemy's decision; and it was a fortunate circumstance that the latter was his determination.

At this time a curious incident occurred, that for a brief space changed the character of the war, and, even on a battlefield covered with the dead and dying, produced a display of kindly feeling between two brave and noble-minded enemies.

A small stream, tributary to the Tagus, flowed through a part of the battle-ground, and separated the combatants. During the pause that the heat, of the weather and the weariness of the troops had produced, both armies went to the banks of the rivulet for water. The men approached each other fearlessly, threw down their caps and muskets, chatted to each other like old acquaintances, and exchanged their brandy-flasks and wine-skins. All asperity of feeling seemed forgotten. To a stranger, they would have appeared more like an allied force, than men hot from a ferocious conflict, and only gathering strength and energy to recommence it anew.

But a still nobler rivalry for the time existed; the interval was employed in carrying off the wounded, who lay intermixed upon the hard-contested field; and, to the honour of both be it told, that each endeavoured to extricate the common sufferers, and remove their unfortunate friends and enemies without distinction. Suddenly, the bugles sounded, the drums beat to arms, many of the rival soldiery shook hands, and parted with expressions of mutual esteem, and in ten

23rd Light Dragoons at Talavera

minutes after they were again at the bayonet's point.

Having ascertained the part of the position, and the extent of it that was occupied by the British brigades, the marshals determined to direct their undivided energies against that portion of the line, and, if possible, crush the British divisions by bearing on them with an overwhelming force. They formed in four columns of attack; the first was destined against that part of the ground where the British and Spaniards united; the second against Sherbrooke and Cameron's brigades; the third was directed against Mackenzie's and the Germans; and the fourth, in great strength, and accompanied by a mass of cavalry, moved up the valley to the left.

A fire from eighty pieces of artillery announced the forward movement of the columns, which soon presented themselves, covered by a cloud of light infantry. A destructive cannonade was borne by the British brigades patiently; in vain the *tirailleurs* kept up a biting fire, but not a shot was returned by the British. Their orders to reserve their fire were strictly obeyed, and the files steadily and quietly closed up, for the men were falling by dozens. Their assailants approached, their officers called "*En avant!*" and the drums beat the *pas de charge*. Nothing could be more imposing than the advance, nothing more complete than their discomfiture. Within twenty paces a shattering volley was delivered from the British line, the word "*Charge!*" was given, and the bayonet did the rest.

Campbell's division, on the right, totally defeated the attack, and charging boldly in return, drove the French back, and captured a battery of ten guns. The enemy endeavoured to retake them, but the Spanish cavalry charged home, the cannon remained with the captors, and the right of the British was victorious everywhere.

The left attack failed totally. The British cavalry were posted in the valley where the hostile movement was being made; and Anson's brigade, consisting of the 23rd Light Dragoons, and the 1st King's German Hussars, were ordered to charge and check the advance. It was gallantly attempted, and though in point of fact the charge failed, and the 23rd were nearly cut to pieces, the daring courage exhibited under circumstances perfectly desperate, so completely astounded the enemy, that their attack on the height was abandoned. If there was an error in the mode that charge was made, it arose from its fearless gallantry; and under common circumstances, its result would have been most glorious. Colonel Napier thus describes the affair:—

The ground upon which this brigade was in line is perfectly level, nor did any visible obstruction appear between it and the columns opposed. The grass was long, dry, and waving, concealing the fatal chasm that intervened. One of General Villatte's columns stood at some distance to the right of the building occupied by the light troops. These were directly in front of the 23rd Dragoons. Another was formed rather to the rear, and more in front of the German Hussars, on the left of the line. Such were the immediate objects of the charge.

For some time, the brigade advanced at a rapid pace, without receiving any obstruction from the enemy's fire. The line cheered. It was answered from the hill with the greatest enthusiasm; never was anything more exhilarating or beautiful than the commencement of this advance. Several lengths in front, mounted on a grey horse, consequently very conspicuous, rode Colonel Elley. Thus, placed he, of course, first arrived at the brink of a ravine, which, varying in width, extended along the whole front of the line. Going half-speed at the time, no alternative was left him. To have checked his horse, and given timely warning, would have been impossible.

With some difficulty he cleared it at a bound, and on gaining the opposite bank, endeavoured by gesture to warn the 23rd of the dangerous ground they had to pass; but advancing with such velocity, the line was on the verge of the stream before his signs could be either understood or attended to. Under any circumstances this must have been a serious occurrence in a cavalry charge; but when it is considered that four or five hundred dragoons were assailing two divisions of infantry, unbroken, and fully prepared for the onset, to have persevered at all was highly honourable to the regiment.

At this moment, the enemy, formed in squares, opened his tremendous fire. A change immediately took place. Horses rolled on the earth; others were seen flying back dragging their unhorsed riders with them; the German Hussars coolly reined up; the line of the 23rd was broken. Still the regiment galloped forward. The confusion was increased; but no hesitation took place in the individuals of this gallant corps. The survivors rushed forward with, if possible, accelerated pace, passing between the flank of the square, now one general blaze of fire, and the building on its left.

Still the remainder of the 23rd, led on by Major Ponsonby, passing under this withering fire, assailed and overthrew a regiment of *chasseurs*; and, though attacked in turn by a squadron of Westphalian horse and some Polish lancers, it cut its way through these, and riding past the intervals of the infantry, reached the base of the mountain, where the Spanish corps of observation secured it. Its loss was awful. In an affair that lasted but a few minutes, nine officers, twelve sergeants, two hundred rank and file, and two hundred and twenty-four horses, were rendered *hors de combat*.

On the centre, the attack was made with great steadiness and determination. The French columns deployed before they attempted to ascend the heights, and, regardless of broken ground, advanced to the charge with imposing gallantry. General Sherbrooke, having fully prepared his men, received them with a volley of musketry, which staggered their resolution, and the whole division rushing forward with the bayonet, the French were driven back with prodigious loss.

But the Guards came loosely on. The French observed it; perceived an opening in the line, and threw in a tremendous fire on the Germans, that caused a momentary confusion. The affair is thus narrated by an officer of the 48th. The celerity with which a mistake, that to other troops might have proved fatal, was remedied by the coolness of the commander and the heroism of his army, could never be better exemplified.

At this period of the battle, and in nearly their last attempt, the enemy had been repulsed and followed. The Guards, carried onwards by victorious excitement, advanced too far, and found themselves assailed by the French reserve, and mowed down by an overwhelming fire. They fell back, but as whole sections were swept away their ranks became disordered, and nothing but their stubborn gallantry prevented a total *déroute*. Their situation was most critical; had the French cavalry charged home nothing could have saved them.

Lord Wellington saw the danger, and speedily despatched support. A brigade of horse was ordered up, and our regiment moved from the heights we occupied to assist our hard-pressed comrades. We came on at double-quick, and formed in the rear by companies, and through the intervals in our line the broken ranks of the Guards retreated. A close and well-directed volley from us arrested the progress of the victorious French, while with amazing celerity and coolness the Guards rallied and reformed, and in a few minutes advanced in turn to support us. As they came on, the men gave a loud huzza. An Irish regiment to the right answered it with a thrilling cheer. It was taken up from regiment to regiment, and passed along the British line, and that wild shout told the advancing enemy that British valour was indomitable. The leading files of the French halted, turned, fell back, and never made another effort.

In every place the British were victorious, and had one forward movement of the Spaniards been made, Talavera would have proved the most decisive defeat that ever the French armies on the Peninsula had sustained, for a rapid flanking march from Cuesta's right upon the Alberche must have compromised half the French Army. But with troops so wretchedly disciplined, it was impossible to change any previous formation in face of an enemy; and thus, the French marshals were enabled to retreat in perfect order, with the greater portion of their baggage, the whole of their wounded, and all their artillery, with the exception of ten guns taken by Campbell's brigade, and seven abandoned in the woods, and afterwards secured.

As victory is ever damped by individual suffering, an event well calculated to increase the horrors of a battlefield occurred, that cannot be recollected without the liveliest sorrow for those who suffered.

From the heat of the weather, the fallen leaves were parched like tinder, and the grass was rank and dry. Near the end of the engagement both were ignited by the blaze of some cartridge-papers, and the whole surface of the ground was presently covered with a sheet of fire. Those of the disabled who lay on the outskirts of the field managed to crawl away, or were carried off by their more fortunate companions who had escaped unhurt; but, unhappily, many gallant sufferers, with "medicable wounds," perished in the flames before it was possible to extricate them.

The battle was ended at about six o'clock, and after that hour scarcely a shot was heard. Both armies occupied the positions of the morning, and the British bivouacked on the field, with little food and no shelter; while the dead lay silently around, and the moans of the wounded broke sadly on the ear, as they were conveyed all through the night to the hospitals in Salamanca.

The French were evidently about to retire, but, from a great inferiority in cavalry, pursuit was impossible. On the next morning, two of their divisions only were seen beyond the river, and these retreated on the night of the 31st, and followed the remainder of the beaten *corps d'armée*.

The British loss was extremely severe, and from the heavy cannonade regiments not otherwise exposed, suffered much. The whole force, exclusive of the Spaniards, did not exceed nineteen thousand, and of these fully four thousand men were killed and wounded. The Spanish loss was inconsiderable, as they were never seriously engaged, not reaching altogether to a thousand *hors de combat*.

The casualties of Joseph Buonaparte's army it would be difficult to ascertain with anything like correctness. It has been stated at six, eight, and even ten thousand. The intermediate estimate would probably be the truest, and certainly the French loss exceeded the allied by a third if not a half.

On the morning after the battle, the light brigade were reinforced by three splendid regiments, the 43rd, 52nd, and 95th, under General Craufurd, who reached the army accompanied by a, troop of horse artillery. Its march was remarkable—sixty-three English miles were accomplished in twenty-seven hours. Advancing under a burning sun, over a sandy country, badly supplied with water, with bad rations and scarcely any bread, the movement was extraordinary. When the weight a soldier in heavy marching order carries is considered, the distance these splendid regiments achieved was certainly a surprising effort.

Aware that the armies were in presence of each other, and apprised that a battle was inevitable, an ardent wish to share the glory of the field stimulated these soldiers to exertions that hunger, fatigue, and thirst could not abate; and though efforts, almost beyond belief failed to bring them to the battleground before the struggle terminated, the rapidity of their march, and the fine condition in which they joined the army, justly obtained for them the admiration of the victors of Talavera.

Chapter 9

The Battle of Busaco, 1810

Soult, who had collected thirty-five thousand men, on learning the defeat of Talavera, made a flank movement to assist Joseph Buonaparte, and reached Placentia by the pass of Banos. Lord Wellington, on being apprised of the French marshal's advance, instantly determined to march forward and engage him; while Cuesta observed the line of the Tagus, and protected the stores and hospitals at Talavera. Accordingly, on the 3rd of August, the British moved to Orapesa; but on that evening information was received that Soult had cut off Lord Wellington's communication with the bridge of Almarez, and that Cuesta was about to evacuate Talavera.

This intelligence made an immediate change in Lord Wellington's plans indispensable, and it became necessary to cross the Tagus instantly. A passage was effected by the bridge of Arzabispo, and the whole artillery and stores were safely brought off, over horrible roads, which hitherto had been deemed impracticable for anything but mules and the rude carriages of the country. After a short stay, the British fell back on Badajoz, early in September.

Cuesta's sudden retreat from Talavera had not only endangered Lord Wellington, but nearly caused the total destruction of the Portuguese corps commanded by Sir Robert Wilson. In obedience to orders, Sir Robert had advanced within twelve miles of the capital before he was recalled, and after narrowly escaping the French armies, by the ill-judged retirement of the Spanish general from Talavera, he found himself completely cut off from the Tagus. With considerable difficulty, the Portuguese general crossed the Sierra de Liana, and seized the pass of Banos, whither Soult, on falling back from Placentia to Leon, was rapidly advancing, nothing remaining for him but to defend the pass, and risk a battle with numbers immensely superior to his own. This determination, was gallantly carried into effect. After a desperate resistance of nine hours, Wilson was at last forced from the position, with a loss of eight hundred men; while the remainder of his corps dispersed, and succeeded in reaching Castello Branco.

Following up this success, Soult, with fifty thousand men, was despatched by Joseph against the southern provinces, and succeeded in crossing the Sierra Morena, though the whole range had been strongly fortified, and thirty thousand men under Ariezaga, intrusted with its defence. So quickly, and with such trifling loss was this dangerous operation achieved, that it was a question whether the marshal was more indebted for his success to treachery or cowardice. Cadiz was preserved by the prompt decision of the duke of Albuquerque, the gates closed against the French, and the city secured against bombardment, except from one point occupied by Fort Matagorda.

All else had gone favourably for the French. Sebastiani defeated Ariezaga on his retreat to Grenada, and that city and Malaga, after a faint effort at defence, fell. Gerona surrendered after a brave and protracted resistance. Hostalrich was also taken; and Astorga capitulated in the middle of April. In fact, the French were everywhere victorious, and Spain once more lay nearly at their feet. This, as Colonel Jones observes, was:

> The second crisis in the affairs of the Peninsula, as, by a succession of desultory and ill-planned enterprises on the part of the Spaniards, all their armies had been annihilated, their fortresses reduced, and three-fourths of the kingdom subdued.

Affairs certainly wore a gloomy aspect. Napoleon had openly announced his determination to drive the British into the sea; and his means, relieved as he was by an alliance with Austria, seemed amply sufficient to realise the threat. Circumstances had increased his resources, and left him a large disposable force to direct on Portugal.

But still, notwithstanding the gloomy prospects of the British, it was surprising what a number of desertions took place from the enemy's corps. Between the commencement of 1810 and the month of May, nearly five hundred men, chiefly Germans and Italians, arrived, time after time, at the British outposts; while desertions from the British regiments were extremely rare.

Early in May, Massena prepared for active operations, and invested the fortress of Rodrigo, the inferiority of Lord Wellington's force rendering any attempt on his part to prevent it impossible. All that could

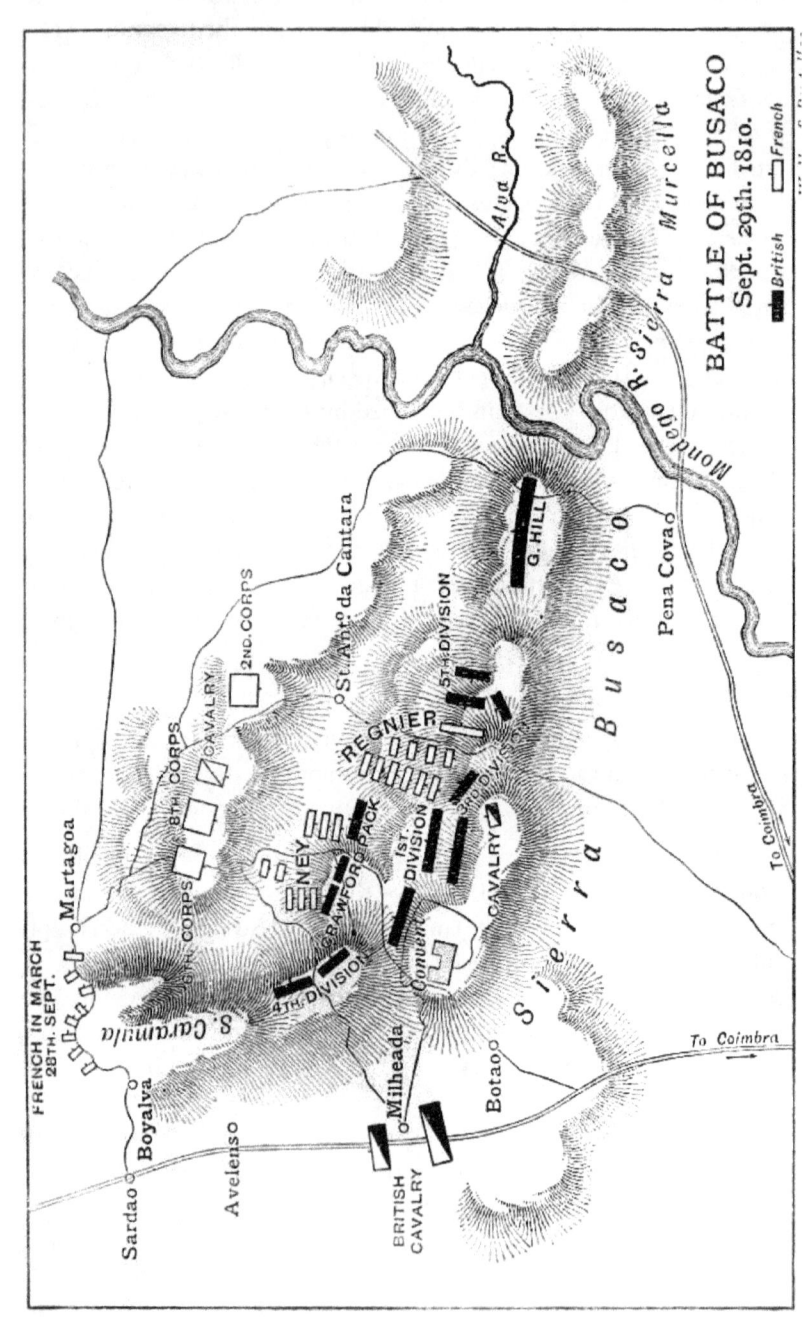

be done was to observe the enemy closely; and for this purpose, headquarters were transferred to Almeida, which, after a few days, were farther retired to Alverca, six leagues in the rear.

The investment of Rodrigo, which occasional advances of the British had partially relaxed, became new more serious, for Ney determined that the place should fall, and taking post on a range of high grounds with thirty thousand men, he covered effectually the operations carried on by Junot, whose separate force amounted to forty thousand more.

It was now ascertained that Matagorda had fallen, that Cadiz, of course, must yield, that divisions of the guards had entered Madrid, and that Napoleon was absolutely across the Pyrenees.

The siege of Rodrigo continued; a gallant resistance was made, for the garrison disputed every inch of ground, rallying frequently, and maintaining a well-directed fire that occasioned the besiegers considerable loss. The old governor, Hervasti, did wonders, and with a garrison of four thousand men, and fortifications in bad condition, many parts of the wall having its breaches only stopped loosely with rubbish, he kept seventy thousand men at bay, provided with siege stores in abundance, and a numerous corps of active and scientific engineers to direct the labours of the thousands who composed their working parties. On the 30th of June, the breach was practicable, and stormed, but the French were repulsed, after suffering an enormous loss in killed and wounded.

Though the British Army looked on, they could not save the fortress. The siege was pressed, and the outposts of the two armies came occasionally in contact with each other.

On the 4th of July, the French made a strong reconnaissance with five regiments of cavalry, a corps of infantry, and some guns. A spirited affair ensued, and Gallegos and Almeida were given up, and a position taken by the British in rear of Fort Conception.

Time passed without any affair of moment occurring, until Ciudad Rodrigo capitulated, after a noble defence of a full month with open trenches. Julian Sanchez, finding the place must fall, quitted the city at midnight with his lancers, and cut his way through the enemy's posts.

Ney, it is said, annoyed at the obstinacy with which the fortress held out, until the breach was found by Hervasti indefensible, and the troops for the assault were actually formed in the trenches, declined all terms but unconditional surrender. Massena, however, with more generosity, conceded the honours of war to the brave and resolute *commandant*.

Consequent on the fall of Rodrigo, numerous movements took place. It was impossible to guess in what way Massena would follow up his success, and the last arrangements were made by Lord Wellington to meet every probable contingency.

When the fall of Almeida was known, Lord Wellington, who had advanced when Massena broke ground, fell back to the position on which he had previously retired; and anxious to get into closer communication with General Hill, he retreated leisurely on Gouvea. By this movement, he checked any attempt that might have been intended from Sabugal by Covilhos, and effectually secured the fortified position of Zezere from being turned.

Yet the situation of the allies was truly critical. The fall of Almeida permitted Massena to advance with confidence, while in numbers, the French marshal was immensely superior; and of the allied force, a great portion of the Portuguese had never been, under fire. The news of Romana's defeat by Mortier, made matters still more alarming; as the latter, might come up in sufficient time to threaten the right of the allies by Alcantara or Abrantes.

But Massena's movements ended this suspense, and Wellington was about to achieve one of his most splendid victories.

It was impossible to avoid a battle. Wellington crossed the Mondego, while the French were concentrated at Viseu. The first division had been placed in observation of the Oporto road, the light on the road of Viseu; but the French having passed the Criz, Lord Wellington changed his position, and fell back upon the heights of Busaco.

The mountain range, upon which the British retired, was about eight miles long; its right touching the Mondego, and the left stretching over very difficult ground to the Sierra de Caramula. There was a road cresting the Busaco ridge, and a ford at Pena Cova, communicating with the Murcella ridge, and the face of the position was steep, rugged, and well defended by the allied artillery. Along the front a sweeping fire could be maintained, and on a part of the summit cavalry might act if necessary.

To an assailing enemy, a position like that of Busaco must present most serious difficulties; and, therefore, it was generally believed that Massena would not risk a battle. But Lord Wellington thought differently, and coolly added, "If he does, I shall beat him."

Pack's division had fallen back on the 22nd September, and on the

23rd Massena drove in the British cavalry. The third division took a position at Antonio de Contara, and the fourth at the convent; while the light division bivouacked in a pine wood. On the 24th it fell back four miles, and some skirmishing of no particular importance took place.

The 25th had nearly brought on a second affair between Craufurd and the enemy. Immense masses of the French were moving rapidly forward, and the cavalry had interchanged a pistol fire, when Lord Wellington arrived, and instantly retired the division. Not a moment could be lost; the enemy came on with amazing rapidity, but the British rear-guard behaved with its usual determination; and after a series of quick and beautifully-executed manoeuvres, secured their retreat on the position. Both armies that evening bivouacked in each other's presence, and sixty-five thousand French infantry, covered by a mass of *voltigeurs*, formed in the British front, while scarcely fifty thousand of the allies were in line on the Sierra de Busaco, and these, of necessity, were extended over a surface which their numbers were quite incompetent to defend.

Ney and Reynier agreed that the moment of their arrival afforded the best chance for attacking Wellington successfully, and Massena was informed that the allied troops were only getting into their ground, and that their dispositions were accordingly imperfect. But the marshal came up too late; for all the arrangements of Wellington had been coolly and admirably effectuated.

The British brigades were continuously posted. On the right, General Hill's division was stationed. Leith, on his left, prolonged the line, with the Lusitanian legion in reserve. Picton joined Leith, and was supported by a brigade of Portuguese. The brigades of Spencer crested the ridge, and held the ground between the third division and the convent; and the fourth division closed the extreme left, covering the mountain path of Milheada, with part of the cavalry on a flat, and a regiment of dragoons in reserve on the summit of the Sierra. Pack's division formed the advanced guard to the right, and extended halfway down the hill; while in a hollow below the convent, the light brigade and Germans were thrown out. The whole front was covered with skirmishers, and on every point from which the artillery could effectively range, the guns were placed in battery.

While these dispositions were being completed, evening had come on, both armies establishing themselves for the night, and the French lighting fires. Some attempts of the enemy to introduce their *tirail-*

leurs, in broken numbers, among the wooded hollows in front of the light division, indicated an intention of a night attack, and the rifles and *cacadores* drove them back. But no attempt was made, and a mild and warm atmosphere allowed the troops to bivouac without inconvenience on the battleground. A few hours of comparative stillness passed, one hundred thousand men slept under the canopy of heaven; and before the first faint glimmering of light, all stood quietly to arms, and prepared for a bloody day.

Shrouded by the grey mist that still was lingering on the Sierra, the enemy advanced. Ney, with three columns, moved forward in front of the convent, where Craufurd's division was posted; while Reynier, with two divisions, approached by less difficult ground the pickets of the third division, before the feeble light permitted his movements to be discovered. With their usual impetuosity, the French pushed forward, and the British as determinately opposed them. Under a heavy fire of grape and musketry, the enemy topped the heights; and on the left of the third division, gained the summit of the mountain, their leading battalions securing themselves among the rocks, and threatening the ridge of the Sierra.

The disorder of a Portuguese regiment, the 8th, afforded them also a partial advantage. But the fire of two guns with grape opened on their flank; in front, a heavy fusillade was maintained; while, advancing over the crown of the height, the 88th and four companies of the 45th charged furiously with the bayonet, and with an ardour that could not be resisted. Both French and British were intermixed in a desperate *mêlée*, both fought hand to hand, both went struggling down the mountain, the head of the French column annihilated, and covering the descent, from the crown to the valley, with heaps of its dead and dying.

At this time the 45th were engaged with numbers out of proportion, but they gallantly maintained their ground. The 5th, 74th, and 83rd, were likewise attacked; but the 88th, from the nature of their situation, came in contact with the full body of the enemy, and, while opposed to three times their own number in front, were assailed on their left by a couple of hundred riflemen stationed in the rocks. Colonel Wallace changed his front, but had scarcely reached the rocks, when a fire, destructive as it was animated, assailed him.

The moment was a critical one, but he never lost his presence of mind. He ordered his two first companies to attack the rocks, while he pressed forward with the remainder of his regiment against the main body. The 8th Portuguese were close on the enemy, and opened a well-directed fire, while the 45th were performing prodigies of valour. At this moment, the 88th came up to the assistance of their comrades, and the three regiments pressed on; a terrific contest took place; the French fought well, but they had no chance with our men when we grappled close with them; and they were overthrown, leaving half of their column on the heath with which the hill was covered.

The French, ranged, amphitheatrically one above another, took a murderous aim at our soldiers in their advance to dislodge; officers as well as privates became personally engaged in a hand-to-hand fight.

Although they combated with a desperation suited to the situation in which they were placed, the heroes of Austerlitz, Baling, and Wagram, were hurled from the rocks by the Rangers of Connaught.

The 88th arriving to the assistance of their comrades, instantly charged, and the enemy were borne over the cliffs and crags with fearful rapidity, many of them being literally picked out of the holes in the rocks by the bayonets of our soldiers.

Referring to their conduct on this occasion, the Duke of Wellington observes in his despatch that he never witnessed a more gallant attack than that made by these two regiments on the division of the enemy which had then reached the ridge of the Sierra. In addition to this flattering testimony of his Grace, and in further evidence of the gallantry they displayed, it will be sufficient to state that the loss sustained by these two corps on the occasion amounted to sixteen officers, seven sergeants, and two hundred and sixty-one men, being nearly one-half of the whole British loss in the battle.

When a part of the Sierra had been gained, Leith perceiving that the French had occupied it, moved the 38th on their right flank, with the Royals in reserve. The 9th formed line under a heavy fire, and, without returning a shot, fairly deforced the French grenadiers from the rocks with the bayonet. The mountain crest was now secure, Reynier completely repulsed, and Hill, closing up to support, prevented any attempt being made to recover it.

The greater difficulty of the ground rendered Ney's attacks still less successful, even for a time, than Reynier's had proved. Craufurd's disposition of the light division was masterly. Under a dipping of the ground between the convent and plateau, the 43rd and 52nd were formed in line; while higher up the hill, and closer to the convent, the Germans were drawn up. The rocks in front formed a natural battery for the guns; and the whole face of the Sierra was crowded with rifle-

General Crauford ordering the attack at Busaco

men and *cacadores*. Morning had scarcely dawned, when a sharp and scattered musketry was heard among the broken hollows of the valley that separated the rival armies, and presently the French appeared in three divisions, Loisson's mounting the face of the Sierra, Marchand's inclining leftwards, as if it intended to turn the right flank of the light division, and the third held in reserve.

The brigade of General Simon led the attack, and reckless of the constant fusillade of the British light troops, and the sweeping fire of the artillery, which literally ploughed through the advancing column, from its leading to its last section, the enemy came steadily and quickly on. The horse artillery worked their guns with amazing rapidity, delivering round after round with such beautiful precision that the wonder was how any body of men could advance under such a withering and incessant cannonade. But nothing could surpass the gallantry of the assailants. On they came, and in a few moments, their skirmishers, "breathless, and begrimed with powder," topped the ridge of the Sierra. The British guns were instantly retired, the French cheers arose, and, in another second, their column topped the height.

General Craufurd, who had coolly watched the progress of the advance, called on the 43rd and 52nd to "Charge!" A cheer that pealed for miles over the Sierra answered the order, and eighteen hundred British bayonets went sparkling over the brow of the hill. The head of the French column was overwhelmed in an instant; both its flanks were lapped over by the British wings, while volley after volley, at a few yards' distance, completed its destruction, and marked with hundreds of its dead and dying, prostrate on the face of the Sierra, the course of its murderous discomfiture. Some of the light troops continued slaughtering the broken columns nearly to the bottom of the hill, until Ney's guns opened from the opposite side, and covered the escape of relics of Simon's division.

And yet the bravery of the French merited a better result. No troops advanced more gallantly; and when the British steel was glittering in their faces, as with resistless force the fatal rush was made over the crest of the Sierra, every man of the first? section of the French raised and discharged his musket, although before his finger parted from the trigger he knew that a British bayonet would be quivering in his heart. Simon was wounded and left upon the field, and his division so totally shattered as to be unable to make any second attempt.

On the right, Marchand's brigades having gained the cover of a pine wood, threw out their skirmishers and endeavoured to surmount the broken surface that the hill everywhere presented. Pack held them in check, while the Guards, formed on the brow of the Sierra, were seen in such imposing force as to render any attempt on the position useless. Craufurd's artillery flanked the pine wood, and maintained a rapid fire; when, finding his troops sinking under an unprofitable slaughter, Ney, after the effort of an hour, retired behind the rocks.

The roar of battle was stilled. Each side removed their wounded men; and the moment the firing ceased both parties amicably intermingled, and sought and brought off their disabled comrades. When this labour of humanity was over, a French company having taken possession of a village within pistol-shot of General Craufurd, stoutly refused to retire when directed. The commander of the light division turned his artillery on the post, overwhelmed it in an instant with his cannonade, and when the guns ceased firing, sent down a few companies of the 43rd to clear the ruins of any whom his grape might have left alive, the obstinacy of the French officer having drawn upon him most justly the anger of the fiery leader of the light division.

The loss sustained by Massena in his attempt upon the British position at Busaco was immense. A general of brigade, Graind'orge, and above a thousand men, were killed; Foy, Merle, and Simon, with four thousand five hundred, were wounded; and nearly three hundred taken prisoners. The allied casualties did not exceed twelve hundred and fifty men, of which nearly one-half were Portuguese.

No battle witnessed more gallant efforts on the part of the enemy than Busaco; and that the British loss should be so disproportionate to that suffered by the French, can readily be conceived from the superior fire, particularly of cannon, which the position of Busaco enabled Lord Wellington to employ. The Portuguese troops behaved admirably, their steadiness and bravery were as creditable to the British officers who disciplined and led them on, as it was satisfactory to the Commander of the Allies.

CHAPTER 10

The Battle of Barrosa, 1811

Massena had suffered too heavily in his attempt on the British position, to think of attacking the Sierra de Busaco a second time. Early on the 28th September he commenced quietly retiring his advanced brigades, and in the evening, was reported to be marching with all his divisions on the Malhada road, after having set fire to the woods to conceal his movements, which was evidently intended to turn the British left. Orders were instantly given by Lord Wellington to abandon the Sierra; and at nightfall Hill's division was again thrown across the river, the remainder of the brigades, defiling to their left, moved by the shorter road on Coimbra, and resumed the line of the Mondego on the 30th.

The celebrated proclamation to the Portuguese nation was issued by Lord Wellington previous to the commencement of his retreat. Determined to destroy any hope the French might have entertained of subsisting their armies on the resources of the country, the people were emphatically desired, on the approach of the enemy, to abandon their dwellings, drive off their cattle, destroy provisions and forage, and leave the villages and towns deserted of inhabitants and devastated of everything which could be serviceable to the invaders.

Generally, these orders were obeyed with a devotion that seems remarkable. Property was wasted or concealed, and the shrine and cottage alike abandoned by their occupants, the peasant deserting the hearth where he had been nursed, and the monk the altar where he had worshipped from his boyhood. The fugitives accompanied the army on its march, and when it halted in the lines, one portion of the wanderers proceeded to Lisbon, while the greater number crossed the Tagus to seek on its southern shores a temporary retreat from those who had obliged them to sacrifice their possessions, and fly from the dwellings of their fathers.

Nothing could surpass the fine attitude maintained by the British in their retreat on Torres Vedras, and every march was leisurely executed, as if no enemy were in the rear. By the great roads of Leiria and Espinal the receding movement was effected; and, with the exception of some affairs of cavalry, and a temporary embarrassment in passing through Condeixa, occasioned by a false alarm and narrow streets, a retreat of nearly two hundred miles was effected with as little confusion as attends an ordinary march. No portion of the field equipage, no baggage whatever was captured, and still more strange, a greater number of prisoners were taken from the pursuers than lost by the pursued—a fact in the history of retreats without a parallel.

Massena, after a three days' reconnaissance, and under the advice of his chief engineers, abandoned all hope of forcing this singular position. Nothing could surpass the chagrin and surprise that the French commander exhibited to his staff, when, by personal observation, he had ascertained the full extent of the defences with which British skill had perfected what nature had already done so much for. To attempt forcing Torres Vedras must have ensured destruction; and nothing remained, but to take a position in its front, and observe that immense chain of posts, which it was found impossible to carry.

Though by cavalry patrols on the right bank of the Tagus and the detachment of a division to Thomar, the French commander had enlarged the scope of country over which his foragers could operate, supplies failed fast; and even French ingenuity failed in discovering concealed magazines. Nothing remained but to retire from cantonments where provisions were no longer procurable; on the morning of the 15th the French Army broke up, and, favoured by thick weather, retired in beautiful order on Santarem and Torres Novas.

Both armies went into cantonments; the allies with headquarters at Cartaxo, the French having chosen Torres Novas for theirs.

Little of military interest occurred for some time, excepting that the Portuguese militias, under their British officers, were incessant in harassing the French.

Time passed on, nothing of moment occurred, the British remaining quiet, in expectation of a reinforcement of troops from home.

The first movements that took place were an advance on Punhete by the allies, and the sudden retirement from Santarem by the French. Massena chose the left bank of the Mondego aa his line of retreat, falling back on Guarda and Almeida, Wellington followed promptly;

and on the 9th, Massena having halted in front of Pombal, the allies hastened forward to attack him. But the French marshal declined an action, and fell back pressed closely by the British light troops, and covered by a splendid rear-guard which he had formed from his choicest battalions, and intrusted to the command of Marshal Ney.

On the 5th of April Massena crossed the frontier. Portugal was now without the presence of a Frenchman, except the garrison of Almeida, and those who had been taken prisoners in the numerous affairs between the British light troops and the enemy's rear-guard. Nothing could be bolder or more scientific than the whole course of Wellington's operations, from the time he left the lines until Massena "changed his position from the Zezere to the Agueda." (Phrase used by Prince of Esling in his despatches, to evade the plain but unpalatable term of *retreat*). Yet it must be admitted that the French retreat all through was conducted with consummate ability. Ney commanded the rear-guard with excellent judgment; his positions were admirably selected; and when assailed, they were defended as might have been expected from one who had already obtained the highest professional reputation.

In a military view, Massena's retreat was admirable, and reflected infinite credit on the generals who directed it; but, in a moral one, nothing could be more disgraceful. The country over which the retreating columns of the French Army passed, was marked by bloodshed and devastation. Villages were everywhere destroyed, property wasted or carried off, the men shot in sheer wantonness, the women villainously abused, while thousands were driven for shelter to the mountains, where many perished from actual want. With gothic barbarity, the fine old city of Leria, and the church and convent of Alcabaca, with its library and relics, were ordered by Massena to be burned. The order was too faithfully executed; and places, for centuries objects of Portuguese veneration, were given to the flames; and those hallowed roofs, beneath which "the sage had studied and the saint had prayed," were reduced to ashes, to gratify a ruthless and vindictive spirit of revenge.

The French soldiers had been so long accustomed to plunder, that they proceeded in their researches for booty of every kind upon a regular system. They were provided with tools for the work of pillage, and every piece of furniture in which places of concealment could be constructed they broke open from behind, so that no valuables could be hidden from them by any contrivance of that kind. Having satisfied themselves that nothing was secreted above ground, they proceeded

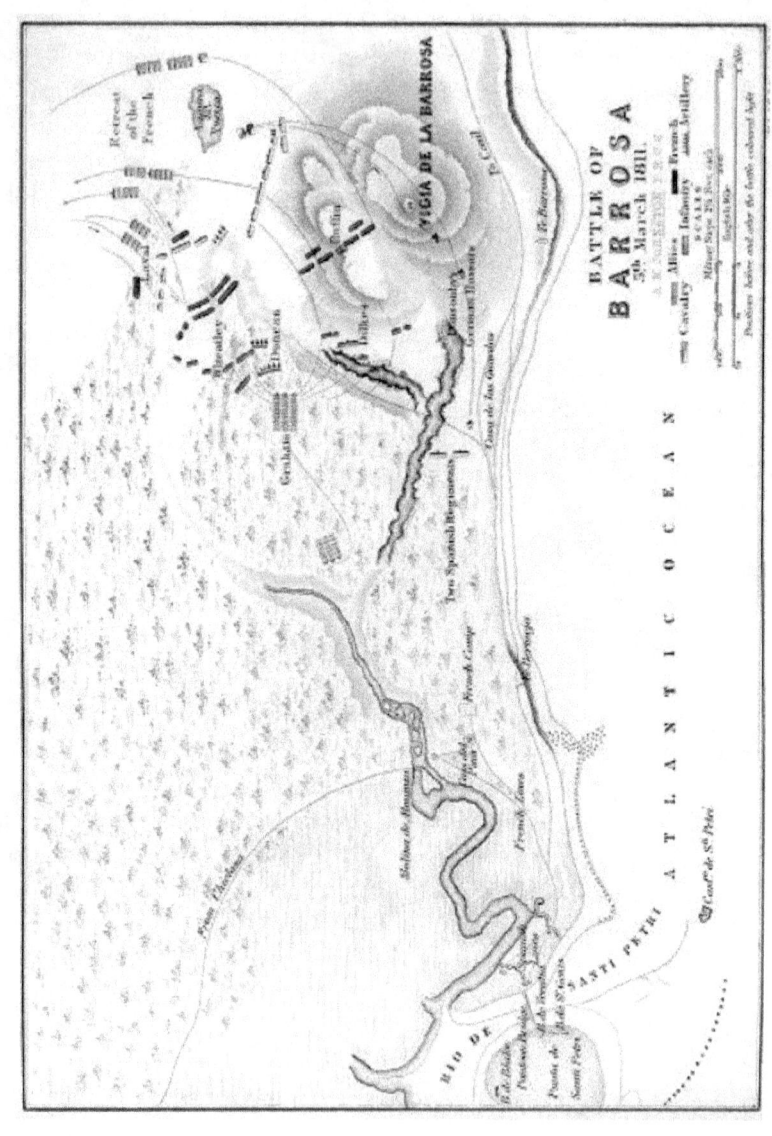

to examine whether there was any new masonry, or if any part of the cellar or ground floor had been disturbed; if it appeared uneven, they dug there; where there was no such indication they poured water, and if it were absorbed in one place faster than another, there they broke the earth.

There were men who at the first glance could pronounce whether anything had been buried beneath the soil, and when they probed with an iron rod, or, in default of it, with sword or bayonet, it was found that they were seldom mistaken in their judgment. The habit of living by prey called forth, as in beasts, a faculty of discovering it; there was one soldier whose scent became so acute that if he approached the place where wine had been concealed, he would go unerringly to the spot.

Wherever the French bivouacked the scene was such as might rather have been looked for in a camp of predatory Tartars than in that of a civilised people. Food and forage, and skins of wine, and clothes and church vestments, books and guitars, and all the bulkier articles of wasteful spoil were heaped together in their huts with the planks and doors of the habitations which they had demolished. Some of the men, retaining amid this brutal service the characteristic activity and cleverness of their nation, fitted up their huts with hangings from their last scene of pillage, with a regard to comfort hardly to have been expected in their situation, and a love of gaiety only to be found in Frenchmen.

Such was the condition of things with the main army when the famous Battle of Barrosa was fought by a different section of the British Army at some distance.

An Anglo-Spanish Army was attempting to raise the siege of Cadiz. All bade fair for success, as the French had scarcely ten thousand men in their lines, while in the city the Spanish force was more than twenty thousand. On this occasion, Graham acted under the command of La Pena, and eleven thousand allied troops were despatched from Cadiz to Tarifa, to operate against the enemy's rear at Chiclana; while it was arranged that Zayas, who commanded in the Isle de Leon, should pass his troops over San Petri near the sea, and unite in a combined attack.

After much delay, occasioned by tempestuous weather, the troops and artillery were safely assembled at Tarifa on the 27th; and when joined by the 28th regiment and the flank companies of the 9th and 82nd, they numbered about four thousand five hundred effective men.

General La Pena arrived the same day with seven thousand Spaniards; and on the next, the united force moved through the passes of the Ronda hills, and halted within four leagues of the French outposts. The commands of the allies were thus distributed—the vanguard to Lardizable, the centre to the Prince of Anglona, the reserve to General Graham, and the cavalry to Colonel Whittingham.

Victor, the French commander, though apprised of the activity of the Spaniards, and the march of General Graham, could not correctly ascertain the point upon which their intended operations would be directed; and therefore, with eleven thousand choice troops, he took post in observation between the roads of Conil and Medina.

On the 2nd April, the capture of Casa Viejas, increased La Pena's force by sixteen hundred infantry, and a number of guerilla horse. Until the 5th, he continued his movements, and, after his advanced guard had been roughly handled by a squadron of French dragoons, he halted on the Cerro de Puerco, more generally and gloriously known as the heights of Barrosa.

Barrosa, though not a high hill, rises considerably above the rugged plain it overlooks, and stands four miles inland from the debouchment of the Santi Petri. The plain is bounded on the right by the forest of Chiclana, on the left by cliffs on the sea-beach, and on the centre by a pine wood, beyond which the hill of Bermeja rises.

The irregularity and tardiness of the Spanish movements gave a portentous warning of what might be expected from them in the field. They occupied fifteen hours in executing a moderate march, passing over the ground in a rambling and disorderly manner, that seemed rather like peasants wandering from a fair, than troops moving in the presence of an enemy. La Pena, without waiting to correct his broken ranks, sent on a vanguard to Zayas; while his rear, entirely separated from the centre, was still straggling over the country, and contrary to the expressed wishes of Graham, who implored him to hold Barrosa, he declined his advice, and ordered the British to march through the pine wood on Bermeja.

Graham, supposing that Anglona's division and the cavalry would continue to occupy the hill, leaving the flank companies of the 9th and 82nd to protect his baggage, obeyed the order, and commenced his march. But the astonishment of the British general was unbounded, when, on entering the wood, he saw La Pena moving his entire corps from the heights of Barrosa, with the exception of three or four battalions and as many pieces of artillery.

Unfortunately, the British general was not the only person who had observed that Barrosa was abandoned. Victor, concealed in the forest of Chiclana, anxiously watched the movements of the allies. He saw the fatal error committed by the Spanish leader, and instantly made dispositions to profit from the ignorance and obstinacy of his antagonist.

The French marshal, having selected three grenadier battalions as reserves, strengthened his left wing with two, and three squadrons of cavalry, while the other was attached to his centre. Ruffin commanded the left, Laval the centre; while Villatte, with two thousand five hundred infantry, covered the camp, and watched the Spaniards at Santa Petri and Bermeja. The cavalry stationed at Medina and Arcos were ordered by Victor to move on Vejer and cut off the allies, for on their certain defeat the French general entertained no doubt.

The time was admirably chosen for a decisive movement. The British corps were defiling through the wood, the strength of the Spaniards posted on the Bermeja, another division pursued a straggling march on Vejer, and a fourth, in great confusion, was at Barrosa, as a protection to the baggage. Making Villatte's division a pivot, Victor pushed Laval at once against the British, and ascending the back of the hill with Ruffin's brigade, he threw himself between the Spaniards and Medina, dispersed the camp followers in an instant, and captured the guns and baggage.

Graham, when apprised of this sudden and unexpected movement, countermarched directly on the plain, to cooperate, as he believed, with La Pena, whom he calculated on finding on the heights, but never was reliance placed by a brave soldier on a more worthless ally. The Spaniard had deceived him; himself was gone, his mob-soldiery were fugitives, Ruffin on the heights, the French cavalry between him and the sea, and Laval close on the left flank of the British.

It was indeed a most perilous situation, and in that extremity the brave old man to whom the British had been fortunately confided, proved himself worthy of the trust. He saw the ruin of retreat; safety lay in daring, and though the enemy held the key of the position with fresh troops, Graham boldly determined to attack them with his wearied ones.

The battle was instantly commenced. Duncan's artillery opened a furious cannonade on the column of Laval; and Colonel Barnard, with the rifles and Portuguese *cacadores* extended to the left and began firing. The rest of the British troops formed two masses, without regard to regiments or brigades; one, under General Dilkes, marched

Chiclana

direct against Ruffin, and the other under Colonel Whately, boldly attacked Laval. On both sides the guns poured a torrent of grape and canister over the field; the infantry kept up a withering fire; and both sides advanced, for both seemed anxious to bring the contest to an issue. Whately, when the lines approached, came forward to the charge; he drove the first line on the second, and routed both with slaughter.

Brown had marched at once on Ruffin, and though half his email number had been annihilated by an overwhelming fire, he held his ground till Dilkes came to his assistance. Never pausing to correct their formation, which the ragged hill had considerably disorganised, on came the British desperately; they were still struggling to attain the summit, and approaching the ridge, breathless and disordered, their opponents advanced to meet them.

A furious combat, hand to hand, ensued; for a moment victory seemed doubtful, but the British fought with a ferocity that nothing could oppose. Whole sections went down, but still the others pressed forward. Ruffin and Rousseau, who commanded the *élite* of the grenadiers, fell mortally wounded. The British never paused, on they went, delivering volley after volley, forcing the French over the heights, and defeating them with the loss of their guns.

The divisions of the French commander, though dreadfully cut up, fell back on each other for mutual support, and endeavoured to rally; but Duncan's guns were moved forward, and opened a close and murderous fire that prevented a possibility of reforming. Nothing could have the shattered battalions from that exterminating cannonade but an instant retreat, and Victor retired, leaving the British in undisputed possession of the field, from which want of food and continued fatigue, while under arms for four-and-twenty hours, of course prevented them from moving in pursuit.

Never was there a shorter, and never a bloodier conflict. Though it lasted scarcely an hour and a quarter, out of the handful of British troops engaged, a loss was sustained of fifty officers, sixty sergeants, and eleven hundred rank and file. The French, besides two thousand killed and wounded, lost six guns, an eagle, and two generals, with nearly five hundred prisoners.

Nothing could exceed the dastardly duplicity with which the Spanish general abandoned his gallant ally. La Pena never made a movement towards the succour of the British, and although the French cavalry scarcely exceeded two hundred men, and the Spanish, under Whittingham, amounted to more than six, the latter never drew a sabre. Never was there a finer field for cavalry to act upon with effect; Ruffin's left was perfectly open, and even a demonstration of attack must have turned defeat to ruin. Three troops of German hussars, under Ponsonby, reached the field at the close of the battle, just as the beaten divisions were attempting to unite. They charged through the French squadrons, overthrew them, captured two guns, and sabred many of Ruffin's grenadiers, while endeavouring to regain their ranks.

To paint the character of Barrosa in a few words, Napier's will best describe it:

> The contemptible feebleness of La Pena furnished a surprising contrast to the heroic vigour of Graham, whose attack was an inspiration rather than a resolution—so wise, so sudden was the decision, so swift, so conclusive was the execution.

CHAPTER 11

The Battle of Fuentes d'Onoro, 1811

Massena having taken the field again, with the object of raising the blockade of Almeida, then closely invested by Lord Wellington, the British commander, determined that this important fortress should not be relieved, resolved, even on unfavourable ground and with an inferior force, to risk a battle.

The River Coa flows past Almeida, its banks are dangerous and steep, and its points of passage few. Beside the bridge of the city, there is a second, seven miles up the stream, at Castello Bom; and a third, twenty miles farther still, at Sabugal. To fight with the river in his rear was hazardous; but Wellington had decided on his course of action, and accordingly he selected the best position which a district of no great military strength would afford.

The Duas Casas runs in a northerly course and nearly parallel with the Coa, having on its left bank the village of Fuentes d'Onoro. It is a sweet hamlet, and prettily situated in front of a sloping hill of easy access, here and there intersprinkled with woods of cork and ilex. The village was a feature of considerable military importance, the channel of the Duas Casas being rocky and broken, and its banks generally steep. Fuentes was occupied by the light troops, the third division were posted on a ridge crossing the road to Villa Formosa, the brigades of Craufurd and Campbell had formed behind the village of Almeida, to observe the bridge over the Duas Casas; Pack's division observed Almeida closely, and shut in the garrison; Erskine held the great road that crosses the Duas Casas by a ford, while the guerilla cavalry were placed in observation, two miles on the right, at the village of Nava-de-Aver. The position was very extensive, covering, from flank to flank, a surface of nearly six miles.

The military attitude which the allied commander held, compared

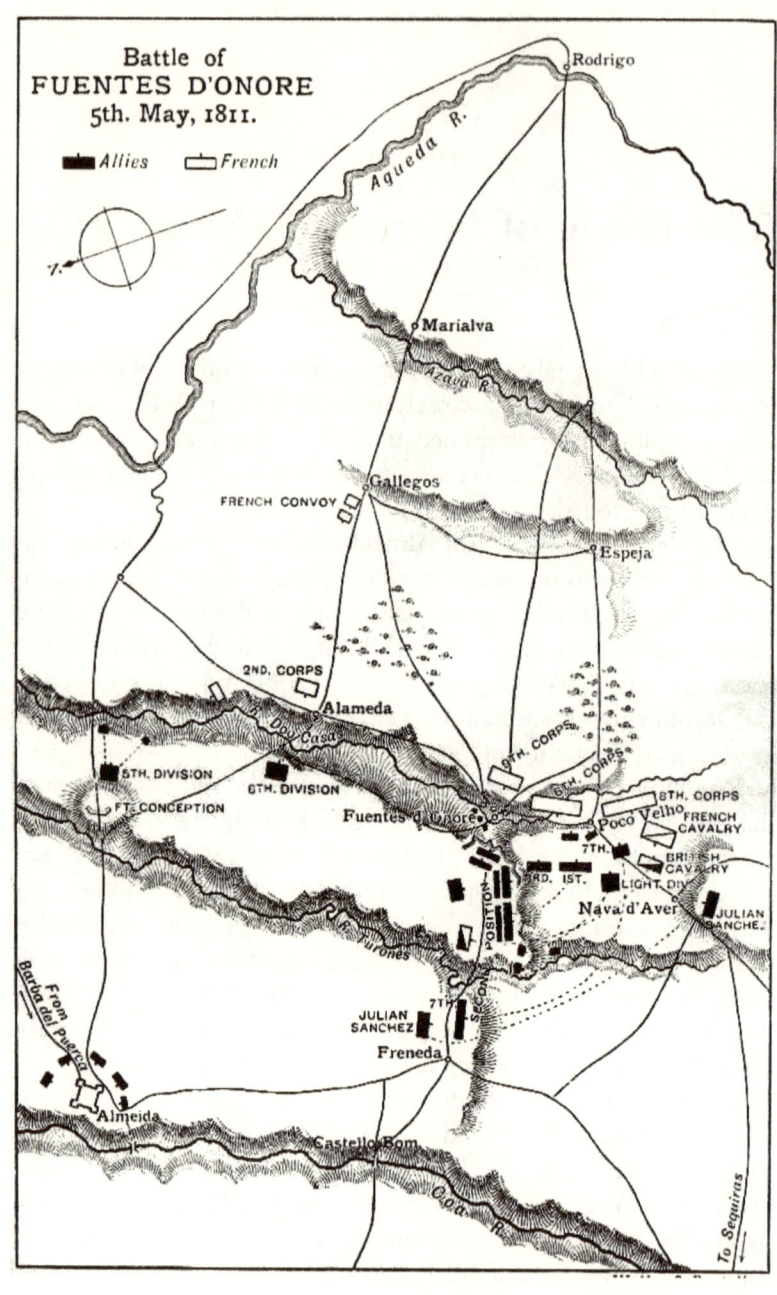

with that of the preceding year, was singularly changed. Then, his being able to maintain himself in the country was more than questionable; now, and in the face of those corps who had driven him on Torres Vedras, he stood with a most effective force.

On the 1st and 2nd of May, Massena, with an immense convoy, passed the Rivers Agueda and Azava, with the intention of relieving Almeida, and providing it with every means for insuring a protracted defence. On the 3rd, in the evening, the French sixth corps appeared on the heights above Fuentes d'Onoro, and commenced a lively cannonade, followed up by a furious assault upon the village. The light companies, who held Fuentes, sustained the attack bravely, until they were supported by the 71st, and, as the affair grew warmer, by the 79th and 24th also.

Colonel Williams was wounded, and the command devolving on Colonel Cameron, he remedied a temporary disorder that had been occasioned by the fall of several officers, and again restored the battle. The ground for a time gained by the French was inch by inch recovered; and, probably, during the Peninsular conflicts, a closer combat was never maintained, as, in the main street particularly, the rival troops fought fairly hand to hand.

The French were finally expelled from the village. Night was closing; undismayed by a heavy loss, and unwearied by a hardly-contested action, a cannon—as it appeared to be—being seen on the adjacent heights, the 71st dashed across the rivulet, and bearing down all resistance, reached and won the object of their enterprise. On reaching it, however, the Highlanders discovered that in the haze of evening they had mistaken a tumbrel for a gun; but they bore it off, a trophy of their gallantry.

The British regiments held the village. The next day passed quietly over, while Massena carefully reconnoitred the position of his opponent. It was suspected that he intended to change his plan of attack, and manoeuvre on the right; and to secure that flank, Houston's division was moved to Posa Velha, the ground there being weak, and the river fordable. As had been anticipated, favoured by the darkness, Massena marched his troops bodily to the left, placing his whole cavalry, with Junot's corps, right in front of Houston's division. A correspondent movement was consequently made; Spencer's and Picton's divisions moved to the right, and Craufurd, with the cavalry, marched to support Houston.

At daybreak, the attack was made. Junot carried the village of Posa

Velha, and the French cavalry drove in that of the allies. But the infantry, supported by the horse artillery, repulsed the enemy and drove them back with loss.

A difficult and a daring change of position was now required; and Lord Wellington, abandoning his communication with the bridge at Sabugal, retired his right, and formed line at right angles with his first formation, extending from the Duas Casas, towards Frenada on the Coa.

This necessary operation obliged the seventh and light divisions, in the face of a bold and powerful cavalry, to retire nearly two miles; and it required all the steadiness and rapidity of British light infantry to effect the movement safely. Few as the British cavalry were, they charged the enemy frequently, and always with success; while the horse artillery sustained their well-earned reputation, acting with a boldness that at times almost exposed them to certain capture.

At one place, however, the fury of the fight seemed for a time to centre. A great commotion was observed among the French squadrons; men and officers closed in confusion towards one point where a thick dust was rising, and where loud cries and the sparkling of blades and flashing of pistols indicated some extraordinary occurrence. Suddenly the multitude was violently agitated, a British shout arose, the mass was rent asunder, and Norman Ramsay burst forth at the head of his battery, his horses breathing fire, and stretching like greyhounds along the plain, his guns bounding like things of no weight, and the mounted gunners in close and compact order protecting the rear.

The infantry, in squares of battalions, repelled every charge; while the Chasseurs Brittanique kept up a flanking fire, that, while the retrogression of the British was being effected, entailed a considerable loss on the assailants who were pressing them closely.

The new position of the British was most formidable. The right *appuied* upon a hill, topped by an ancient tower, and the alignment was so judiciously taken up that Massena did not venture to assail it.

While these operations were going on, a furious attack was repeated on Fuentes d'Onoro. Infantry, cavalry, and artillery, all were brought to bear, a tremendous cannonade opened on the devoted village, and the assault was made at the same moment on flanks and front together. Desperate fighting in the streets and churchyard took place. The French feeding the attacking troops with fresh numbers, pressed the three regiments that held the upper village severely, but alter one of the closest and most desperate combats that has ever been

Royal Horse Artillery saving the guns

maintained, a bayonet charge of the 88th decided the contest; and the assailants, notwithstanding their vastly superior force, were driven with prodigious slaughter from Fuentes, the upper village remaining in possession of its gallant defenders, and the lower in the silent occupation of the dead.

Evening closed the combat. Massena's columns on the right were halted, and his sixth division, with which he had endeavoured to storm Fuentes d'Onoro, withdrawn, the whole French army bivouacking in the order in which they had stood when the engagement closed. The British lighted their fires, posted their pickets, and occupied the field they had so bravely held; and both parties lay down to rest, with a confident assurance on their minds, that the battle was only intermitted till the return of daylight.

A brigade of the light division relieved the brave defenders of Fuentes, and preparatory to the expected renewal of attack, they threw up some works to defend the upper village and the ground behind it. But these precautions were unnecessary; Massena remained for the next day in front of his antagonist, exhibiting no anxiety to renew the combat. The 7th found the British, as usual, under arms at dawn, but the day passed as quietly as the preceding one had done. On the 8th, however, the French columns were observed in full retreat, marching on the road to Ciudad Rodrigo. Massena, with an army reinforced by every battalion and squadron he could collect from Gallicia and Castile, had been completely beaten by a wing of the British army, consisting of three divisions only.

With that unblushing assurance, for which the French marshals have been remarkable, of changing defeat into conquest, Massena did not hesitate to call Fuentes d'Onoro a victory. But the object for which the battle was fought was unattained—he failed in succouring the beleaguered city, and Almeida was left to its fate.

In a close and sanguinary contest, like that of Fuentes d'Onoro, the loss on both sides must necessarily be immense. The British had two hundred killed, one thousand and twenty-eight wounded, and two hundred and ninety-four missing. The French suffered much more heavily; and it was computed that nearly five thousand of Massena's army were rendered *hors de combat*. In the lower village of Fuentes alone, two hundred dead bodies were reckoned.

In the conduct of an affair which terminated so gloriously for the divisions engaged, the system of defence adopted by Lord Wellington was very masterly. Every arm of his force was, happily employed, and all were well combined for mutual protection. Massena had every advantage for arranging his attack, for thick woods in front enabled him to form his columns unseen, and until the moment of their debouchment, none could tell their strength, or even guess the place on which they were about to be directed. Hence, the French marshal had the means of pouring a mass of infantry on any point he pleased, and of making a serious impression before troops could be moved forward to meet and repel the assault.

His superiority in cavalry and artillery was great. He might, under a cannonade that the British guns could not have answered, have brought forward his cavalry *en masse*, supported by columns of infantry, and the allied line, under a masked movement of this kind, would in all probability have been penetrated. Or, by bringing his cavalry round the right of the British flank, and crossing the Coa, he might have obliged Lord Wellington to pass the river under the greatest disadvantages. Indeed, this was apprehended on the 5th, and there was but one alternative, either to raise the blockade of Almeida, or relinquish the Sabugal road. The latter was done. It was a bold measure, but it was not adopted without due consideration; and it received an ample reward in the successful termination of this hard-fought battle.

CHAPTER 12

The Battle of Albuera, 1811

While Marshal Beresford was endeavouring to reduce Badajoz, intelligence reached him that Soult was marching from Larena. Beresford, of course, at once abandoned the siege, removed the artillery and stores, and having united himself with Blake, Castanos, and Ballesteros, the combined armies took position behind the Albuera, where the Seville and Olivenca roads separate.

On the westward of the ground where the allies determined to abide a battle, the surface undulated gently, and on the summit, and parallel with the river, their divisions were drawn up. The village of Albuera was in front of the left, and the right was formed on a succession of knolls, none of them of any strength, and having no particular *appui*. On the eastern side of the river, an open country extends for a considerable distance, terminating in thick woods; and in these Soult bivouacked on the night of the 15th, and there made his dispositions for attack.

The French Army, though numerically weaker, was composed of veteran troops, and amounted to twenty thousand infantry, three thousand cavalry, and forty pieces of cannon. The allies numbered twenty-seven thousand infantry, two thousand cavalry, and thirty-two guns; but of this force, fourteen thousand were Spanish.

These last were formed in a double line upon the right, Stewart's division was in the centre, a Portuguese division on the left. The light infantry, under Alten, held the village, and the dragoons, under Lumley, were placed on the right flank of the Spaniards. Cole's division (the fusiliers) and a Portuguese brigade, which came up after the action had commenced, were formed in rear of the centre.

Beresford's was a medley of three nations. He had thirty thousand men in position, but not a fourth was British; while nearly one-half

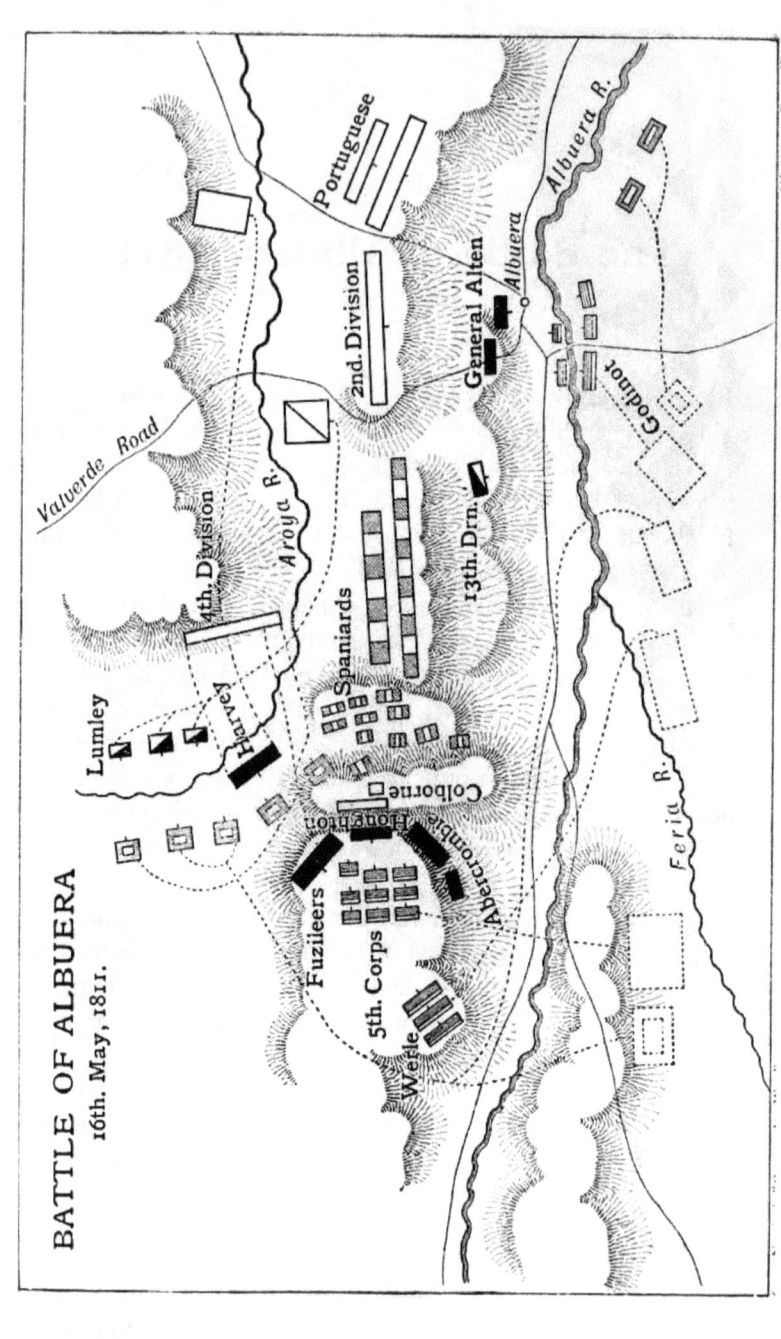

was composed of that worst of military mobs—the Spaniards; nor were these even brought up in time to admit of their being properly posted. Blake had promised that his corps should be on the hill of Albuera before noon on the 15th May, and, with but a few miles to march, with excellent roads to traverse, the head of his columns reached the ground near midnight, and the rear at three on the morning of the 16th.

Bad as Beresford's army was, had it been in hand, more might have been done with it. It was three o'clock on the 16th before Blake was fairly up, and six before the fourth division reached the ground; while three fine British regiments under Kemmis, and Madden's Portuguese cavalry, never appeared. As the event showed, a few British soldiers would have proved invaluable, and these troops, though immediately contiguous during the long and doubtful struggle that ensued, remained *non-combattant*.

Beresford's position had been carefully reconnoitred by Soult on the evening of the 15th, and aware that the fourth British division was still before Badajoz, and Blake not yet come up, he determined to attack the marshal without delay. A height, commanding the Valverde road, if a front attack were made, appeared on his examination of the ground to be the key of the position; and as Beresford had overlooked its occupation, Soult ably selected it as the point by which his principal effort, should be made.

A wooded hill behind the Albuera, and within cannon-shot of the allied right, afforded the French marshal the means of forming a strong column for attack, without his design being noticed by his opponent. Covered by the darkness, he brought forward the artillery of Ruty, the fifth corps under Girard, with the cavalry of Latour Maubourg, and formed them for his intended assault; thus, concentrating fifteen thousand men and forty guns within ten minutes' march of Beresford's right wing, and yet that general could neither see a man, nor draw a sound conclusion as to the real plan of attack. The remainder of his corps was placed in the wood on the banks of the Feria, to bear against Beresford's left, and by carrying the bridge and village sever the wings of the allied army.

The engagement commenced by Godinot debouching from the wood, and making a feint on the left, while the main body of the French ascended the heights on the right of the Spaniards. On perceiving the true object of Soult's attack, Beresford, who had vainly endeavoured, through an *aide-de-camp*, to persuade Blake to change

his front, rode to the Spanish post, pointed out the heads of the advancing columns, and induced his ally to take up a new alignment. It was scarcely done until the French bore down upon the Spanish infantry; and though at first, they were stoutly opposed, the battalions gradually began to yield ground; and, being farther forced back, Soult commenced deploying on the most commanding point of the position. A serious attack was to be dreaded; the French cavalry sweeping round the allies, threatened their rear, and Godinot's column made fresh demonstrations of vigorously assailing the left.

All this was most alarming; the Spanish line confusedly endeavouring to effect the difficult manoeuvre of changing its front, while two-thirds of the French, in compact order of battle, were preparing to burst upon the disordered ranks, and insure their total destruction. The French guns had opened a furious cannonade, the infantry were firing volley after volley, the cavalry charging where the Spanish battalions seemed most disordered. Already their ranks were wavering, and Soult determined to complete the ruin he had begun, ordered up the reserve, and advanced all his batteries.

At this perilous moment, when the day seemed lost, General Stewart pushed the leading brigade of the fourth division up the hill under Colonel Colborne, and it mounted by columns of companies. To form line on gaining the top, under a withering fire, was difficult; and while in the act of its being effected, a mist, accompanied by a heavy fall of rain, shut every object out from view, and enabled the whole of the light cavalry of Godinot's division to sweep round the right flank, and gallop on the rear of the companies at the time they were in loose deployment. Half the brigade was cut to pieces—the 31st, who were still fortunately in column, alone escaping the lancers, who, with little resistance, were spearing right and left a body of men surprised on an open flat, and wanting the necessary formation which can alone enable infantry to resist a charge of horse.

This scene of slaughter, by a partial dispersion of the smoke and fog that had hitherto concealed the battleground, was fortunately observed by General Lumley, and he ordered the British cavalry to gallop to the relief of the remnant of Colborne's brigade. They charged boldly; and, in turn, the lancers were taken in rear, and many fell beneath the sabres of the British.

The weather, that had caused the destruction of the British regiments, obscured the field of battle, and prevented Soult from taking an immediate advantage by exterminating that half-ruined brigade.

Stewart brought up Houghton's corps; the artillery had come forward, and opened a furious cannonade on the dense masses of the French; and the 31st resolutely maintained its position on the height. Two Spanish brigades were advanced, and the action became hotter than ever. For a moment, the French battalions recoiled, but it was only to rally instantly, and come on with greater fury. A raging fire of artillery on both sides, sustained at little more than pistol range, with reiterated volleys of musketry, heaped the field with dead, while the French were vainly endeavouring to gain ground, and the British would not yield an inch.

But the ranks of the island soldiery were thinning fast, their ammunition was nearly exhausted, their fire slackened, and notwithstanding the cannonade checked the French movement for a time, Soult formed a column on the right flank of the British, and the French lancers charging furiously again, drove off the artillerymen and captured six guns. All now seemed lost, and a retreat appeared inevitable. The Portuguese were preparing to cover it, and the marshal was about to give the order, when Colonel Hardinge suggested that another effort should be made, and boldly ordered General Cole to advance, and then riding to Colonel Abercrombie, who commanded the remaining brigade of the second division, directed him also to push forward into the fight.

The order was instantly obeyed; General Harvey, with the Portuguese regiments of the fourth division, moved on between the British cavalry and the hill; and though charged home by the French dragoons, he checked them by a heavy fire and pushed forward steadily; while General Cole led on the 7th and 23rd Fusiliers in person,

In a few minutes, more the remnant of the British must have abandoned the hill or perished. The French reserve was on its march to assist the front column of the enemy, while, with the allies all was in confusion; and as if the slaughter required an increase, a Spanish and a British regiment were firing in mutual mistake upon each other. Six guns were in possession of the French, and their lancers, riding furiously over the field, threatened the feeble remnant of the British still in line, and speared the wounded without mercy.

At this fearful moment, the boundless gallantry of British officers displayed itself; Colonel Arbuthnot, under the double musketry, rushed between the mistaken regiments, and stopped the firing; Cole pushed up the hill, scattered the lancers, recovered the guns, and passed the right of the skeleton of Houghton's brigade, at the same instant that

British regiments at Albuera

Abercrombie appeared upon its left. Leaving the broken regiments in its rear, the fusilier brigade came forward with imposing gallantry, and boldly confronted the French, now reinforced by a part of its reserve, and who were, as they believed, coming forward to annihilate the "feeble few" that had still survived the murderous contest.

From the daring attitude of the fresh regiments, Soult perceived, too late, that the battle was not yet won; and, under a tremendous fire of artillery, he endeavoured to break up his close formation and extend his front. For a moment, the storm of grape poured from Ruty's well-served artillery, staggered the fusiliers; but it was only for a moment. Though Soult rushed into the thickest of the fire, and encouraged and animated his men, though the cavalry gathered on their flank and threatened it with destruction, on went these noble regiments; volley after volley falling into the crowded ranks of their enemy, and cheer after cheer pealing to Heaven in answer to the clamorous outcry of the French, as the boldest urged the others forward.

Nothing could check the fusiliers; they kept gradually advancing, while the incessant rolling of their musketry slaughtered the crowded sections of the French, and each moment embarrassed more and more Soult's efforts to open out his encumbered line. The reserve, coming to support their comrades—now forced to the very edge of the plateau—increased the crowd without remedying the disorder. The British volleys rolled on faster and more deadly than ever; a horrid carnage made all attempts to hold the hill vain, and uselessly increased an unavailing slaughter. Unable to bear the withering fire, the shattered columns of the French were no longer able to sustain themselves, the mass were driven over the ridge, and trampling each other down, the shattered column sought refuge at the bottom of the hill.

On that bloody height stood the conquerors. From fifteen hundred muskets, a parting volley fell upon the routed column as it hurried down the Sierra. Where was the remainder of the proud army of Britain, that on the morning had exceeded six thousand combatants? Stretched coldly in the sleep of death, or bleeding on the battleground!

During the time this desperate effort of the fusilier brigade had been in progress, Beresford, to assist Hardinge, moved Blake's first line on Albuera, and with the German light troops, and two Portuguese divisions, advanced to support the 7th and 23rd, while Lautour Maubourg's flank attack was repelled by the fire of Lefebre's guns, and a threatened charge by Lumley. But the fusiliers had driven the French over the heights before any assistance reached them, and Beresford was

Captain Fawcett of the 57th at Albuera

enabled to form a fresh line upon the hill, parallel to that by which Soult had made his attack in the morning. For a short time, the battle continued at Albuera, but the French finally withdrew from the village, and at three o'clock in the evening the firing had totally ceased.

There is not on record a bloodier struggle. In four hours' fighting fifteen thousand men were *hors de combat*. The allied loss was frightful; it amounted to nearly seven thousand in killed, wounded, and missing. Almost all its general officers were included in the melancholy list; Bought on, Myers, and Duckworth in the killed; and Cole, Stewart, Ellis, Blakeney, and Hawkshaw among the wounded.

The loss of some regiments was terrible; the 57th came into action with five hundred and seventy bayonets, and at the close it had lost it colonel (Inglis), twenty-two officers, and four hundred rank and file. The proportion of the allied casualties told how fatal Albuera had proved to the British; two thousand Spaniards, and six hundred German and Portuguese, were returned as their killed and wounded, leaving the remainder to be completed from the British regiments. Hence, the unexampled loss of more than four thousand men, out of a corps little exceeding six, was sustained in this sanguinary battle by the British.

Never was more heroism displayed than by the British regiments engaged in the murderous conflict of Albuera. The soldiers dropped by whole ranks, but never thought of turning. When a too ardent wish to succour those pressed upon the hill induced Stewart to hurry Colborne's brigade into action, without allowing it a momentary pause to halt and form, and in the mist, that unluckily favoured the lancer charge the companies were unexpectedly assailed, though fighting at dreadful disadvantage, the men resisted to the last. Numbers perished by the lance-blade; but still the dead Poles that were found intermingled with the fallen British, showed that the gallant islanders had not died without exacting blood for blood.

The French exceeded the British by at least a thousand. Of their worst wounded, eight hundred were left upon the field. Their loss in superior officers, like that of the British, had been most severe—two generals having been killed, and three severely wounded.

To a victory both sides laid claim—the French resting theirs on the capture of some colours, the taking of a howitzer, with some five hundred prisoners whom they had secured unwounded. But the British kept the battleground, and though neither cannon nor eagle remained with them, a field covered with carcases, and heaped with bleeding enemies, was the best trophy of their valour, and clearly established to whom conquest in reality belonged.

Much military controversy has arisen from the fight of Albuera, and Marshal Beresford has received some praise and more censure. Probably the battle should not have been fought at all; or, if it were unavoidable, greater care might have been bestowed in taking the position.

If Beresford's judgment be open to censure, his personal intrepidity must be admitted and admired. No man could make greater exertions to retrieve the day when defeat appeared all but certain. When Stewart's imprudence, in loosely bringing Colborne's brigade into action, had occasioned it a loss only short of annihilation, and the Spaniards, though they could not be induced to advance, fired without ceasing, with a British regiment in their front, Beresford actually seized an ensign and dragged him forward with the colours, hoping that these worthless troops would be inspirited to follow.

Not a man stirred, and the standard-bearer, when the marshal's grasp relaxed, instantly flew back to herd with his cold-blooded associates. In every charge of the fight, and on every part of the field, Beresford was seen conspicuously; and whatever might have been his failing as a general, his bravery as a man should have commanded the respect of many who treated his arrangements with unsparing severity.

A painful night succeeded that sanguinary day. The moaning of the wounded and the groans of the dying were heard on every side; and it was to be dreaded that Soult, who had still fifteen thousand troops fit for action, would renew the battle.

On the next day, however, three fresh British regiments joined the marshal by a forced march; and on the 18th, Soult retreated on the road of Solano, covered by the heavy cavalry of Lautour Maubourg. He had previously despatched such of his wounded as could bear removal towards Seville, leaving the remainder to the generous protection of the British commander.

Soult continued retreating, and Beresford followed him, by order of the allied commander.

CHAPTER 13

The Siege of Ciudad Rodrigo, 1812

A campaign highly honourable to the British arms had ended, and the rival armies had taken up cantonments for the winter months, each covering an extensive range of country, for the better obtaining of forage and supplies. Active operations for a season were suspended, and officers whose private concerns or bad health required a temporary leave of absence, had asked and received permission to revisit Britain. The restoration of the works of Almeida, which the French had half destroyed, occupied the leisure time of the British and Portuguese artificers, while, for the ostensible purpose of arming that fortress, siege stores and a battering train were conveyed thither by water carriage—the Douro having been rendered navigable by the British engineers for an extended distance of forty miles.

But the arming of Almeida was but a feint—the reduction of Ciudad Rodrigo was the real object of Lord Wellington, and with indefatigable zeal he applied himself to obtain the means. A waggon train was organised—six hundred carts, on an improved construction, were built; and while the French marshal, supposing that the weakness of Lord Wellington was a security against any act of aggression upon his part, detached Montbrun to Valencia, and Dorsenne to the Asturias and Montana, the British general was quietly preparing to strike a sudden and unexpected blow, and completed his necessary arrangements for investing Rodrigo the 6th of January.

Considering the season of the year, and the nakedness of the country for many miles around the threatened fortress, the intended operation was bold to a degree. The horses had scarcely any forage, and the men were literally destitute of bread or shelter. The new year came in inclemently, rain fell in torrents, and though the investment was delayed two days, the brigade (Mackinnon's) that marched from Aldea

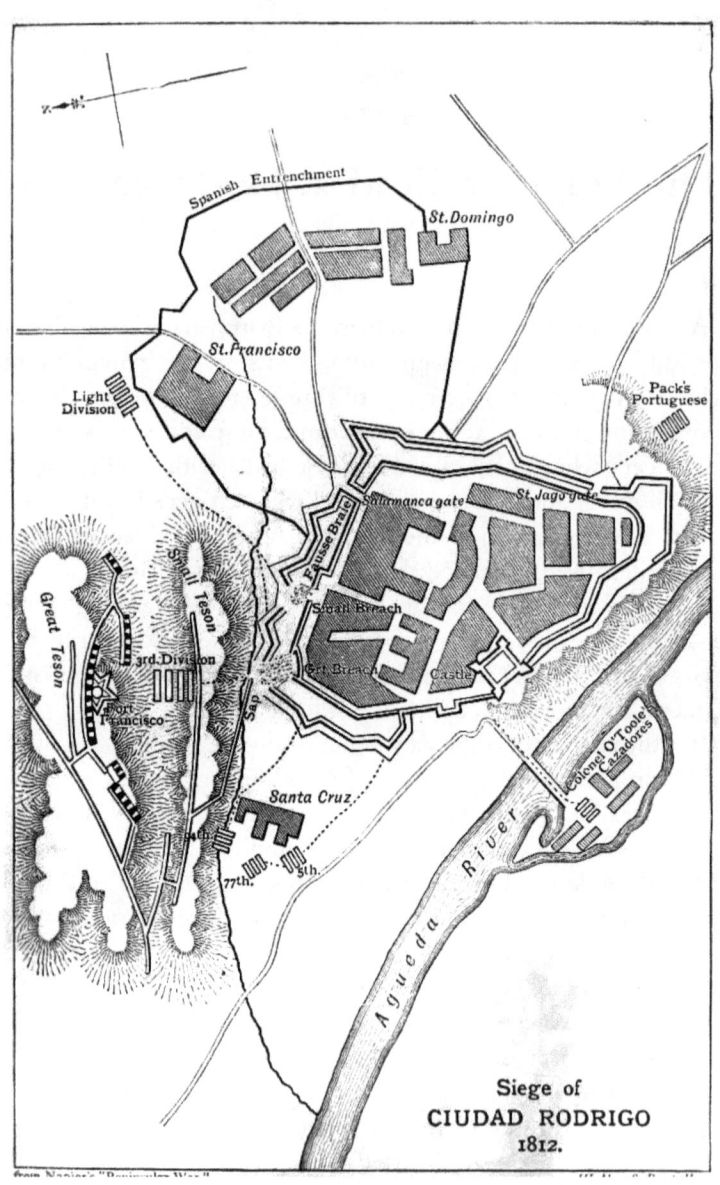

de Ponte, left nearly four hundred men behind, in a route of only four-and-twenty miles, numbers of whom perished on the line of march, or died subsequently from the fatigue they had endured.

Ciudad Rodrigo stands on high ground, in the centre of an extensive plain it domineers. The city is; erected on the right bank of the Agueda, which there branches into numerous channels, and forms a number of small islands. The citadel commands the town, and standing on an elevated mound is difficult of access on every side. Since their late occupation, the French had added considerably to the strength of the place. The suburbs were secured against a *coup de main*, by fortifying two convents on their flanks, and another nearly in the centre.

On the north side the ground rises in two places; that furthest from the works is thirteen feet above the level of the ramparts, from which it is distant six hundred yards. The other, of lesser altitude, is scarcely two hundred paces. On the former the enemy had erected a redoubt; it was protected by a fortified convent called San Francisco, as well as the artillery of the place, which commanded the approaches from the hill.

The Agueda is fordable in several places, the best passage being within pistol-shot of the walls. In winter, from the sudden floodings of the river, these fords cannot be relied upon, and a bridge of eighteen trestles, with a platform four hundred feet long, was secretly constructed in the citadel of Almeida and conveyed to Salices.

Four divisions were entrusted with the duties of the siege. They took their turns in course, each for twenty-four hours furnishing the requisite guards and working parties.

On the night of the 8th of January, the investment was regularly commenced, and the redoubt on the upper Teson stormed by three companies of the 52nd with trifling loss. Ground was broken on its flank, and by the morning the trench was four feet wide and three in depth. On the following night, the first parallel was opened; and the outlines of three batteries for eleven guns each were traced.

The weather continued dreadfully inclement, and as it was believed that Marmont would endeavour to raise the siege, Wellington decided on rapid operations, and resolved to attempt a storm even with the counterscarps entire. Both the besiegers and the besieged were active in their operations. On the night of the 13th, the convent of Santa Cruz was taken; and on the 14th, while the division was coming to relieve the working parties, the garrison made a sortie, overturned the gabions in advance of the parallel, and would have succeeded in spik-

Second Siege at Ciudad Rodrigo

ing the guns, but for the spirited opposition of a few workmen and engineers, who checked the attempt, until the head of the division closing up obliged the French to retire.

On the morning of the. 14th, the batteries were nearly ready for breaching, mounted with twenty-three 24-pounders and two eighteens. At four o'clock in the afternoon their fire commenced, and a spectacle more strikingly magnificent, it has rarely been the good fortune even of a British soldier to witness.

The evening chanced to be remarkably beautiful and still; there was not a cloud in the sky, nor a breath of wind astir, when suddenly the roar of artillery broke in upon its calmness, and volumes of smoke rose slowly from the batteries. These floating gently towards the town, soon enveloped the lower part of the hill, and even the ramparts and bastions in a dense veil, while the towers and summits lifting their heads over the haze, showed like fairy buildings, or those substantial castles which are sometimes seen in the clouds on a summer's day. The flashes from the British guns, answered as they were from the artillery in the front, and the roar of their thunder reverberating among the remote mountains of the Sierra de Francisca; these, with the rattle of the balls against the walls, proved altogether a scene which, to be rightly understood, must be experienced.

That night the convent of San Francisco was escaladed by a wing of the 40th, and the French having abandoned the suburbs, they were occupied by the besiegers.

At daybreak on the 15th the batteries resumed their fire, and at sunset the walls of the main scarp and *fausse braye* were visibly shaken. Under cover of a fog on the 16th, the second parallel was prolonged; but the front of the works was so limited, and the fire of the enemy so concentrated and correct, that it required immense time to throw up a battery. The difficulty may be readily imagined, from the fact of the French having discharged at the approaches, upwards of twenty thousand shot and shells. Another battery of seven guns was opened on the 18th. On the 19th, two breaches were distinctly visible from the trenches, and on being carefully reconnoitred, they were declared practicable. Lord Wellington examined them in person, decided on storming them that evening, and from behind the reverse of one of the approaches, issued written orders for the assault.

The French were not inactive. The larger breach, exposing a shattered front of more than one hundred feet, had been carefully mined—the base of the wall strewn with shells and grenades, and the top, where troops might escalade, similarly of ended. Behind, a deep retrenchment was cut, to insulate the broken rampart, in the event of its being carried by storm. The lesser breach was narrow at the top, exceedingly steep, with a four-and-twenty pounder turned sideways, that blocked the passage up, except an opening between the muzzle and the wall, by which two files might enter.

Early in the evening, the third and light divisions were moved from their cantonments. At six, the third moved to the rear of the first parallel, two gun-shots from the main breach, while the light formed behind a convent, three hundred yards in front of the smaller one. Darkness came on, and with it came the order to "Stand to arms." With calm determination, the soldiers of the third division heard their commanding officer announce the main breach as the object of attack; and every man prepared himself promptly for the desperate struggle. Off went the packs, the stocks were unbuckled, the cartouche box arranged to meet the hand more readily, flints were screwed home, every one after his individual fancy fitting himself for action. The companies were carefully told off, the sergeants called the rolls, and not a man was missing.

The town clock struck seven, and its sonorous bell knelled the fate of hundreds. Presently the forlorn hope formed under the leading of the senior subaltern of the 88th, William Mackie; and Picton and Mackinnon rode up and joined the division. The former's address to the Connaught Rangers was brief, it was to "Spare powder, and trust entirely to cold iron," The word was given, "Forward!" was repeated in under tones, the forlorn hope led the way, the storming party, carrying bags filled with dry grass, followed the division in column succeeded, all moved on in desperate silence, and of the third division not a file hung back.

The fifth regiment joined from the right, and all pressed forward to the breach. The bags, thrown into the ditch by the sappers, reduced the depth, one half; ladders were instantly raised, the storming party mounted, and after a short but severe struggle, the breach was won.

Before the storming party had entered the ditch, the shells and combustibles had been prematurely exploded, occasioning but trifling loss to the assailants. The French instantly abandoned the breach, sprang the mines, and fell back behind the retrenchment, from which, and from the neighbouring houses, they maintained a murderous fire.

In the meantime, the light division had stormed the lesser breach. It was most gallantly carried; and the loss would not have been severe, but for the accidental explosion of a service magazine behind the traverse, by which several officers and a number of men were destroyed. Directed by the heavy fire at the main breach, part of the 43rd and 95th rushed along the ramparts to assist their comrades of the third division; and Pack's brigade, having converted their feint upon the southern face of the works into a real attack, entered the *"fausse braye,"* and drove the French before them with the bayonet. Thus, threatened in their rear, the enemy abandoned the retrenchment; and, still resisting, were driven from street to street, until they flung down their arms and asked and received that quarter which the laws of war denied and the fury of an excited soldiery left them but little hope of obtaining.

The first men that surmounted the difficulties the breach presented were a sergeant and two privates of the 88th. The French, who still remained beside the gun, whose sweeping fire had hitherto been so fatal to those who led the storm, attacked these brave men furiously; a desperate hand-to-hand encounter succeeded. The Irishmen, undaunted by the superior number of their assailants, laid five or six of the gunners at their feet. The struggle was observed, and some soldiers of the 5th regiment scrambled up to the assistance of their gallant comrades, and the remnant of the French gunners perished by their bayonets.

Lieutenant Mackie, who led the forlorn hope, had miraculously escaped without a wound, and pressing "over the dying and the dead," he reached the further bank of the retrenchment, and found himself in solitary possession of the street beyond the breach, while the battle still raged behind him.

The town was won; but alas! many of the best and bravest had fallen. General Craufurd was mortally wounded in leading the light division to the lesser breach, and General Mackinnon was killed after having gained the ramparts of the greater breach.

During the siege, the allies lost three officers and seventy-seven killed; twenty-four officers and five hundred men wounded; while in the storm six officers and one hundred and forty men fell, and sixty officers and nearly five hundred men were wounded. The French loss was severe; and the commandant, General Barrie, with eighty officers and seventeen hundred men, were taken prisoners. There were found upon the works one hundred and nine pieces of artillery, a battering train of forty-four guns, and an armoury and arsenal filled with military stores.

Thus, fell Rodrigo. On the evening of the 8th the first ground was broken—on that of the 19th the British colours were flying on the ramparts. Massena, after a tedious bombardment, took a full month to reduce it; Wellington carried it by assault in eleven days. No wonder that Marmont, in his despatch to Berthier, was puzzled to account for the rapid reduction of a place, respecting whose present safety and ultimate relief, he had previously forwarded the most encouraging assurances.

After all resistance had ceased, the usual scene of riot, plunder, and confusion, which by prescriptive right the stormers of a town enjoy, occurred. Every house was entered and despoiled; the spirit stores were forced open; the soldiery got desperately excited, and in the madness of their intoxication committed many acts of silly and wanton violence. All plundered what they could, and in turn they were robbed by their own companions. Brawls and bloodshed resulted, and the same men who, shoulder to shoulder, had won their way over the "imminent deadly breach," fought with demoniac ferocity for some disputed article of plunder. At last, worn out by fatigue, and stupefied with brandy, they sank into brutal insensibility; and on the second day, with few exceptions, rejoined their regiments; the assault and sacking of Rodrigo appearing in their confused imaginations, rather like some troubled dream than a desperate and bloodstained reality.

On the second day, order was tolerably restored; stragglers had returned to their regiments; the breaches were repaired, the trenches filled in, and the place being once more perfectly defensible, was given up by Lord Wellington to Castanos, the captain-general of the province, who had been present at the siege. Additional honours were deservedly conferred upon the conqueror of Rodrigo. Wellington was created a British earl and a Spanish duke, and a farther annuity of £2000 a year was voted by a grateful country, to support the dignities she had so deservedly conferred.

But another and a bolder blow was yet to be struck. Again, the troops were put in motion, and the order was obeyed with pleasure, all being too happy to quit a place where every supply had been exhausted, and every object recalled the loss of relatives and friends. Leaving a division of infantry on the Agueda, the remainder of the army moved rapidly back upon the Tagus, and, crossing the river, headquarters were established at Elvas, on the 11th. There every preparation was completed for one of the boldest of Lord Wellington's attempts, for on the 16th, a pontoon bridge across the Guadiana was traversed by the light, third, and fourth divisions, and Badajoz regularly invested.

CHAPTER 14

The Siege of Badajoz, 1812

The town of Badajoz contained a population of about 16,000, and, within the space of thirteen months, experienced the miseries attendant upon a state of siege three several times. The first was undertaken by Lord Beresford, towards the end of April, 1811, who was obliged to abandon operations by Soult advancing to its relief, and which led to the Battle of Albuera on the 16th of May.

The second siege was by Lord Wellington in person, who, after the Battle of Fuentes d'Onoro, directed his steps towards the south with a portion of the allied army. Operations commenced on the 30th of May, and continued till the 10th of June, when the siege was again abandoned, Soult having a second time advanced in combined operation with the army of Marmont from the north. The allies continued the blockade of the town till the 17th, when they recrossed the Guadiana, and took up a position on the Caya,

The secrecy and despatch with which Lord Wellington had formed or collected all necessary *matériel* for besieging this formidable place on whose reduction he had determined, was astonishing. The heavy guns had been brought by sea from Lisbon, transhipped into craft of easy draught of water, and thus conveyed up the river until they reached the banks of the Guadiana. Gabions and fascines, (small branches of trees bound together, used for filling ditches, masking batteries, &c.), were prepared in the surrounding woods, entrenching tools provided, the pontoon bridge brought up from Abrantez, and the battering train, comprising sixteen 24 and twenty 18-pounders, with sixteen 24-pound howitzers, were forwarded from Almeida, and parked upon the glacis of Elvas, in readiness for the opening of the siege.

Though not entirely aware of the extent of these hostile preparations, Philippon, the governor of Badajoz, had apprised Marshal Soult

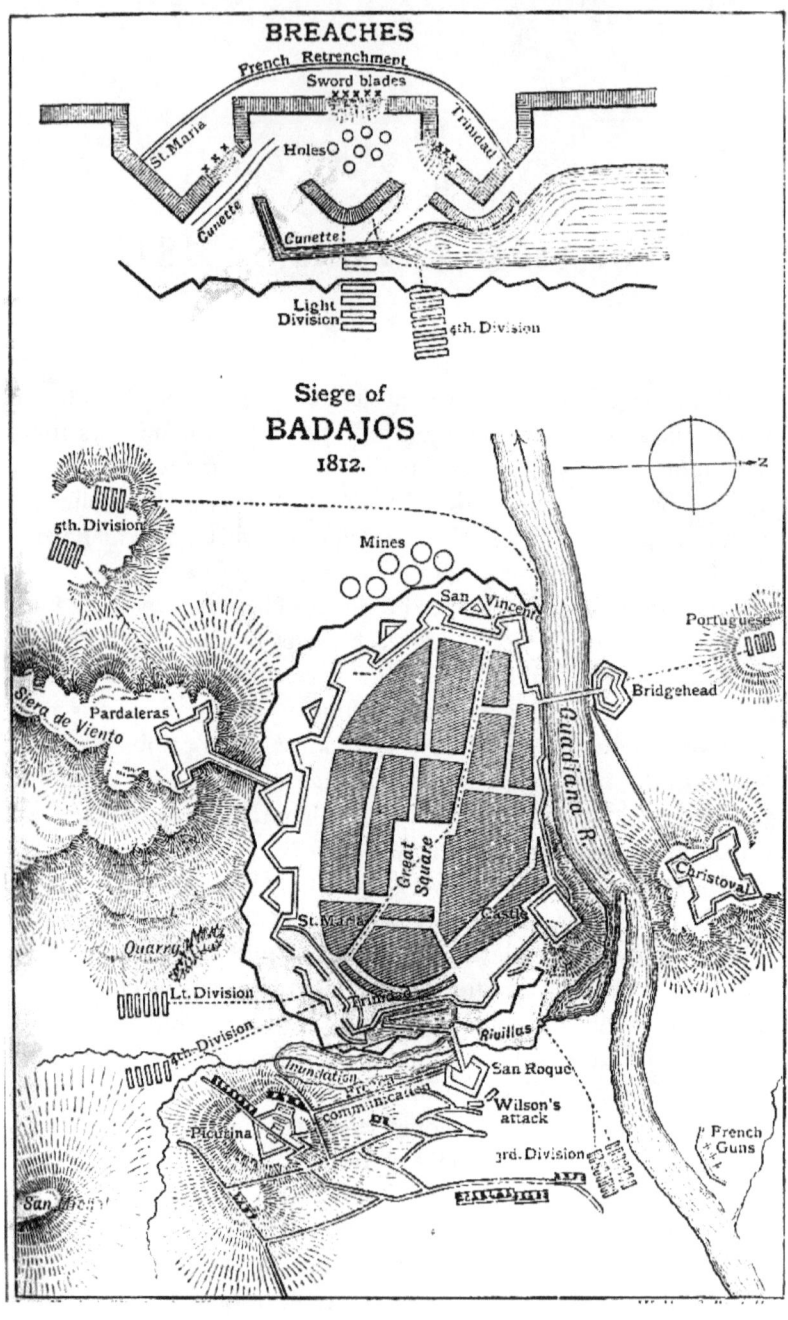

that the fortress was threatened, and demanded a supply of shells and gunpowder. This requisition, though immediately complied with, was not obtained, for Sir Rowland Hill, with his characteristic activity, prevented the convoy from reaching its destination.

Indeed, nothing which could secure the place had been forgotten or neglected by its governor. The forts of San Christoval and Pardelaras had been considerably strengthened and enlarged, the former by a lunette, (work on either side of a ravelin, with one perpendicular face, sometimes thrown up beyond the second ditch, opposite the places of arms), magazine and bomb-proof, and the latter by a general repair. Badajoz was provisioned for five weeks, the garrison was numerous and well appointed, and, confident in his own resources and skill, Philippon, after two successful defences, resolutely prepared himself for a third, and with a perfect conviction that, like the others, it, too, would prove successful.

Badajoz is easily described. Round one portion of the town, the rivulets Calamon and Rivellas sweep, and unite with the Guadiana, which flows in the face of the works, and in front of the heights of San Christoval. The castle stands above the union of these rivers. The fortifications are exceedingly strong, the bastions and curtains regular, while formidable outworks, the forts of Pardelaras, Picarina, and San Christoval, complete the exterior defences.

A close reconnaissance at once convinced Lord Wellington that the defences had been amazingly improved and, as time pressed, and the means of regular investment were but indifferent, he determined that the bastion of La Trinidad, from its unfinished counterguard, (small ramparts, with parapets and ditches, erected in front of a bastion or ravelin, to secure the opposite flanks from being open to the covertway), should be battered. To effect this, the Picarina redoubt, forming nearly an angle with the bastion, and the lunette of San Rocque, must necessarily be carried.

The night of the 16th March was bad enough to mask any daring essay, and rain, darkness, and storm favoured the bold attempt. Ground was accordingly broken, and though but one hundred and seventy yards from the covered way, the working parties were neither heard nor molested. The 17th and 18th were similarly employed, but under a heavy fire from the Picarina fort, and such of the guns upon the works as could be turned by the garrison on the approaches.

The evening of the 18th, however, produced a very different scene, for the enemy became assailant, and a sortie was made with fifteen

hundred men, accompanied by some forty cavalry. To the works, this sudden assault occasioned but little mischief. The gabions, (large circular baskets, filled with earth or sand, and used for forming parapets, covering working parties, &c.), were overturned, some entrenching tools captured, and great confusion caused among the working parties; but the French were speedily driven back, after causing much alarm, and a loss of one hundred and fifty in killed and wounded. Colonel Fletcher, the chief of the engineers, was unfortunately among the latter.

The weather was in every way unfavourable for prosecuting the siege, and elemental influences seemed to have united with Philippon against the allied commander. The rain fell in torrents, the river rose far beyond its customary height, the pontoons swamped at their moorings, and all were swept away. From the violence of the current, the flying bridges worked but slowly, and serious apprehensions were entertained lest the communications should be interrupted with the other side, and, of necessity, that the siege must be raised. To forward the works required incredible fatigue; the ground was soaked with moisture, the trenches more than knee-deep with mud and rain, the *revêtements* of the batteries, (exterior front, formed of masonry or fascines, which keeps the bank of the work from falling), crumbled away under any pressure, and it was almost impossible to lay platforms for the guns.

Indeed, had the works been ready for their reception, the task of transporting heavy artillery across a surface, rendered a perfect swamp by the incessant torrents which had fallen for days without any intermission, would have been a most laborious duty.

Fortunately, the weather changed, the ground dried partially, and the works were carried on with additional spirit. By employing teams of oxen, assisted by numerous fatigue parties, the guns were brought forward, and the batteries armed, and on the 25th they opened on the Picarina and the place itself, with excellent effect, while Philippon returned the fire from every gun upon the ramparts that could be brought to bear.

Perceiving the true object of the besiegers, and certain that the Picarina would be assailed, ample measures were taken for its defence. The ditch was deepened, the gorge secured by an additional palisade; under the angles of the *glacis, fougasses,* (*glacis* is the part beyond the covert-way to which it forms the parapet, *fougasse* is a small mine, sir or seven feet underground, generally formed in the glacis or dry ditch), were placed, and shells and grenades laid along the parapet, to roll down upon the storming party at the moment of attack. The ditch was exposed to a flanking fire, and two hundred spare muskets were ranged along the banquet. Every means, in short, were adopted that could insure a vigorous and successful resistance.

That night, at ten o'clock, the fort was attacked and carried by five hundred men of the third division, under Major-General Kempt. One party was directed to attempt the gorge, another prevented the place from being succoured from the city, and at the same time cut off the garrison from retreat; and a third were to distract the attention of the French, and assist their comrades by making a front attack.

The first detachment reached the gorge undiscovered, but failed in forcing the palisades, from the heavy fire of musketry poured on them by the garrison. Retiring from a place where success was hopeless, the storming party moved round the left flank, and escaladed and won the parapet; while another forced the salient angle simultaneously. The French retreated to a guardhouse, which they barricaded and defended most obstinately.

Alarmed by a false report that a large body of the besieged had sallied from the town to relieve the fort, the troops were about to abandon these advantages, and quit a place their bravery had already won; but General Kempt dispelled the panic, led them forward, and attacked the garrison again, who fought to the very last; and, with the exception of some seventy, perished while desperately resisting. The taking of Picarina was gallantly effected, but it cost the British dear, the casualties in killed and wounded, being nineteen officers and upwards of three hundred men.

The capture of the fort enabled the second parallel to be pushed on, and breaching batteries to be completed. The guns maintained a heavy fire on the bastion of La Trinidad; and the sappers directed their efforts against the lunette of San Rocque. The progress of the siege was slow; and though two breaches were made, the certainty that both were retrenched, (in fortification this means the isolating of a breach by forming inner defences), and secured by interior defences, rendered an assault too hazardous an experiment to be ventured.

Lord Wellington was critically circumstanced, as Marmont had made some forward movements in front of Beira, and Soult was advancing, determined to relieve the place. His light troops were already at Larena; the covering army under Hill had been obliged to retreat; and after blowing up two arches of the bridge of Merida, had taken post in front of Talavera,

In consequence, the fifth division was ordered to advance, leaving the observation of San Christoval to the Portuguese cavalry; the British general having decided on leaving a corps of ten thousand men to protect the trenches, and with the remainder of his force bring Soult to action.

At noon, on the 5th April, the breaches were reconnoitred and declared practicable; but the assault was deferred for another day to allow the artillery time to batter down the curtain, connecting the bastion with an unfinished ravelin. The concentrated fire of the British batteries fell upon the old wall with irresistible force; it was breached in a single day, and thus three points for assault were thrown open. The report of the engineers was encouraging; the mam breach was sufficiently wide, and the ascent to all three easy enough for troops to mount.

Ten o'clock on the night of the 6th was appointed for the assault to be attempted, and the necessary orders were issued accordingly. The castle was to be attacked by the third division, the bastion of La Trinidad by the fourth, that of Santa Maria by the light division, the lunette of San Rocque by a party from the trenches; while the fifth should distract the garrison by a false attack on the Pardelaras, and the works contiguous to San Vicente.

Philippon, well aware that an assault might be expected, had employed every resource that skill and ingenuity could devise to render the attempt a failure. As Lord Wellington had neither time nor means to destroy the counterscarps, the French were enabled to raise the most formidable obstructions at their foot, and insulate the breaches effectually. At night, the rubbish was removed, retrenchments formed, and the battered parapets repaired by sand-bags, casks, and woolpacks. Powder-barrels and grenades were laid along the trenches, and at the foot of the breach sixty fourteen-inch shells, communicating with hoses and bedded in earth, were placed ready for explosion. A *chevaux-de-frieze*, was stretched across the rampart, and planks studded with spikes covered the slopes of the breaches.

★★★★★★

Chevaux-de-frieze are wooden spars, spiked at one end, and set into a piece of timber. They were originally used as a defence against cavalry, but are now commonly employed in strengthening outworks and stopping breaches.

★★★★★★

Every species of combustible was employed, and a cartridge specially prepared for the musketry, formed of buck-shot and slugs; and when the distance was so close, nothing would prove more mischievous.

The day was remarkably fine, and the troops, in high spirits, heard the orders for the assault, and proceeded to clean their appointments, as if a dress parade only was intended. Evening came, darkness shut distant objects out, the regiments formed, the roll was called in an under voice, the forlorn hope stepped out, the storming party was told off, all were in readiness and eager for the fray.

Shortly before ten, a beautiful firework rose from the town, and showed the outline of Badajoz and every object that lay within several hundred yards of the works. The flame of the carcase died gradually away, and darkness, apparently more dense, succeeded this short and brilliant illumination.

The word was given, the forlorn hope moved forward, the storming parties succeeded, and the divisions, in columns, closed the whole. Of these splendid troops, now all life and daring, how many were living in an hour?

At that moment, the deep bell of the cathedral of St. John struck ten; the most perfect silence reigned around, and except the softened footsteps of the storming parties, as they fell upon the turf with military precision, not a movement was audible. A terrible suspense, a horrible stillness, darkness, a compression of the breathing, the dull and ill-defined outline of the town, the knowledge that similar and simultaneous movements were making on other points, the certainty that two or three minutes would probably involve the forlorn hope in ruin, or make it the beacon-light to conquest—all these made the heart throb quicker and long for the bursting of the storm, when victory should crown daring with success, or hop and life should end together.

On went the storming parties; one solitary musket was discharged beside the breach, but none answered it. The light division moved forward, rapidly closing up in columns at quarter distance. The ditch was gained, the ladders were lowered, on rushed the forlorn hope, with the storming party close behind them. The divisions were now on the brink of the sheer descent, when a gun boomed from the parapet. The earth trembled, a mine was fired, an explosion, and an infernal hissing from lighted *fusees* succeeded, and, like the rising of a curtain on the stage, in the hellish glare that suddenly burst out around the breaches, the French lining the ramparts in crowds, and the British descending the ditch, were placed as distinctly visible to each other as if the hour were noontide!

A tremendous fire from the guns, a number of which had been laid upon the approaches to the breach, followed the explosion; but, all undaunted, the storming party cheered, and undauntedly the French answered it. A murderous scene ensued, for the breach was utterly impassable. Notwithstanding the withering fire of musketry from the parapets, with light artillery directed immediately on the breach, and grape from every gun upon the works that could play upon the assailants and the supporting columns, the British mounted. Hundreds were thrown back, and hundreds as promptly succeeded them.

Almost unharmed themselves, the French dealt death around; and secure within defences, that even in daylight and to a force unopposed, proved afterwards nearly insurmountable, they ridiculed the mad attempt; and while they viewed from the parapets a thousand victims writhing in the ditch, they called in derision to the broken columns, and invited them to come on.

While the assaults upon the breaches were thus fatally unsuccessful, the third and fifth divisions had moved to their respective points of attack. Picton's, to whom the citadel was assigned, found difficulties nearly equal to those encountered at the breaches. Thither Philippon had determined to retire, if the assault upon the other defences should succeed, and, in that event, hold the castle and San Christoval to the last. To render the place more secure, he had caused the gates to be built up, and the ramparts were lined with shells, cart-wheels, stones, and every destructive missile.

Fireballs betrayed the movements of the assailants; and, for a time, every attempt at escalade failed with prodigious loss. At last one ladder was planted, a few daring spirits gained the ramparts, crowds followed them, and in an incredibly short time the castle was won. Philippon heard of the disaster too late to redeem its loss. The troops despatched from the breaches and elsewhere were unable to recover it, a British jacket waved from the flag-staff, and in the first dawn of morning announced the downfall of Badajoz.

The fifth division were equally successful; though General Leith had to delay his attack till eleven o'clock, from the party who had charge of the ladders losing their way.

The attempt on San Vicente succeeded, notwithstanding every preparation had been made for its defence; Major-general Walker overcame all opposition, and established himself securely in the place.

And yet it is astonishing, even in the spring-tide of success, how the most trivial circumstances will damp the courage of the bravest, and check the most desperate in their career. The storming party of the fifth had escaladed a wall of thirty feet with wretched ladders, forced an uninjured palisade, descended a deep counterscarp, crossed the lunette behind it, and this was effected under a converging fire from the bastions, and a well-sustained fusillade, while but a few of the assailants could force their way together, and form on the rampart when they got up. But the leading sections persevered until the brigade was completely lodged within the parapet; and now united, and supported by the division who followed fast, what could withstand their advance?

They were sweeping forward with the bayonet, the French were broken and dispersed, when at this moment of brilliant success, a portfire, which a retreating gunner had flung upon the rampart was casually discovered. A vague alarm seized the leading files, they fancied some mischief was intended, and imagined the success, which their own desperate gallantry had achieved, was but a ruse of the enemy to lure them to destruction.

"It is a mine, and they are springing it!" shouted a soldier.

Instantly the leaders of the storming party turned, and it was impossible for their officers to undeceive them. The French perceived the panic, rallied and pursued, and friends and foes came rushing back tumultuously upon a supporting regiment (the 38th) that was fortunately formed in reserve upon the ramparts. This momentary success of the besieged was dearly purchased; a volley was thrown closely in, a bayonet rush succeeded, and the French were scattered before the fresh assailants, never to form again.

The fifth division rushed on; everything gave way that opposed it, the cheering rose above the firing, the bugles sounded an advance, the enemy became distracted and disheartened, and again the light and fourth divisions, or, alas! their skeletons, assisted by Hay's brigade, advanced to the breaches. No opposition was made; they entered, and Badajoz was their own! Philippon, finding that all was lost, retired across the river to San Christoval; and early next day, surrendered unconditionally.

The loss sustained by the allies in the reduction of this well defended fortress was awful. In the assault alone, the British casualties were fifty-nine officers and seven hundred and forty-four men killed.

Two hundred and fifty-eight officers, and two thousand six hundred men wounded!

Lord Wellington had stationed himself on the high ground behind San Christoval, to view the progress of the assault. During a contest, so doubtful and protracted, his anxiety was painfully acute. What a period of dreadful suspense must have ensued, from the time the striking of the town clock announced the marching of the divisions, until the thunder of artillery told the British leader that the conflict had begun! For a minute the fireworks thrown from the place showed the columns at the breaches. Darkness followed, stillness more horrible yet, and then the sudden burst of light, as shells and mines exploded. The main breach was literally in a blaze—sheets of fire mounted to the sky, accompanied by a continued roaring of hellish noises, as every villainous combustible was ignited to discover or destroy the assailants.

The wounded came fast to the rear, but they could tell little how matters were progressing. At last a mounted officer rode up. He was the bearer of evil tidings; the attack upon the breaches had failed, the majority of the officers had fallen, the men, left without leaders to direct them, were straggling about the ditch, and unless instant assistance was sent, the assault must fail entirely. Pale but collected, the British general heard the disastrous communication, and issued orders to send forward a fresh brigade (Hay's) to the breaches. Half an hour passed, and another officer appeared. He came from Picton to say the castle had been escaladed, and that the third division was actually in the town.

Instantly staff officers were despatched to the castle with orders that it should be retained, and that the divisions, or rather their relics, should be withdrawn from the breaches.

Though the regular assaults had been sanguinary failures, the detached attacks upon the castle and San Vicente were brilliantly successful, and either of them must have next day produced the fall of Badajoz. In fact, the city was doubly won; and had Leith's division obtained their ladders in proper order, the place would have fallen in half the time, and a frightful loss of life have been consequently avoided.

It may be readily imagined that such a fierce resistance as that made by the French would provoke a desperate retaliation from the victors. For a day and two nights the city presented a fearful scene of rapine and riot. The streets were heaped with the drunken and the dead, and very many of the conquerors, who had escaped uninjured in the storm, fell by the bayonets of their comrades.

No language can depict the horrors which succeed a storm. A few hours made a frightful change in the condition and temper of the soldiery. In the morning, they were obedient to their officers, and preserved the semblance of subordination; now they were in a state of furious intoxication—discipline was forgotten, and the splendid troops of yesterday had become a fierce and sanguinary rabble, dead to every touch of human feeling, and filled with every demoniac passion that can brutalise the man. The town was in terrible confusion, and on every side frightful tokens of military license met the eye.

Streets were almost choked up with broken furniture, for the houses had been gutted from the cellar to the garret, the partitions torn down, and even the beds ripped and scattered to the winds, in the hope that gold might be found concealed. Brandy and wine casks were rolled out before the stores; some were full, some half drunk, but more staved in mere wantonness, and the liquors running through the kennel. All within that devoted city was at the disposal of an infuriated army, over whom for the time control was lost, aided by an infamous collection of camp followers, who were, if possible, more sanguinary and pitiless even than those who had survived the storm! It is useless to dwell upon a scene from which the heart revolts.

Strict measures were taken on the second day by Lord Wellington to repress these desperate excesses and save the infuriated soldiery from the fatal consequences their own debauchery produced. A Portuguese brigade was brought from the rear, and sent into the town, accompanied by the provost marshal and the gallows. This demonstration had its due effect, and one rope carried terror to rioters whom the bayonets of a whole regiment could not appal.

CHAPTER 15

The Battle of Salamanca, 1812

Early in June, the British divisions began to concentrate; and on the 13th the cantonments on the Agueda were broken up, and Lord Wellington crossed the frontier.

The condition of the army was excellent, and the most exact discipline was preserved, while all unnecessary parades were dispensed with. The march ended, the soldier enjoyed all the comforts he could command; if foot-sore, he had rest to recruit: if untired, he had permission to amuse himself. His arms and appointments were rigidly inspected, his supper cooked, his bivouac formed, and at sunrise he rose at the *reveille*, to resume, with light heart and "gallant hope," the march that was to lead to victory.

The weather was fine, and as the route lay principally through forest lands, nothing could be more picturesque and beautiful than the country which the line of march presented. The wooded landscape displayed its verdure under the sunny influence of a cloudless sky, and singularly contrasted its summer green with the snow-topped pinnacles of the Sierra de Gata. No enemy appeared; for days, the march was leisurely continued, until, on clearing the forest at Valmasa. the German Hussars in advance, had a alight skirmish with a French picket in front of Salamanca.

This city, celebrated for its antiquity, and noted in the middle ages as foremost among the most celebrated schools of learning, was destined to witness a fresh triumph of British bravery. The situation of Salamanca is bold and imposing, standing on high ground on the right bank of the Tormes, and surrounded by a fine Champaign country, divested of wood, but interspersed with numerous clay-built villages. A Roman road can still be traced without the town, while a portion of the bridge across the Tormes, consisting of twenty-seven arches, is

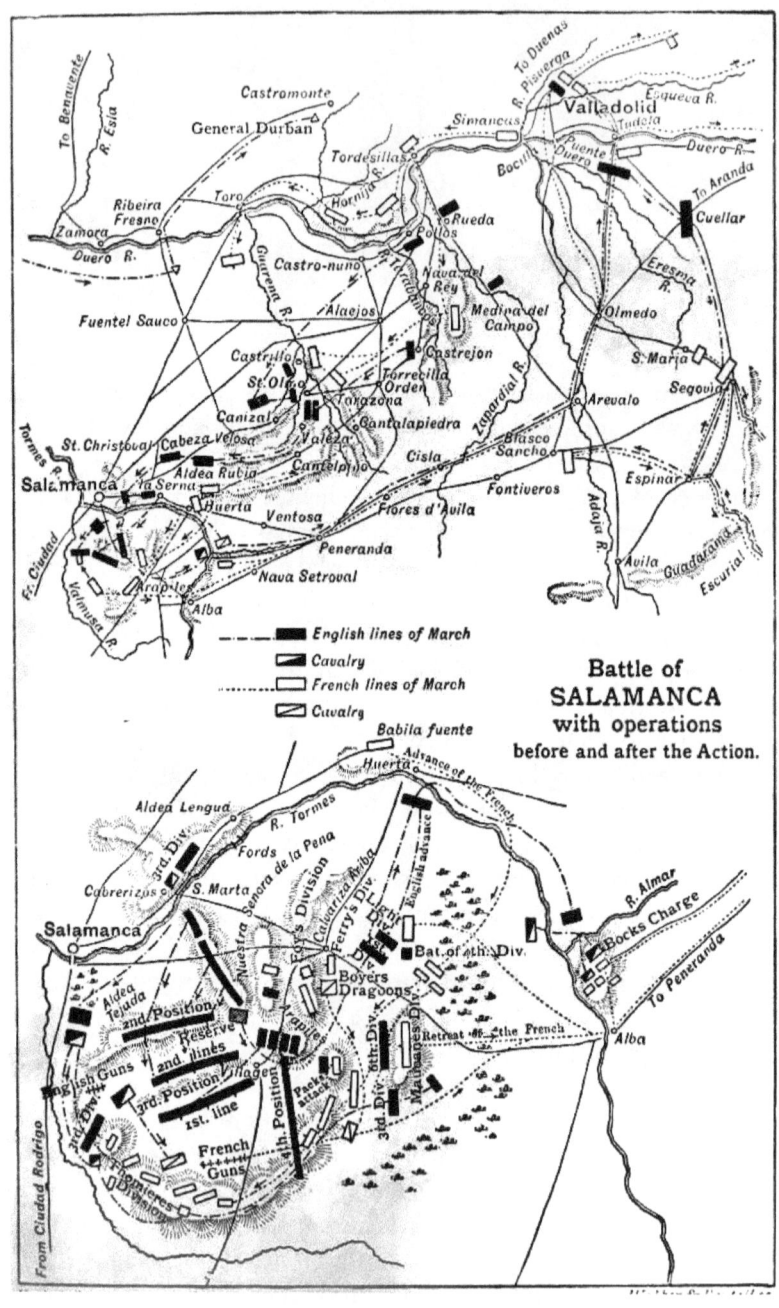

supposed to have been constructed when the Eternal City was mistress of the world.

Ultimately it was generally believed that a battle on the plains of Valesa was inevitable; and the troops bivouacked in two lines, and before daybreak were under arms. But with the first light, Marmont was seen extending by his left, and the allies moved consequently in a parallel direction. Either commander might provoke an action, but neither seemed inclined to risk one. The French marshal's design was very apparent. He kept the high ground, manoeuvred to outflank his opponent, and, should opportunity permit, attack him at advantage.

His able antagonist, however, never gave the chance. Some time passed in manoeuvring, and the French held Babila, Fuente, and Villamesa; the allies, Cabesa and Aldea Lingua.

The 21st July was also spent in flank marching, during which both commanders crossed the Tormes; the French by the fords of Alba and Huerta, and the allies by Santa Martha and the bridge of Salamanca. The hostile armies bivouacked again that right, and such a night can scarcely be imagined.

The evening was calm and sultry, but the extreme verge of the horizon became heavily overcast, and persons conversant with "skyey influences" might have easily foretold a coming storm. Suddenly a torrent fell, the wind rose and swept across the open hills with amazing violence, the thunder-clouds burst, and, by the glare of lightning, the sparkling arms of infantry masses were visible over the whole extent of the position, as the last brigades pressed through the tempest to occupy their ground. No shelter the allied army could obtain could have averted a summer shower, and all in a few minutes were drenched to the skin; while the cavalry horses, scared by the lightning, broke from their picketings, and trampling upon their riders rushed madly to and fro, occasioning indescribable confusion.

Nothing could be more imposing than, the parallel movements of the rival armies during the last three days. Far as the eye could range, masses, apparently interminable, pursued their march with beautiful regularity, now displayed in brilliant sunshine as they swept over a contiguous height, now lost where an accidental dipping of the ground for a time concealed the column. Generally, both armies abstained from hostile collision, by a sort of mutual consent; and excepting where the line of march brought the light troops into immediate proximity, or the occupation of a village produced a trifling fusillade, the grand movements of the rival hosts exhibited a "ceaseless march," the leading columns pressing forward toward the Tormes, and the rear hidden from view "by dust and distance."

The whole system of manoeuvres which marked the operations of the French marshal since Bonnet's division had joined him on the Douro, showed clearly that he only waited for a fitting moment to attack. The French Army were in high spirits: while in numerical force they were formidable indeed, numbering forty-five thousand men, of whom four thousand were cavalry. Other circumstances were favourable to the commencement of active aggression by the French. The communications with the capital were open, reinforcements constantly arriving, while a powerful accession of strength had approached the immediate neighbourhood of the scene of operations from the army of the North; a part of its cavalry and horse-artillery having already reached Polios.

If Marmont was anxious to offer battle, the British general, for obvious reasons, was as willing to accept it. Aware of his opponent's abilities in tactics, and apprised of the fine *matériel* of the army he commanded, Lord Wellington was as confident in his own resources as in the indomitable courage of that soldiery which, under his leading, had been frequently assailed and never beaten. His own position was daily becoming more unsafe. For security, the stores deposited at Salamanca had been removed to the rear, consequently the maintenance of his army was endangered, as supplies from the depots were tardily obtained

No difficulty, however, was experienced by the French in provisioning their army; every procurable necessary was exacted from the wretched inhabitants, who might curse, while they durst not oppose those who despoiled them of their property.

Both commanders were anxious to try the issue of a contest. Vanity, in the one, urged Marmont to offer battle upon ground favourable for the movements of a force superior in number and perfect in every arm. Prudence, in Lord Wellington, aimed at results only to be effected by a victory. No wonder, then, that with such dispositions a conflict was inevitable. The decree had gone forth; a fiery trial of skill and valour must ensue, and well did a fearful night harbinger "a bloody morrow."

The morning was cloudy and threatening, and the dawn was ushered in by a sharp fusillade, in the direction of Calvarasa de Arriba. The enemy's tirailleurs had occupied the heights of Senora de la Pena in considerable force, and part of the seventh division, with the light cavalry of Victor Alten, were opposing their farther advance.

The British right was *appuied* upon the nearest of the Arapiles, and united itself with the extremity of a ridge, on which the divisions had taken their position on the preceding evening. Another hill, similarly named, rose from the plain at a distance of five hundred yards, and as it commanded the right of the alignment, it was deemed advisable to possess it.

The French marshal, however, had entertained a similar design; and a wood favouring the unobserved advance of part of Bonnet's division, the summit was occupied by the French with their 122nd regiment, and a brigade of guns.

Meanwhile the enemy commenced extending to the left, in the rear of the Arapiles, and formed on the skirts of a wood. As the movement of the columns brought them within cannon range, General Leith advanced a battery to a height in front of his position, and it opened with considerable effect. The French, obliged to retire, brought up a brigade of artillery to check the British guns. Their diagonal fire silenced the British battery, and it was necessary, without delay, to retire the guns, and withdraw a troop of the 16th light dragoons, which, for their protection, had been drawn up under shelter of the hill. This perilous evolution was executed with complete success, the ravine was passed at speed, and with little loss, the artillery and light cavalry regained the position.

The day wore on; the late tempest apparently had cleared the atmosphere, all was bright and unclouded sunshine, and over a wide expanse of undulating landscape, nothing obscured the range of sight but dust from the arid roads, or wreathing smoke occasioned by the spattering fire of the light troops. Marmont was busily manoeuvring, and Lord Wellington coolly noticing from a height the dispositions of his opponent, which as he correctly calculated would lead to a general engagement.

At noon, a combination of at least eight thousand men, moved from the rear of the Arapiles, and formed in front of the fifth division. Lord Wellington rode to the ground, and there found the division in perfect readiness for the anticipated attack. Perceiving at once that this movement was only a demonstration of the French marshal to mask his real designs, his lordship returned to the right, which was now the interesting point of the position.

Finding his feint upon the fifth division unsuccessful, Marmont put his columns into motion, and marching rapidly by his left, endeav-

oured to turn the right of the allies, and thus interpose between them and Ciudad Rodrigo. Under a heavy cannonade, his front and flank, covered by a cloud of skirmishers, and supported by a cavalry force that drove in the British dragoons and light troops, pressed forward to gain the Rodrigo road. But that hurried movement was badly executed by Marmont's generals of division. Their extension was made with careless haste, the line consequently weakened, and this false manoeuvre brought on the crisis of the day. The moment for action had come, and Lord Wellington seized the opportunity and struck the blow.

At two o'clock, when the French commenced extending by their left, the allied army was thus disposed. On the right, the fifth division (Leith's) had moved behind the village of Arapiles, and had taken ground on the right of the fourth (Cole's); the sixth and seventh, under Generals Clinton and Hope, formed a reserve; the third division (Pakenham's), D'Urban's cavalry, two squadrons of the 14th Light Dragoons, and a corps of Spanish infantry, were in position near Aldea Tejada. Bradford's brigade, with Le Marchant's heavy cavalry, were formed on the right, and in the rear of the fifth. The light division (Barnard's) and the first (the Guards and Germans) were drawn up between the Arapiles and the Tonnes, in reserve. Cotton's cavalry were formed in the rear of the third and fifth divisions; an artillery reserve, posted behind the dragoons, and in the rear of all the Spaniards, under Don Carlos D'Espana, appeared in the extreme distance, but entirely out of fire.

Marmont had remarked, and rode forward to correct the irregularity of his flank movement, and personally direct the debouchment of his third and fourth divisions from the wood that had partially concealed them. At that moment, Lord Wellington was seated on the hillside, eating his hurried meal, while an *aide-de-camp* in attendance watched the enemy's movements with a glass. The bustle then perceptible in the French line attracted his lordship's notice, and he quickly inquired the cause.

"They are evidently in motion," was the reply.

"Indeed! what are they doing?"

"Extending rapidly to the left," was answered.

Lord Wellington sprang upon his feet, and seized the telescope; then muttering that Marmont's good genius had deserted him, he mounted his horse, and issued the orders to attack.

All was instantly on the alert. The staff went off at speed to bring up the fifth and sixth divisions. The infantry stood to arms, primed and loaded, fixed bayonets, uncased the colours, and abandoning the defensive system, hitherto so admirably employed, prepared for an immediate attack.

Pakenham commended the action by advancing in four columns along the valley, assailing the left flank of the enemy, and driving it before him in great confusion. D'Urban's Portuguese dragoons, and Harvey's light cavalry (the 14th), protected the flank during tire movement, and, when the French became disordered, charged boldly in and sabred the broken infantry. Nothing could be more brilliant than Pakenham's advance. A level plateau of nearly eight hundred yards was to be crossed before the assailants could reach the heights, whither Fox's division were marching hastily to occupy the ground.

A heavy fire from the French guns was showered on the advancing columns, while the British batteries, under Captain, Douglass, replied by a furious cannonade. Wallace's brigade—the 45th, 74th, and 88th—formed the first line, and moved forward in open column. The face of the height was covered with *tirailleurs*, who kept up an incessant fusillade, while grape and canister ploughed the ground, occasioning a heavy loss, and more particularly to the centre.

They suffered, but they could not be checked; not waiting to deploy, the companies brought forward their right shoulders in a run, forming line from open column without halting, while the wings of the brigade, having moved up the hill with less impediments than the centre, were more advanced, and the line thus assumed rather the figure of a crescent. All the mounted officers, regardless of a withering fusillade, were riding in front of the battalions, and the men following with their muskets at the rest.

At last they reached the brow. Foy's division, beating the *pas de charge*, advanced, and threw in a murderous volley. Half the British front rank went down. Staggered by that deadly fire, the brigade recoiled a step or two, but, instantly recovering, the rear rank filled the places of the fallen. On it went with imposing steadiness, regardless of the irregular fusillade, for the French continued to pour in their fire with more rapidity than effect.

Foy's division, alarmed by this movement, became unsteady. The daring advance of an enemy, whom the concentrated fire of five thousand muskets could not arrest, was indeed astounding. All that brave men could do was done by the French officers. They strove to confirm the courage of their troops, and persuade them to withstand an assault that threatened their wavering ranks. The colonel of the 22nd

Légère, seizing a musket from a grenadier, rushed forward, and mortally wounded Major Murphy of the 88th. Speedily his death was avenged; a Ranger shot the Frenchman through the head, who tossing his arms wildly up, fell forward and expired. The brigade betrayed impatience; the 88th, excited to madness by the fall of a favourite officer, who passed dead along the front, as his charger galloped off with his rider's foot sticking in the stirrup, could scarcely be kept back.

Pakenham marked the feeling, and ordered Wallace "to let them loose." The word was given, down came the bayonets to the charge, the pace quickened, a wild cheer, mingled with the Irish slogan, rent the skies, and unable to stand the shock, the French gave ground. The Rangers, and the supporting regiments, broke the dense mass of infantry, bayoneting all whom they could overtake, until, run to a regular standstill, they halted to recover breath and stayed the slaughter.

Nor were the operations of the fifth division less marked and brilliant. For an hour, they had been exposed to a heavy cannonade, sheltering occasionally on the ground from the shot and shells, which fell in showers upon the height they occupied, and ricochet ted through their ranks. At last the order to advance was given. They moved in two lines, the first entirely British, the second composed of the Portuguese infantry of General Spry. Bradford's brigade, having united itself for the attack, formed on the right of the fifth.

In mounting the height where the French division was posted, the assailing columns were annoyed by a sharp discharge of artillery, and the fire of a swarm, of sharpshooters, who in extended order occupied the face of the hill. The British light infantry pushed on to clear the line of march, and, if practicable, make a dash at the enemy's artillery. The *tirailleurs* were speedily driven back, the cannon removed from the crest of the height to the rear, and unimpeded, the division moved up the hill with a perfect regularity in its formation, and the imposing steadiness of men who marched to victory. In the front of the centre of that beautiful line rode General Leith, directing its movements, and regulating its advance.

The enemy were preparing for the struggle. He retired his columns from the ridge, and formed continuous squares, fifty paces from the crest of the heights, which the assailants must crown previous to attacking. The artillery from the French rear cannonaded the advancing columns, but nothing could check the progressive movement of the British. The men marched with the same orderly steadiness as at first; no advance in line at a review was ever more correctly executed; the dressing was admirable; and spaces were no sooner formed by casualties than closed up with the most perfect regularity, and without the slightest deviation from the order of march.

When General Leith reached the summit of the hill, the enemy were observed formed in supporting squares, with their front rank kneeling. Their formation was complete, their fire reserved, and till the drum rolled, not a musket was discharged. Nearly at the same moment, the French squares and the British delivered their volleys. A dense smoke hid all for a time from view. A loud and sustained cheer pealed from the British ranks; no shout of defiance answered it; while, rushing forward, the British broke the squares, and pressing on with dauntless impetuosity, every attempt at opposition ceased, and what just now had appeared a disciplined body, almost too formidable to be assailed, became a disorganised mass, flying at headlong speed from the fury of its conquerors. To increase the confusion, a portion of Foy's division crossed the *déroute*, and mingled with it, while the rush of advancing cavalry was heard, and that sound, so ominous to broken infantry, confirmed the panic.

Presently the heavy brigade—the 3rd and 4th Dragoons, and 5th Dragoon Guards—galloped across the interval of ground, between the heights where the third division had made its flank attack, and the fifth its more direct one. Sweeping through a mob of half-armed fugitives, the brigade rode boldly at the three battalions of the French 66th, which had formed in six supporting lines to check the advance of the conquerors, and afford time for the broken divisions to have their organisation restored.

Heedless of its searching fire, the British dragoons penetrated and broke the columns; numbers of the French were sabred; while the remainder were driven back upon the third division and made prisoners. Still pressing on, another regiment, in close order, presented itself; this, too, was charged, broken, and cut down. Nothing arrested the victorious career until the ground became gradually obstructed with trees, embarrassing the movements of the cavalry, while it afforded a broken infantry ample time to rally, and engage horsemen at evident advantage.

Although the regiments of the heavy brigade in the course of these brilliant charges had of necessity become intermixed, and their line crowded, without intervals between the squadrons, they still pushed forward without confusion to charge a brigade that had formed under cover of the trees. The French steadily awaited the attack, within twenty yards their reserved fire was thrown in, and on a concentrated body of horse and at this short distance, its effect was fatal. General Marchant was killed, Colonel Elley badly wounded, while one-third of the brigade were brought to the ground by that close and murderous volley. Still, those of the heavy dragoon who could keep their saddles sustained nobly the reputation they had earned that day, and charging the French column home, penetrated and dispersed it. A furious *mêlée* succeeded, the scattered infantry fighting desperately to the last, while the long straight sword of the trooper proved in British hands irresistible.

While the remnant of the cavalry brigade continued their pursuit, a small battery of five guns was seen upon the left. Lord Edward Somerset instantly galloped down, charged, and brought them off. The brigade was then retired, after a continued succession of brilliant charges that had lasted nearly an hour.

Of course, the loss sustained was great. From three splendid regiments that had ridden into action, at least one thousand strong, with difficulty three squadrons were formed in the evening, such being the number of men and horses rendered *hors de combat* during its late scene of brilliant but dear-bought success.

With such decided advantages, the battle might have been considered gained, and the French defeat inevitable. But the splendid successes attendant on the third and fifth divisions, with Bradford's Portuguese brigade, and the light and heavy cavalry, were nearly counterbalanced by the total failure of Pack's attack on the Arapiles, and the repulse of Cole's division by that of Bonnet.

The 1st and 16th Portuguese advanced to carry the height; it was occupied by a French battalion, and protected by a battery of trims. A force of nearly two thousand men, led on in person by a "fighting general," should have wrested the hill from such inferior force, no matter how strong the ground might naturally have been. On this occasion, however, the attack proved totally unsuccessful; the Portuguese regiments recoiled from the fire, and their officers endeavoured to rally them in vain.

The attack on the Arapiles was consequently abandoned, the French left in undisturbed possession, and, unassailed themselves, they turned their musketry and cannon upon the flank and rear of Cole's division, who, under the impression that Pack's assault must have succeeded, had fearlessly advanced across the plain, driving Bonnet's corps before it, with the promise of as glorious results as had attended the gallant operations of the third and fifth.

At that moment, even when the fourth division believed itself victorious, its position was most dangerous—its very existence more than doubtful. Bonnet perceiving Pack's failure, reformed his division, still numerically superior to his opponent's, advanced boldly against the fourth, and furiously attacked it, while from the crest of the Arapiles, the French troops poured upon the now retreating columns a withering fire of grape and musketry.

General Cole was carried off the field; Beresford, who had come to his relief, with a Portuguese brigade of the fifth, was also badly wounded. The British were falling fast; while the French heavy cavalry, under Boyer, moved rapidly to support Bonnet, who was momentarily gathering strength from the junction of the scattered soldiers who had escaped the slaughter of the fourth and seventh French divisions already *dérouted* on the left.

Wellington marked the emergency, and ordered Clinton's division to advance. This fine and unbroken corps, numbering six thousand bayonets, pushed rapidly forward, confronted the victorious enemy, who, with loud cheers, were gaining ground on every point, as the hard-pressed fourth division was driven back by overwhelming numbers. Bonnet, determined to follow up his temporary success, met Clinton's division manfully, and for a time neither would give ground, and a close and furious conflict resulted. The ceaseless roll of musketry, and the thunder of fifty guns told how furiously the battleground was disputed. Both fought desperately, and though night was closing, the withered grass, blazing on the surface of the hill, threw an unearthly glare upon the combatants, and displayed the alternations that attended the "heady fight."

But the British bayonet at last opened the path to victory. Such a desperate encounter could not endure. The French began to waver, the sixth division cheered, pushed forward, gained ground, while, no longer able to withstand an enemy who seemed determined to sweep everything before it, the trench retired in confusion, leaving the hard-contested field in undisputed possession of the island conquerors.

Darkness fell. The remains of Bonnet's division found shelter in the woods, or crossed the Tonnes at the ford of Alba, which, from its natural strength, the Spaniards could have easily defended. The conflict, at different points, had raged six hours with unabated fury; and those of the divisions which had been engaged, exhausted with fatigue and suffering dreadfully from heat and thirst, rested on the battleground.

The guards, Germans, and light brigade, who had been in reserve during the day, however, pushed forward in pursuit. Distant musketry was heard occasionally, gradually this spattering fire ceased, and the groans of dying men and wounded horses succeeded the headlong rush of cavalry, the thunder of a, hundred guns, the shout of proud defiance, and, wilder still, the maddening cry of victory!

Salamanca, whether considered with regard to its merits as a battle, or its results as a victory, probably stands foremost among the Peninsular contests, and many and peculiar traits distinguish it from every precious encounter. It was coolly and advisedly fought, by commanders confident in themselves, satisfied with the strength and *matériel* of their armies, jealous of each other's reputation, and stimulated by every longing after military glory, to exhaust the resources of their genius and experience to secure a successful issue. Nothing could surpass Marmont's beautiful manoeuvring for consecutive days while moving round the British flank, except the countervailing rapidity with which his talented opponent defeated every effort to outflank him, and held the marshal constantly in check.

At two on the 22nd, the French marshal threatened an attack; at four, he was himself the assailed, and the same mistake that lost Marengo, involved ruin and defeat at Salamanca. One false movement that might have been easily corrected before a slower leader could see and seize the momentary advantage, brought on a crisis that clouded the French destinies in Spain by removing the delusory belief that their arms should eventually prove invincible.

A conflict, close and desperate, like that of Salamanca, conferred a sanguinary victory, while it involved a still bloodier defeat. The allied loss, in killed and wounded, exceeded five thousand men, and this, of course, fell chiefly on the British. The Portuguese, comparatively suffered little, and the Spaniards, being entirely non-combatant, had very few casualties to record. The only post intrusted—and that most unhappily—to their charge, was the castle of Alba; and this was abandoned without a shot, leaving Clausel a safe retreat, while its vigorous occupation must have involved its total ruin.

The French loss was never correctly ascertained. Two eagles, eleven pieces of cannon, seven thousand prisoners, and as many dead soldiers left upon the field, were the admitted trophies of British victory. Among the commanding officers of both armies the casualties were immense; of the British, Le Marchant was killed; Beresford, Cole, Leith, Cotton, and Alten wounded. The French were equally unfortunate—the generals of brigade, Thomières, Ferrey, and Desgraviers were killed; Marmont, early in the day, mutilated by a howitzer shell; Bonnet severely, and Clausel slightly wounded.

Clausel, who commanded *en chef* after Marmont was disabled, retreated with great rapidity. Viewed from the summit of La Serna, the French exhibited a countless mass of all arms, confusedly intermingled. While the range permitted it, the horse-artillery annoyed them with round shot, but by rapid marching they gradually disappeared, while, opportunely, a strong corps of cavalry and a brigade of guns joined from the army of the North, and covered the retreat until they fell back upon their reserves.

Although Salamanca was in every respect a decisive battle, how much more fatal must it not have proved, had darkness not shut in, and robbed the conquerors of half the fruits of victory? The total demolition of the French left was effected by six o'clock, and why should the right attack have not been equally successful? Had such been the case, in what a hopeless situation the broken army must have found itself!

Salamanca was a great and influential victory. Accidental circumstances permitted Clausel to withdraw a beaten army from the field, and a fortunate junction of those arms which alone could cover his retreat enabled him, with little loss, to outmarch his pursuers, preserve his communications, and fall back upon his reserves. But at Salamanca the delusory notion of French superiority was destroyed.

The enemy discovered that they must measure strength with opponents in every point their equals. The confidence of wavering allies was confirmed; while the evacuation of Madrid, the abandonment of the siege of Cadiz, the deliverance of Andalusia and Castile from military occupation, and the impossibility of reinforcing Napoleon during his northern campaign, by sparing any troops from the corps in the Peninsula all these great results were among the important consequences that arose from Marmont's defeat upon the Tonnes.

CHAPTER 16

The Siege of Burgos, 1812

The occupation of Madrid was among the most brilliant epochs of Peninsular history, and, from circumstances, it was also among the briefest. The conquest of the capital was certainly a splendid exploit. It told that Wellington held a position and possessed a power that in Britain many doubted and more denied; and those, whose evil auguries had predicted a retreat upon the shipping, and finally an abandonment of the country, were astounded to find the allied leader victorious in the centre of Seville, and dating his general orders from the palace of the Spanish kings. The desertion of his capital by the usurper, proclaimed the extent of Wellington's success; and proved that his victories were not, as had been falsely asserted at home, "conquests only in name."

Without entering into military history too extensively, it will be necessary to observe, that on many expected events which should have strengthened his means, and weakened those of his opponents, Lord Wellington was miserably disappointed. Maitland's diversion on Catalonia had proved a failure. Ballasteros exhibited the impotent assumption of free action, and refused obedience to the orders of the British general, and Hill was therefore obliged to leave Estremadura, to cover the three roads to Madrid. The Cortes, instead of straining their energies to meet the exigencies of the moment, wasted time in framing new constitutions, and in desultory and idle debates.

While Wellington, removed from his supplies, his military chest totally exhausted, and his communications menaced, was imperatively obliged to open others, and secure assistance from the only place on which reliance could be reposed—the mother country. To quote Lord Wellington's own words aptly illustrates the real case:—

I likewise request your lordship not to forget horses for the cavalry and artillery, and money. *We are absolutely bankrupt.* The troops are now five months in arrears, instead of being one month in advance. The staff have not been paid since February; the muleteers not since June, 1811; and we are in debt in all parts of the country. I am, obliged to take the money sent to me by my brother for the Spaniards, in order to give my own troops a fortnight's pay, who are really suffering for want of money.

It was, indeed, full time to move. The Spanish Army were driven from Gallicia, and Clausel threatened to interrupt the communications of the allies with Portugal. Lord Wellington, therefore, decided on marching against the army he had beaten at Salamanca; and leaving Hill's division to cover the capital, he left Madrid on the 1st of September, and crossing the Douro on the 6th, moved on Burgos by Valencia.

That night Clausel abandoned Valladolid, and after crossing the Pisuerga, destroyed the bridge of Berecal. Anxious to unite with Castanos, Wellington waited for the Gallician Army to come up, while Clausel leisurely retreated through the valleys of Arlanzan and Pisuerga, as remarkable for beauty and fertility as for the endless succession of strong posts which they afforded to a retiring army.

Clausel, after an able retreat, took a position at Cellada del Camino, and to cover Burgos, offered battle to the allied commander. The challenge was promptly accepted; but the French general, discovering that a junction of twelve thousand Spaniards had strongly reinforced his antagonist, prudently declined a combat, retired, and united his own to Souham's corps, which numbered above eight thousand men. This reserve had been organised by Napoleon's special orders—and was intended to remedy any discomfiture which might befall Marmont in the event of his being defeated by the allies.

The British entered the city of Burgos, from which the French had previously retired, after garrisoning the castle with two thousand five hundred men, under the command of General Dubreton. Twelve thousand allied troops, comprising the first and sixth British divisions, with two Portuguese brigades, sat down before the place; while the remainder of Lord Wellington's army, amounting to twenty-five thousand effective troops, formed the covering army of the siege.

The castle of Burgos was a weak fortress, on which trench inge-

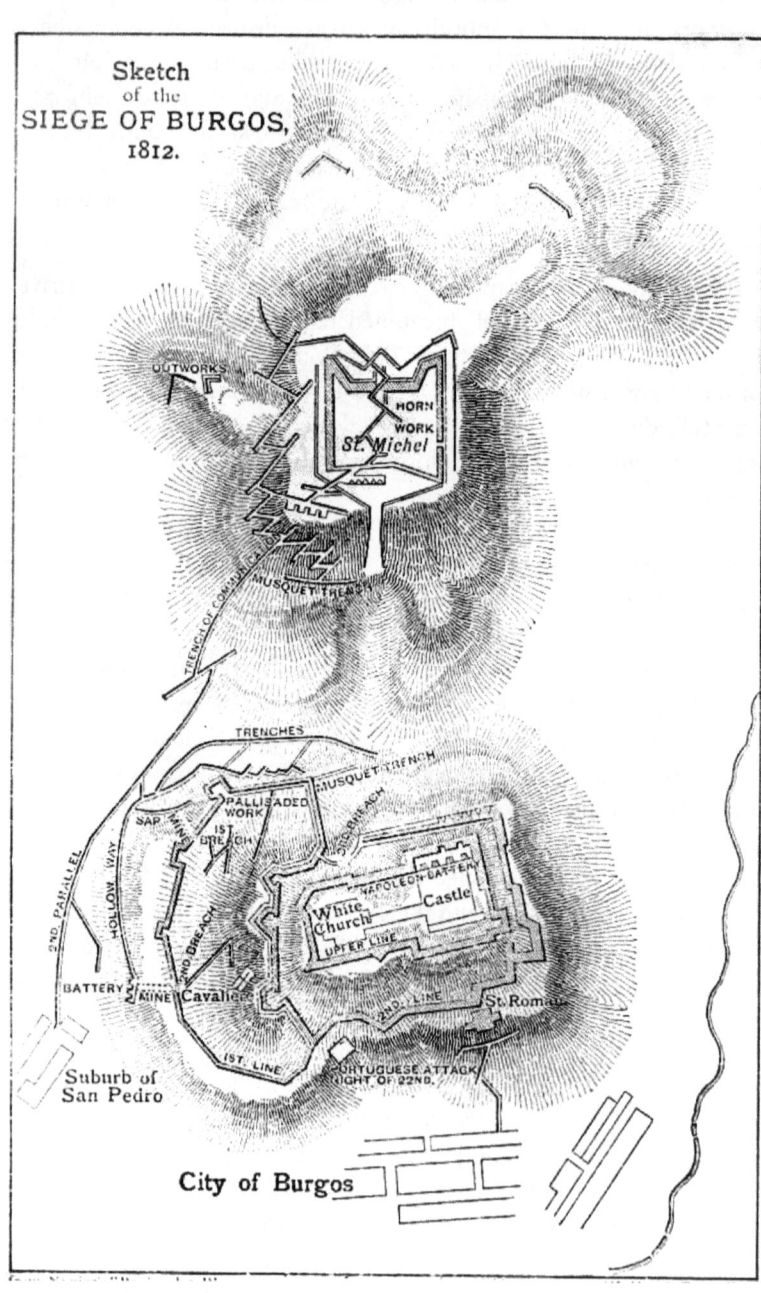

nuity had done wonders in rendering it defensible at all. It stood on a bold and rocky height, and was surrounded by three distinct lines, each placed within the other, and variously defended.

The lower and exterior line consisted of the ancient wall that embraced the bottom of the hill, and which Caffarelli had strengthened by the addition of a modern parapet, with salient, (the salient angle is that which turns from the centre of a place; while the re-entering points directly towards it), and re-entering flanks. The second was a field retrenchment, strongly palisaded.

The third, a work of like construction, having two elevated points, on one of which the ancient keep of the castle stood, and on the other, a well-entrenched building called the White Church; and that being the most commanding point, it was provided with a casemated work, and named in honour of Napoleon. This battery domineered all around, excepting on its northern face, where the hill of St. Michael rising nearly to a level with the fortress, was defended by an extensive horn-work, having a sloping scarp and counter scarp, the former twenty-five feet in height, the latter, ten. (A horn-work is a work having a front and two branches. The front comprises a curtain and two half-bastions. It is smaller than a crown-work, and generally employed for effecting similar purposes).

Although in an unfinished state, and merely palisaded, it was under the fire of the castle and the Napoleon battery. The guns, already mounted, comprised nine heavy cannon, eleven fieldpieces, and six mortars and howitzers; and, as the reserve artillery and stores of the army of Portugal were deposited in the castle of Burgos, General Dubreton had the power of increasing his armament to any extent he thought fit.

Two days passed before the allies could cross the river. On the 19th August, the passage was effected, and the French outposts on St. Michael were driven in. That night, the horn-work itself was carried after a sanguinary assault, the British losing in this short and murderous affair upwards of four hundred men.

From the hill, now in possession of the allies, it was decided that the future operations should be carried on, and the engineers arranged that each line in succession should be taken by assault. The place, on a close examination, was ascertained to be in no respect formidable; but the means to effect its reduction, by comparison, were feebler still. Nothing, indeed, could be less efficient; three long 18-pounders, and five 24-pound howitzers, formed the entire siege artillery that Lord

Wellington could obtain.

The headquarters were fixed at Villa Toro. The engineering department intrusted to Colonel Burgoyne, and the charge of the artillery to Colonels Robe and Dickson.

The second assault, that upon the exterior wall, was made on the night of the 22nd by escalade. Major Laurie of the 79th, with detachments from the different regiments before the place, formed the storming party. The Portuguese, who led the attack, were quickly repulsed, and though the British entered the ditch, they never could mount a ladder. Those who attempted it were bayoneted from above, while shells, combustibles, and cold shot were hurled on the assailants, who, after a most determined effort for a quarter of an hour, were driven from the ditch, leaving their leader, and half the number who composed the storming party, killed and wounded.

After this disastrous failure, an unsuccessful attempt to breach the wall was tried, in effecting which, of the few guns in battery, two were totally disabled by the commanding fire of the castle, and the engineers resorted, from sheer necessity, to sap and mine. The former, from the plunging fire kept up from the enemy's defences, and which occasioned a fearful loss, was speedily abandoned; but the latter was carried vigorously on, and the outward wall mined, charged, and, on the 29th, exploded.

At twelve o'clock at night the hose was fired, the storming party having previously formed in a hollow way some fifty paces from the gallery. When the mine was sprung, a portion of the wall came down, and a sergeant and four privates, who formed the forlorn hope, rushed through the smoke, mounted the ruins, and bravely crowned the breach. But in the darkness, which was intense, the storming party and their supporting companies missed their way, and the French recovering from their surprise, rushed to the breach, and drove the few brave men who held it back to the trenches. The attack consequently failed, and from a scarcity of shot no fire could be turned on the ruins. Dubreton availed himself of this accidental advantage, and by daylight the breach was rendered impracticable again.

Still determined to gain the place, Lord Wellington continued operations, although twelve days had elapsed since he had sat down before it. A singular despondency, particularly among the Portuguese, had arisen from those two failures; while insubordination was creeping into the British regiments, which produced a relaxed discipline that could not be overlooked, and which, in general orders, was consequently strongly censured. The siege continued; and, on the 4th of October, a battery opened from Saint Michael's against the old breach, while the engineers announced that a powerful mine was prepared for springing. At five o'clock that evening the *fusee* was fired. The effect was grand and destructive; one hundred feet of the wall was entirely demolished, and a number of the French, who happened to be near it, were annihilated by the explosion. The 24th regiment, already in readiness to storm, instantly rushed forward, and both breaches were carried, but, unfortunately, with heavy loss.

A lodgement was immediately effected, and preparations made for breaching the second line of defence where it joined the first.

On the 5th October, early in the evening, the French with three hundred men. The attack was too successful; one hundred and fifty of the guard and working party were killed or wounded, the gabions overturned, the works at the lodgement injured, and the entrenching tools carried off.

That night, however, the damage was repaired; the sap was rapidly carried forward, and at last the British had got so close to the wall that their own howitzers ceased firing lest the workmen should be endangered by their shot. The guns on Saint Michael's battery had also breached with good effect, and fifty feet of the parapet of the second line was completely laid in ruins. But, in effecting these successes, a heavy loss was inflicted on the besiegers, and of their originally small means for carrying on a siege, the few pieces of artillery they possessed at first, were now reduced to one serviceable gun.

The weather had also changed, and rain fell in quantities and filled the trenches. A spirit of discontent and indifference pervaded the army. The labour was unwillingly performed, the guards loosely kept, and Dubreton again sallied furiously, drove off the working party, destroyed the new parallel, carried away the tools, and occasioned a loss of more than two hundred men. Among the killed, none was lamented more than Colonel Cocks, who having obtained promotion most deservedly for previous gallantry, died at the head of his men, while rallying the fugitives and repelling the sally.

Three assaults had failed; but still the allied commander did not quit the place in despair. Preparations for another attempt were continued, and the exertions of the engineers, of whom one-half had fallen, were redoubled. Heated shot was tried against the White Church unsuccessfully; while that of San Roman was marked a the more vulnerable

point, and a. gallery commenced against it.

On the 17th, the great breach was again exposed by the fire of the British guns, and the ramparts on either side extensively damaged. A mine beneath the lower parallel was successfully exploded, and a lodgement effected in a cavalier, (work in the body of a place, domineering the others by ten or twelve feet), from whence the French had kept up a destructive fire on the trenches. It was held but for a short time, as the enemy came down in force, and drove the besiegers from it. On the 18th, the breach was reported practicable, and an assault decided on, the signal arranged being the springing of the mine beneath the church of San Roman. That building was also to be assailed, while the old breach was to be attempted by escalade, and thus, and at the same moment, three distinct attacks would occupy the enemy's attention.

At half-past four the explosion of the mine gave the signal. A countermine was immediately sprung by the French, and between both, the church was partially destroyed, and Colonel Browne, with some Portuguese and Spanish troops, seized upon the ruined building. The Guards, who had volunteered a detachment, rushed through the old breach, escaladed the second line, and, in front of the third, encountered the French in considerable force, while two hundred of the German Legion, under Major Wurmb, carried the new breach, pushing up the hill, and fairly gaining the third line of the defences. Unfortunately, however, these daring and successful efforts were not supported with the promptness that was needed. The French reserves were instantly advanced; they came on in overwhelming force, cleared the breaches of the assailants, and drove them beyond the outer line, with the loss of two hundred officers and men.

San Roman was taken the following night by the French, and recovered again by the British. But with this affair the siege virtually terminated, and Lord Wellington, by an imperious necessity, was obliged to retire from a place of scarcely third-rate character, after four attacks by assault, and a loss of two thousand men.

In war, the bravest and the most prudent measures are frequently marred or made by fortune. Lord Wellington, with very insufficient means, attempted the reduction of Burgos; and although skill and gallantry were displayed in every essay, obstacles arose which checked the most daring efforts; and all that science and determination could effect were vainly tried to overcome difficulties physically insurmountable. Had Wellington possessed the requisite *matériel* for the conduct of a siege, Burgos must have been taken in a week.

But let justice be done to its defenders. Much was expected from them, and assuredly, the governor and garrison of the castle of Burgos realised the high reliance placed upon their skill and heroism by their countrymen.

On the 18th, the British corps united. On the 20th some trifling affairs occurred between the outposts, and on the 21st the siege of Burgos was regularly raised, and Lord Wellington issued orders for retiring from before the place.

CHAPTER 17

The Battle of Vitoria, 1813

Winter passed away, the army recovered from its hardships, and Lord Wellington was indefatigable in perfecting the equipment of every department, to enable him to take the field efficiently when the season should come round, and active operations could be again renewed. In its minuter details, the interior economy of the regiments underwent a useful reformation. The large and cumbrous camp-kettles hitherto in use were discarded, and small ones substituted in their place; while three tents were served to each company, affording, particularly to the sick and disabled, a means of shelter in the field which hitherto had been wanting.

Nothing could surpass the splendid state of discipline that this period of inactivity had produced, while the allied army was reposing in winter quarters. Its *matériel* was now truly magnificent; powerful reinforcements having arrived from the mother country. The Life and Horse Guards had joined the cavalry; and that arm, hitherto the weakest, was increased to nineteen efficient regiments. The infantry had been recruited from the militias at home, the artillery was complete in every requisite for the field, while a well-arranged commissariat, with ample means of transport, facilitated the operations of the most serviceable force which had ever taken the field under the leading of a British general.

Previous to the opening of the campaign in May, 1813, the Anglo-Portuguese Army numbered close upon seventy thousand men of all arms, and were cantoned in the neighbourhood of the Douro. Morillo's corps occupied Estremadura; Giron held the frontier of Gallicia; O'Donel was stationed in Andalusia; Elio on the frontiers of Murcia and Valencia; and the Duc del Parque, with a strong corps, held possession of La Mancha.

The French, at that time, might have probably mustered one hundred and fifty thousand men in Spain. Madrid and Toledo were in the occupation of the armies of the centre and the south, whose corps were spread over the central provinces. Valladolid had the headquarters of the army of Portugal; the line of the Douro was carefully observed, while Suchet occupied Valencia and Catalonia; and a part of the army of the north was quartered in Aragon and Biscay.

Never did a leader take the field under more promising auspices than those with which the allied commander opened the campaign of 1813. The Spanish troops were strong in numbers, and considerably improved in discipline; while the guerilla leaders were in great force, and ready for daring enterprise. Summer was coming fast, a rich and luxurious country was before him, every requisite prepared for his march, his troops flushed with victory, and his opponents dispirited by constant discomfiture. Even the opening movements tended to increase these feelings, for the British were preparing to advance, and the French already retrograding.

No wonder, then, that the brilliant hopes of a country were fully realised; that the career of British conquest continued almost without a check; and the fields of France saw her banners float in victory until the last struggles at Orthes and Toulouse, attested the invincibility of Wellington and his island soldiery!

While the allies were preparing to march, Joseph Buonaparte put the army of the centre into motion, and, followed by those of the south and Portugal, retired slowly on the Ebro. As they were not pressed by the British light troops, the enemy's corps moved leisurely towards the frontier, accompanied by enormous trains of equipage and baggage.

The appearance of the French Army was more picturesque than military. It was crowded in its march, and too fanciful both in the character of its equipment and the variety of its costume. The line and light infantry excepted, few of the regiments were similarly dressed. The horse artillery wore uniforms of light blue, braided with black lace. The heavy cavalry were arrayed in green coats with brass helmets. The chasseurs and hussars, mounted on slight and active horses, were showily and variously equipped.

The "*gendarmerie* à *cheval*," a picked body chosen from the cavalry at large, had long blue frocks, with cocked hats and buff belts; while the *élite* of the dragoons, selected for superior size and general appearance, were distinguished by bearskin caps, and wore a look of martial determination, that their past and future bearing in the battlefield, did

not belie. Each regiment of the line had its company of grenadiers and *voltigeurs*, even the light regiments having a company of the former. The appearance of the whole force was soldiery and imposing; the cavalry was indeed superb, and the artillery, as to guns, caissons, and appointments, most complete; and, better still, their horses were in excellent condition.

Both armies were in the highest state of efficiency, for to both the undivided attention of their commanding officers had been directed, and yet in their respective equipments a practised eye would detect a marked dissimilarity. With the British, everything was simple, compact, and limited, as far as its being serviceable would admit, while the French were sadly encumbered with useless equipages and accumulated plunder. Those of the Spanish *noblesse* who had acknowledged the usurper, now accompanied his retreat; state functionaries, in court dresses and rich embroidery were mingled with the troops; *calashes*, carrying wives or mistresses, moved between brigades of guns: while nuns from Castile and ladies from Andalusia, attired *en militaire* and mounted on horseback, deserted castle and convent, to follow the fortunes of some soldier or *employ*é. Excepting that of his great brother while retreating from Moscow, no army since the days of Xerxes, was so overloaded with spoil and baggage as that of Joseph Buonaparte.

Although this abuse had not escaped the observation of many of the best officers in the army of the usurper, the facility with which these enormous ambulances were transported encouraged rather than repressed the evil. Looking on Spain as a conquered country, the means necessary to forward their convoys were unscrupulously seized, and every horse and mule was considered the property oi the finder. The roads were good, the retreat unmolested; on the 10th no enemy had appeared, and the allies were remaining quietly in their quarters. The fancied apathy of the British general was extraordinary, and prisoners were asked by their French escort, "Was Lord Wellington asleep?"

But nothing could exceed the astonishment of Joseph, when, on the evening of the 18th May, he was informed that the allies in considerable force, were actually on the left bank of the Ebro! The French dispositions were rendered useless, and an immediate night march became unavoidable. The drums beat to arms, the baggage was put in motion, and the entire of the French corps which had occupied Pancorbo or bivouacked in its vicinity, were hastily collected, and moved rapidly towards Vitoria.

That city on the evening of 19th May, displayed a singular spectacle of hurry and alarm, confusion and magnificence. Joseph Buonaparte, with his staff and guards, the entire of his court, and the headquarters of the army of the centre, accompanied by an endless collection of equipages, intermingled with cavalry, artillery, and their numerous ambulances, occupied the buildings and crowded the streets, while an unmanageable mass of soldiers and civilians were every moment increased by fresh arrivals, all vainly seeking for accommodation in a town unequal to afford shelter to half their number.

While the city was brilliantly illuminated in honour of the pseudo-king—and a gayer sight could not be fancied than its sparkling interior presented beyond the walls, an army was taking a position, and a multitude of the peasants, forced by the French engineers, were employed in throwing up field defences, and assisting those who had ruled them with an iron hand to place their guns in battery, and make other military dispositions to repel the army of the allies, who were advancing to effect their deliverance.

Vitoria is a city of great antiquity, and the capital of the province of Alava. It stands in a valley surrounded on every side by high grounds, while in the distance a lesser range of the Pyrenees is visible. Its name is derived from some forgotten victory, or, as some assert, from one achieved by its founder, Sacho VII. In front of this city Joseph Buonaparte concentrated his *corps d'armée* on the night of the 19th, to cover the town and hold the three great roads leading from Lagrona, Madrid, and Bilboa, to Bayonne.

The day of the 20th May was occupied by Lord Wellington in bringing forward his detached brigades, and making a careful reconnaissance of the enemy. Although, generally, the position selected by Marshal Jourdan was strong, and certainly well chosen to effect the objects for which he risked a battle, still it had one material defect. Its great extent would permit many simultaneous efforts to be made by an attacking army; and accordingly, on the following day, the allied leader, with admirable skill, availed himself of this advantage, and a most decisive victory was the result.

In point of strength, the contending armies were nearly equal, each numbering from seventy to seventy-five thousand men, the allies exceeding the French, probably by five thousand. Perfect in every arm, more splendid troops were never ranged upon a battlefield. Both armies were ably commanded; nominally, Joseph was *général-en-chef*, but Jourdan chose the ground, and directed every disposition.

The morning of the 21st broke in glorious sunshine. The atmo-

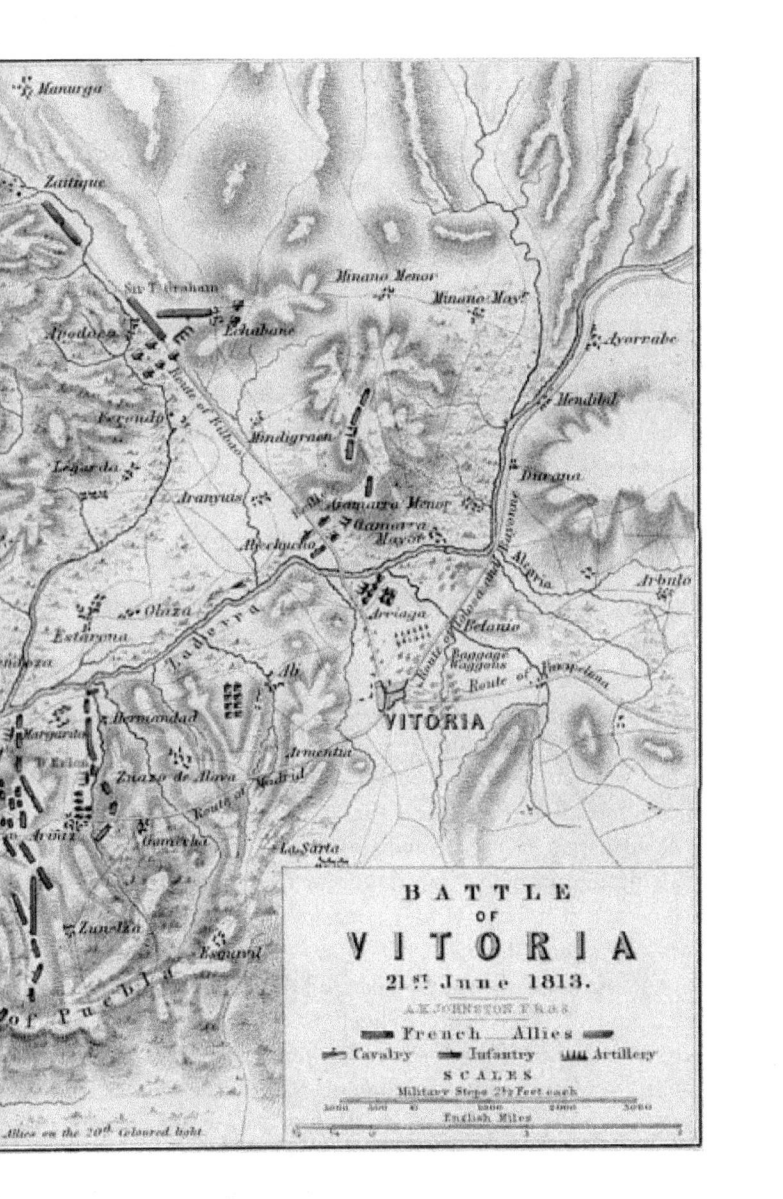

sphere was cloudless, and from the adjacent heights the progress of the battle could be distinctly viewed, except when smoke-wreaths for a time hid the combatants from many an anxious looker-on.

The French corps occupied a line of nearly eight miles—the extreme left placed upon the heights of La Puebla, and the right resting on an eminence above the villages of Abechuco and Gamarra Mayor. The centre was posted along a range of hills on the left bank of the river; while a strong corps, resting its right flank upon the left centre, was formed on the bold high grounds which rise behind the village of Sabijana. The reserve was placed at the village of Gomecha; and the banks of the Zadorra, and a small wood between the centre and the right, were thickly lined with tirailleurs.

The first line consisted of the armies of the south; and the army of the centre, with the greater portion of the cavalry, formed the reserve. That part of the position near the village of Gomecha, having been considered by Jourdan his most vulnerable point, was defended by a numerous artillery. The bridges were fortified, the communications from one part of the position to the other were direct, a deep river ran in front, the great roads to Bayonne and Pamplona in the rear, while, to arrest Wellington's career and preserve the immense convoys within the city or on the road to France, loaded with the plunder of a despoiled capital and a denuded country, the pseudo-king determined to accept the battle, which the British leader was now prepared to deliver.

During the Peninsular campaigns, there was no battle fought that required nicer combinations, and a more correct calculation in time and movement, than that of Vitoria. It was impossible for Lord Wellington to bring up, to an immediate proximity for attack, every portion of his numerous army, and hence many of his brigades had bivouacked on the preceding night a considerable distance from the Zadorra. Part of the country before Vitoria was difficult and rocky; and hamlets, enclosures, and ravines, separated the columns from each other; hence some of them were obliged to move by narrow and broken roads, and arrangements, perfect in themselves, were liable to embarrassment from numerous contingencies. But the genius, that directed these extended operations, could remedy fortuitous events, should such occur.

At daybreak, on the 21st, Wellington's dispositions were complete, and the allied army in motion. Sir Rowland Hill, with the second British, Amarante's Portuguese, and Morillo's Spanish divisions, was ordered to storm the heights of La Puebla, occupied by the enemy's left. The first and fifth divisions, with Pack's and Bradford's brigades, Bock's and Anson's cavalry, and Longa's Spanish corps, were directed to turn the French right, cross the Zadorra, and seize on the Bayonne road. The third, fourth, seventh, and light divisions were to advance in two columns and attack Vitoria in front and flank, and thus oblige Jourdan either to come to a general engagement, or abandon the city and sacrifice his valuable convoys.

At dawn of day, Joseph placed himself upon a height that overlooked his right and centre. He was attended by a numerous staff, and protected by his own bodyguard. Wellington chose an eminence in front of the village of Arinez, commanding the right bank of the Zadorra, and continued there, observing through a glass the progress of the fight, and directing the movements of his divisions, as calmly as he would have inspected their movements at a review.

The attack commenced by Hill's division moving soon after daylight by the Miranda road, and the detaching of Morillo's Spanish corps to carry the heights of La Puebla, and drive in the left flank of the enemy. The latter task was a difficult one, as the ground rose abruptly from the valley, and towering to a considerable height, presented a sheer ascent, that at first sight appeared almost impracticable.

The Spaniards, with great difficulty, although unopposed, reached the summit; and there, among rocks and broken ground, became sharply engaged with the French left. Perceiving that they were unable to force the enemy from the heights, Sir Rowland Hill advanced a British brigade to Morillo's assistance, while, alarmed for the safety of his flank, Jourdan detached troops from his centre to support the division that held La Puebla.

A fierce and protracted combat ensued; the loss on both sides was severe, and Colonel Cadogan fell at the head of his brigade. But gradually and steadily the British gained ground; and while the eyes of both armies were turned upon the combatants and the possession of the heights seemed doubtful still, the eagle glance of Wellington discovered the forward movement of the Highland tartans, and he announced to his staff that La Puebla was carried.

The village of Sabijana was the next object of attack, and a brigade of the second division stormed it after a short but determined resistance. As that village covered the left of their line, the French made many efforts to recover its possession; but it was most gallantly retained until the left and centre of the allies moved up, and the attack on the enemy's line became general.

While Sabijana. was repeatedly assaulted, the light division was formed in close columns under cover of some broken ground, and at a short distance from the river. The hussar brigade, dismounted, were on the left; and the fourth division in position on the right, waiting the signal for advancing. The heavy cavalry formed a reserve to the centre, in event of its requiring support before the third and seventh divisions had come up; and the first and fifth, with a Spanish and Portuguese corps, were detached to occupy the road to San Sebastian, and thus intercept the enemy's retreat.

Presently, an opening cannonade upon the left announced that Sir Thomas Graham was engaged, and Lord Dalhousie notified his arrival with the third and seventh divisions at Mendonza. The moment for a grand movement had come; Lord Wellington saw and seized the crisis of the day, and ordered a general attack on the whole extent of the French position.

The light division moved forward under cover of a thicket, and placed itself opposite the enemy's right centre, about two hundred paces from the bridge of Villoses, and on the arrival of Lord Dalhousie, the signal was given to advance. At this critical moment, an intelligent Spaniard opportunely came up, and announced that one of the bridges was undefended. The mistake was quickly seized upon. A brigade, led by the first rifles, crossed it at a run, and, without any loss, established itself in a deep ravine, where it was completely protected from the enemy's cannonade.

Nothing could be more beautiful than the operations which followed. The light division carried the bridge of Nanclaus, and the fourth that of Tres Puentes; the divisions of Picton and Dalhousie followed, and the battle became general. The passage of the river, the movement of glittering masses from right to left, far as the eye could range, the deafening roar of cannon, the sustained fusillade of infantry, all was grand and imposing; while the English cavalry, displayed in glorious sunshine and formed in line to support the columns, completed a spectacle, grand and magnificent beyond description.

Immediately after crossing the Zadorra, Colville's brigade became seriously engaged with a strong French corps, and gallantly defeated it. Pressing on with characteristic impetuosity, and without halting to correct the irregularity a recent and successful struggle had occasioned, the brigade encountered on the brow of the hill, two lines of French infantry regularly drawn up, and prepared to receive their assailants. For a moment, the result was regarded with considerable apprehension, and means actually adopted for sustaining the brigade when—as that event seemed inevitable—it should be repulsed by the enemy. But valour overcame every disadvantage, and the perfect formation of the French could not withstand the dashing onset of the assailants. Their rush was irresistible; on went these daring soldiers, "sweeping before them the formidable array that, circumstanced, as they were, appeared calculated to produce annihilation."

While the combined movements of the different divisions were thus in every place successful, the attack on the village of Arinez failed, and the 88th were repulsed in an attempt to storm it. Here, the French fought desperately, and here alone the fortune of the day wavered for a moment. Nothing could exceed the obstinacy with which the village was defended; but, under a severe fire, Lord Wellington in person directed a fresh assault. The 45th and 74th ascended the height; the French were fairly forced out at the point of the bayonet, and Arinez, after a sanguinary struggle, was won.

Meanwhile the flank movements on Gamarra Mayor and Abechuco were effected with splendid success. Both villages, having bridges across the river, were filled with troops and vigorously defended. Gamarra Mayor was stormed with the bayonet by Oswald's division without firing a shot; and, under cover of the artillery, Halket's German light infantry, and Bradford's Portuguese *cacadores*, advanced against Abechuco. Nothing could be more gallant than their assault; the French were dislodged from the village with heavy loss, and the bridges left in the undisputed possession of the victors.

The whole of the enemy's first line were now driven back, but they retired in perfect order, and reforming close to Vitoria, presented an imposing front, protected by nearly one hundred pieces of artillery. A tremendous fire checked the advance of the left, centre; and the storm of the guns on both sides raged with unabated fury for an hour. Vitoria, although so near the Combatants, was hidden from view by the dense smoke, while volley after volley from the French infantry thinned, though it could not shake, Picton's "fighting third."

It was a desperate and final effort. The allies were advancing in beautiful order; while confusion was already visible in the enemy's ranks, as their left attempted to retire by *eschelons* of divisions—a dangerous movement when badly executed. Presently the cannon were abandoned, and the whole mass of French troops commenced a most disorderly retreat by the road to Pamplona.

The sun was setting, and his last rays fell upon a magnificent spectacle. Red masses of infantry were seen advancing steadily across the plain—the horse artillery at a gallop to the front, to open its fire on the fugitives—the hussar brigade charging by the Camino Real—while the second division, having overcome every obstacle, and driven the enemy from its front, was extending over the heights upon the right in line, its arms and appointments flashing gloriously, in the fading sunshine of "departing day."

Never had an action been more general, nor the attacks on every part of an extended position more simultaneous and successful. In the line of operations six bridges over the Zadorra were crossed or stormed—that on the road to Burgos enabled Lord Hill to pass; the fourth division crossed that of Nanclares; the light, at Tres Puentes; Picton and Dalhousie passed the river lower down; while Lord Lynedoch carried Abechuco and Gamarra Mayor, though both were strongly fortified, and both obstinately defended.

Driven completely through Vitoria, the French never made an attempt to rally. The formation of their army was totally destroyed, and its disorganisation completed. Indeed, no defeat could have been more decisive—the *déroute* was general; and an army, at sunrise perfect in every arm, had become at evening a mixed and helpless mob. Even at Ocana and Medellin, the raw, undisciplined, and ill-commanded Spaniards had never been more completely routed. Very few of the infantry retained their muskets, and many threw away their whole accoutrements in order to expedite their flight. All were abandoned to the conquerors, and the travelling carriage of the pseudo-king, with his wardrobe, plate, wines, and private correspondence, were found among the spoils. Indeed, Joseph himself narrowly escaped from being added to the list; for Captain Wyndham made a bold dash at "The Intruder," with a squadron of the 10th Hussars, and firing into the coach, obliged him to leave it, and ride off at speed under the protection of a strong escort of cavalry.

Night closed upon the victors and the vanquished, and darkness and broken ground favoured the escape of battalions flying from the field in mob-like disorder, and incapable of any resistance, had they been overtaken and attacked. Two leagues from Vitoria, however, the pursuit was reluctantly given up, but the horse artillery, while a shot could reach the fugitives, continued to harass the retreat.

The whole baggage and field equipage of three distinct armies fell on this occasion into the hands of the conquerors. One hundred and fifty pieces of cannon, four hundred caissons, twelve thousand rounds of ammunition, and two millions of musket-cartridges, with a thousand prisoners, were taken. The casualties on both sides were heavy. The British lost five hundred killed, two thousand eight hundred wounded; the Portuguese one hundred and fifty killed, nine hundred wounded; and the Spaniards eighty-nine of the former, and four hundred and sixty of the latter. The French loss, of course, was infinitely greater, and even by their own returns it was admitted to amount to eight thousand; but, prisoners included, it must have exceeded that number considerably.

On the morning of the 22nd, the field of battle, and the roads for some miles in the rear, exhibited an appearance it seldom falls within human fortune to witness. There lay the wreck of a mighty army; while plunder, accumulated during the French successes, and wrung from every part of Spain with unsparing rapacity, was recklessly abandoned to any who chose to seize it. Cannon and caissons, carriages and tumbrels, waggons of every description, were overturned or deserted—and a stranger *mélange* could not be imagined, than that which these enormous convoys presented to the eye. Here, was the personal baggage of a king; there, the scenery and decorations of a theatre. Munitions of war were mixed with articles of *virtù*, and scattered arms and packs, silks, embroidery, plate, and jewels, mingled together in wild disorder.

One waggon would be loaded with money, another with cartridges, while wounded soldiers, deserted women, and children of every age, everywhere implored assistance, or threw themselves for protection on the humanity of the victors. Here, a lady was overtaken in her carriage—in the next *calash* was an actress or *fille-de-chambre*—while droves of oxen were roaming over the plain, intermingled with an endless quantity of sheep and goats, mules and horses, asses and cows.

That much valuable plunder came into the hands of the soldiery is certain; but the better portion fell to the peasantry and camp-followers. Two valuable captures were secured—a full military chest, and the baton of Marshal Jourdan.

Were not the indiscriminating system of spoliation pursued by the French armies recollected, the enormous collection of plunder abandoned at Vitoria would appear incredible. From the highest to the lowest, all were bearing off some valuables from the country they had overrun; and even the king himself had not proved an exception, for, rolled in the imperials of his own coach, some of the finest pictures from the royal galleries were discovered. To secure or facilitate their transport, they had been removed from their frames, and deposited in the royal carriage, no doubt, destined to add to the unrivalled collection, that by similar means had been abstracted from the Continent, and presented to the Louvre. Wellington, however, interrupted the Spanish paintings in their transit, and thus saved the trouble and formality of a restoration.

CHAPTER 18

The Battles of the Pyrenees: Part First, 1813

Wellington was now in possession of the passes of the Pyrenees; and in the short space of two months had moved his victorious army across the kingdom of Spain, and changed his cantonments from the frontier of Portugal to a position in the Pyrenees, from which he looked down upon the southern provinces of France.

Napoleon received intelligence of Lord Wellington's success with feelings of undissembled anger and surprise. To recover the line of the Ebro was his instant determination, for he knew the dangerous effect the presence of a British Army on the frontier of "beautiful France" must of necessity produce.

Like the tidings of Marmont's disaster at Salamanca, the news of Joseph's defeat reached Napoleon at a crisis, when a. lost battle was a calamity indeed. With him, every previous armistice had obtained concessions; and, had Vitoria terminated differently, battles, in no way decisive, might from a fortunate success in Spain, have produced results similar to those of Marengo, Austerlitz, and Jena, With ominous rapidity, the intelligence reached every European court that Joseph had been driven from his throne, and Wellington overlooked the fields of France and none could gainsay it—a conqueror. With what astonishment these tidings were received, those immediately round the person of Napoleon have since narrated. Nothing could be mere humiliating—nothing, the time considered, more ruinous. His brother no longer prosecuted the war in Spain, but, defeated and shaken in confidence, had sought shelter in the plains of Gascony.

Accustomed as he had been to receive reports from the Peninsula little calculated to give satisfaction, or to confirm his impression of the invincible qualities of those troops which he had personally ever led to certain victory, so extensive and alarming a reverse as that now made must have been as unexpected as it was disastrous; but with all the promptitude of a person born to command, instead of yielding to gloomy circumstances, he issued orders for a bold effort to counteract the tide of war, to recover the ground lost by Vitoria, and to awaken to energy, as he conceived, the dormant spirit of his soldiers.

Marshal Soult was, therefore, specially despatched from Germany to assume the chief command of the beaten army, and, if possible, restore its fallen fortunes.

Wellington foresaw the coming storm, and turned his immediate attention to the reduction of Pamplona and San Sebastian. From the strength of the former, and the excellent condition of its defences, the allied commander decided on a blockade; and it was accordingly closely invested by General Hill. Redoubts were thrown up within fifteen hundred yards of the place, armed with the cannon taken at Vitoria, and to the Spanish Army under O'Donel the conduct of the blockade was entrusted.

Graham, with his corps augmented to ten thousand men, was directed to besiege San Sebastian; and on the 11th of July he sat down before the place.

San Sebastian is built on a peninsula, its western defences washed by the sea, and its eastern by the River Urumea, which at high water rises several feet above the base of the escarp wall. A bold and rocky height, called Monte Orgullo, rises at the extreme point of a narrow neck of land, and on its summit stands the citadel of La Mota.

Eight hundred yards distant from the land-front, the convent of San Bartolemeo, with a redoubt and circular fieldwork, were garrisoned. These advanced posts were strongly fortified, and, as it was determined to breach the eastern wall and storm it afterwards at low water, when the receding tide should permit an advance by the left of the Urumea, it became necessary, as a preliminary step, to dislodge the enemy from the convent.

On the 14th of July, the guns in battery opened a heavy fire on San Bartolemeo; and by the next day the walls of the building were injured considerably. Another battery, erected beyond the Urumea, fired with equal success upon the bastion; and on the 17th both works were carried by assault. Batteries, armed with thirty-two siege guns and howitzers, opened on the town wall from the sandhills; and on the 25th two breaches were effected, one of thirty yards' extent, and the other of ten. A mine was also driven under the glacis, and at its explosion was the appointed signal for an assault upon the breaches.

At first the astounding noise distracted the garrison, and enabled the advance of both storming parties to gain the breaches; but the French recovered from their panic, and poured such a fire of grape and musketry on the assailants, that the breach was heaped with dead and dying, and the allies were driven back to the trenches with a loss of above six hundred men. The loss of the British, from the 7th to the 27th of July, amounted to two hundred and four killed, seven hundred and seventy-four wounded, and three hundred missing.

This severe repulse, added to the certain intelligence that Soult was preparing to strike a grand blow, induced Lord Wellington to issue immediate orders to raise the siege.

Circumstances, indeed, rendered that step unavoidable. The French were already in motion; Soult had forced the passes on the right, penetrated the valleys of the Pyrenees, and was marching to relieve Pamplona.

Lord Wellington had a most extensive, and, consequently, a very difficult position to defend, his *corps d'armée* covering an extent of country extending, from flank to flank, over sixty miles of mountains, without lateral communications, or the means of holding a disposable reserve in the rear of the passes, all of which must be defended, as the loss of one would render the defence of the others unavailing.

After issuing a spirited proclamation to his army, Soult lost no time in commencing operations. His corps had been organised anew, strongly reinforced, and strengthened in every arm, and more particularly in artillery. To relieve Pamplona, it would be necessary to carry the passes of Maya and Roncesvalles; and accordingly, the French marshal suddenly assembled the wings of his army and a division of the centre, at St. Jean Pied de Port; while D'Erlon, with, the remainder of the corps, concentrated at Espaletta.

By feints upon the smaller passes of Espagne and Lereta, D'Erlon masked his real attempt, which was to be made upon that of Maya, by a mountain path from Espaletta. From several suspicious appearances an attack was dreaded by the allies, and some light companies had been ordered up, and, with the pickets, they were assailed at noon in such force that, though supported by the 34th, 50th, and 92nd, they were driven back on a height communicating with Echalar when, reinforced by Barnes's brigade of the seventh division, they succeeded in repulsing the attack and holding their ground again.

RIFLE'S OFFICER

The affair was very sanguinary. One wing of the 92nd was nearly cut to pieces. All the regiments engaged highly distinguished themselves, and the 32nd in particular. The allies lost nearly two thousand men, and four pieces of artillery.

Soult's advance on Roncesvalles was made in imposing force, but his movements were foreseen, and necessary dispositions had been made for defeating them. General Byng, who commanded, sent Morillo's Spanish division to observe the road of Arbaicete, by which the pass of Maya, might have been turned on the right; and descending the heights, placed his own brigade in a position by which that important road might be covered more effectually. Soult, however, directed his true attack upon the left. Cole was overpowered and driven back; but the fusilier brigade sustained him, and the attack throughout being met with steady gallantry, was eventually defeated.

On Byng's division the French marshal directed his next effort; and with a force so superior, that, though obstinately resisted, it proved successful, so far as it obliged the weak brigades of the British general to fall back upon the mountains, and abandon the Arbaicete road, while Morillo's Spaniards were driven on the fourth division. Necessarily the whole fell back at nightfall, and took a position in front of Zubiri.

Picton's division united with the fourth next morning, and both fell leisurely back as the Duke of Dalmatia advanced. Picton continued retiring on the 27th July, and that evening took a position in front of Pamplona to cover the blockade, General Hill having already fallen back on Irurita.

Nearly at this time Lord Wellington had come up; putting in motion the several corps which lay in his route to the scene of action, and at one end of a mountain village he pencilled a despatch, as a French detachment had entered by the other.

Riding at full speed, he reached the village of Sorauren, and his eagle glance detected Clausel's column in march along the ridge of Zabaldica. Convinced that the troops in the valley of the Lanz must be intercepted by this movement, he sprang from his saddle, and pencilled a note on the parapet of the bridge, directing the troops to take the road to Oricain, and gain the rear of Cole's position. The scene that followed was highly interesting. Lord Fitzroy Somerset, the only staff-officer who had kept up with him, galloped with these orders out of Sorauren by one road, the French light cavalry dashed in by another, and the British general rode alone up the mountain to reach his troops.

One of Campbell's Portuguese battalions first descried him, and raised a cry of joy, and the shrill clamour caught up by the next regiments swelled as it run along the line into that stern and appalling shout which, the British soldier is wont to give upon the edge of battle, and which no enemy ever heard unmoved. Lord Wellington suddenly stopped in a conspicuous place; he desired that both armies should know he was there; and a double spy who was present pointed out Soult, then so near that his features could be plainly distinguished.

The British, general, it is said, fixed his eyes attentively upon this formidable man, and speaking as if to himself, said:

> Yonder is a great commander, but he is a cautious one, and will delay his attack to ascertain the cause of these cheers; that will give time for the 6th division to arrive, and I shall beat him.

And certain it is that the French general made no serious attack that day.

Twelve British regiments were embattled on the Pyrenees who had fought at Talavera; and there were present not a few who might recall an incident to memory, that would present a striking but amusing contrast. Cuesta, examining his battleground four years before in lumbering state, seated in an unwieldy coach, and drawn by eight pampered mules; Wellington, on an English hunter, dashing from post to post at headlong speed, and at a pace that distanced the best mounted of his staff.

Having despatched the order, he galloped to the place where Picton's divisions were drawn up—the third, on the right, in front of Heart, and extending to the heights of Olaz, and the fourth, with Byng's and Campbell's brigades, formed on the left; their right on the road from Roncesvalles to Zubiri, and the left commanding that from Ostiz to Pamplona. The reserve was formed of the corps of Morillo and O'Donel, while, on the only ground on which cavalry could act, the British dragoons were formed under Sir Stapleton Cotton.

Soult had occupied the high grounds in the front of those held by the allies, and in the evening he made an effort to possess a hill occupied by a Portuguese and Spanish brigade on the right of the fourth division. These troops steadily resisted the attack, and, supported by a British and Spanish regiment, repulsed the French, until darkness ended the firing on both sides.

Pack's division came up on the 28th, and took a position in the rear

British Infantry sergeant

of the fourth division, covering the valley of the Lanz. The village of Sorauren in their front was held by the French; from which, in considerable force, they moved forward, and attacked the sixth division. But this movement was exposed to a flanking fire, that obliged the enemy to retire after suffering a serious loss. On the left of the division, a regiment of Portuguese *cacadores* was driven back by a simultaneous attack, but Ross's brigade came rapidly forward, and completely repulsed the French. On the right, a renewed effort partially succeeded, as the Spanish regiments were deforced; but the 40th came to the charge, and cleared the hill of the enemy.

The French marshal's efforts had been directed against the whole of the height held by the fourth division. In almost all he was repelled; but on the right of the brigade of Ross, Soult was for a time successful, and Campbell's Portuguese regiments, unable to bear the furious and sustained attack, lost ground, and allowed the enemy to establish a strong body of troops within the allied position. Of necessity, General Ross, having his flank turned, immediately fell back.

Wellington saw the crisis, and the 27th and 48th were directed to recover the ground with the bayonet. Ross moved forward in support, a brilliant and bloody struggle terminated in the total repulse of the French division, which with severe loss, was precipitately driven from the height it had with such difficulty gained. At this period of the fight, Pack's brigade advanced up the hill. The French gave up further efforts on the position, and a long, sanguinary, and determined contest terminated.

The fourth division in this affair had been most gloriously distinguished. The bayonet, in every trying exigency, was resorted to; the charges were frequent, and some regiments, the fusiliers (7th and 23rd), with the 20th and 40th, repeatedly checked an advance, or recovered lost ground, by "steel alone."

Hill's division had marched by Lanz, and Lord Dalhousie from San Estevan on Lizasso, and reached it on the 28th, while the seventh division moved to Marcelain, and covered the Pamplona road. Soult, failing in his efforts on the front of the position, determined to attack Hill's corps, turn the left of the allies, and thus relieve Pamplona.

D'Erlon had reached Ostiz on the 29th, and Soult detached a division from his own position to strengthen him. During the night of the 29th, he crossed the Lanz, and occupied the heights in front of the sixth and seventh divisions, and withdrawing the corps hitherto posted opposite the third British division, his left wing closed in on the main position of the mountain, directly in front of the fourth division. D'Erlon's corps, now considerably strengthened, communicated by the right of the Lanz with the heights occupied by their left.

These dispositions of the French marshal were at once penetrated by Lord Wellington, and he decided on driving the enemy from the main position, which, from its importance, was very strongly occupied.

Picton, crossing the heights from which the French corps had been recently withdrawn, turned the left of their position on the road to Roncesvalles, while Lord Dalhousie advanced against the heights in front of the seventh division, and gained their right flank. Packenham, with the sixth division, turned the village of Sorauren, and, assisted by Byng's brigade, carried that of Ostiz. These flank movements were executed with admirable rapidity, and enabled Cole, with part of the fourth division, to assault the front of the enemy's position. His attack succeeded. The French gave way, a noble chain of posts was forced on every side, as well by the dashing gallantry of the troops as the excellent dispositions of their leader.

The French had endeavoured to outflank General Hill; but Pringle's brigade manoeuvred on the heights above the La Zarza road, and as the enemy extended by the right, they observed a. parallel direction. During these movements, front attacks were frequently and furiously made, and always repulsed by the bayonet. Sir Rowland steadily maintained his position behind Lizasso, until a strong corps, detached by D'Erlon, succeeded in filing round the left flank of the British brigades. No result of any importance ensued, for Hill leisurely retired on a mountain position at Eguarras, a mile in the rear, and every attempt made by D'Erlon to dislodge him proved a failure.

That night, Soult, discomfited in his numerous and well-sustained attacks on every position of the allied lines, fell back, and was vigorously pursued by his opponent. Two divisions were overtaken at the pass of Donna Maria, and brought to action. Although most formidably posted, they were driven from their ground by the second and seventh divisions, while at another point, Barnes's brigade made a daring and successful attack on a corps of much superior strength, formed in a difficult position.

Wellington continued the pursuit to Irurita, the French retiring rapidly towards the frontier, from whence they had so confidently advanced, and on which they were as promptly obliged to recede. In their retreat through the valley of the Bidassao, the enemy's loss in prisoners and baggage was considerable. A large convoy was taken at Elizondo, and on the night of the 1st of August, the entire of the French corps were driven from the Spanish territory, and the British bivouacs once more established on the same ground which they had occupied previous to the advance of the Duke of Dalmatia.

During the continued series of bold operations, and constant and sustained attacks, the loss on both sides could not but be immense. Soult's amounted to at least eight thousand, and Wellington's to eight hundred and eighty-one killed, five thousand five hundred and ten wounded, and seven hundred and five missing. That the French marshal was perfectly confident of succeeding, could be inferred from the tone of his address to the army, and the mass of cavalry and immense pare of guns, with which he had provided himself, and which, as they could not be employed in mountain combats, were evidently designed to assist in future operations that should succeed his deforcement of the allies from the Pyrenees, and the raising of the blockade of Pamplona.

Nothing could have been more annoying to the French marshal, than that he should have actually reached within one league of the blockaded fortress, and never be permitted afterwards to open the slightest communication with its garrison.

CHAPTER 19

The Siege of San Sebastian, 1813

After the retreat of Soult, the British and their allies resumed the positions from which they had been dislodged by the advance of the French marshal, and re-established headquarters at Lezeca. A short period of comparative inactivity succeeded; immediate operations could not be commenced on either side—the enemy had been too severely repulsed to permit their becoming assailants again; while, on the other hand, Wellington would not be justified in crossing the frontier and entering a hostile country, with Pamplona and San Sebastian in his rear, and garrisoned by the French.

Nothing could be more magnificent than the position of the British brigades. For many a mile along the extended line of occupation, huts crowning the heights or studding the deep valleys below them, showed the rude dwellings of the mighty mass of human beings collected in that Alpine country. At night the scene was still more picturesque. The irregular surface of the sierras sparkled with a thousand watch-fires, and the bivouacs of the allies exhibited all the varieties of light and shadow which an artist loves to copy.

To the occupants themselves the views obtained from their elevated abodes were grand and imposing. One while obscured in fog, the hum of voices alone announced that their comrades were beside them, while at another, the sun bursting forth in cloudless beauty, displayed a varied scene, glorious beyond imagination. At their feet the fertile plains of France presented themselves; above, ranges of magnificent heights towered in majestic grandeur to the skies, and stretched into distance beyond the range of sight.

Although no military movements were made, this inactive interval of a vigorous campaign was usefully employed by the allied commander, in organising anew the regiments that had suffered most,

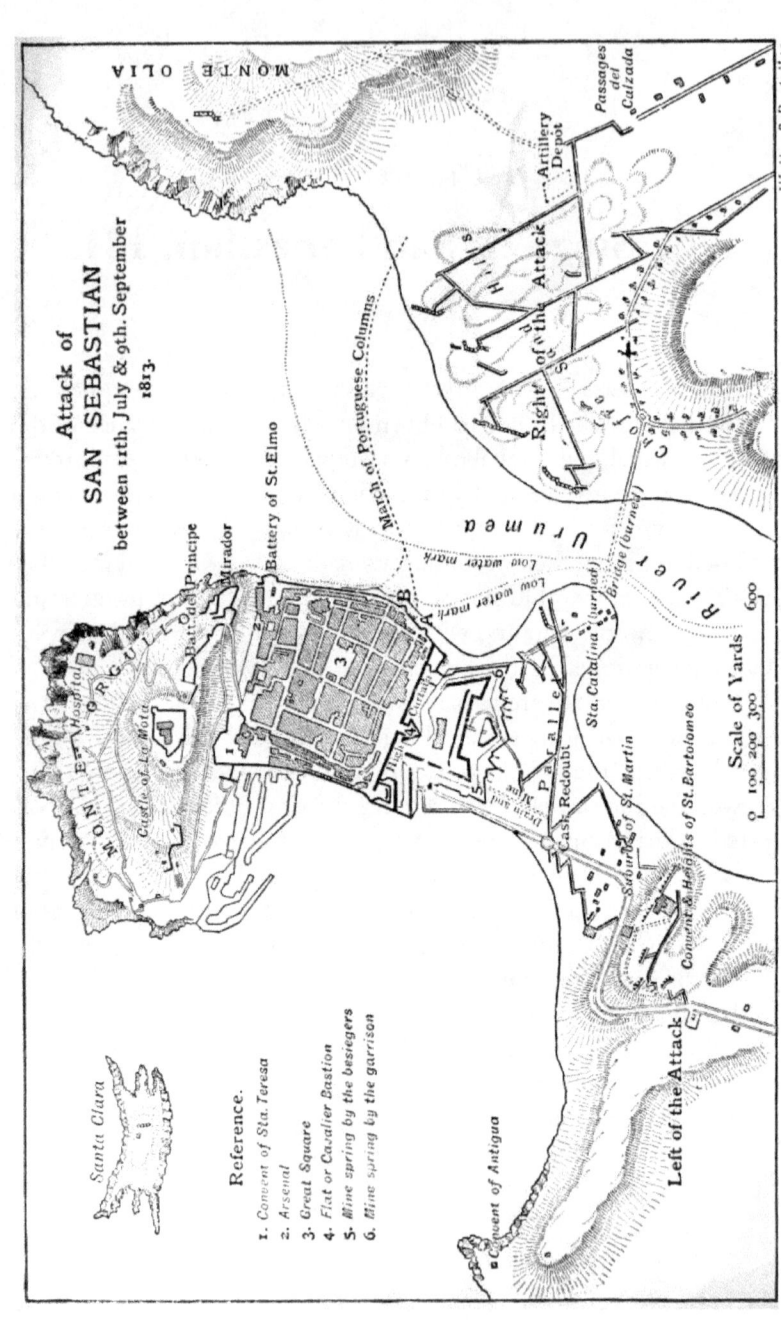

concentrating the divisions, replacing exhausted stores, and perfecting the whole *matériel* of the army. Those of the British near the coast, compared with the corps that were blockading Pamplona, lived comfortably in their mountain bivouacs; indeed, the task of covering a blockade is the most disagreeable that falls to the soldier's lot. Exposed to cold and rain, continually on the alert, and yet engaged in a duty devoid of enterprise and interest, nothing could be more wearying to the troops employed; and desertions, which during active service were infrequent, now became numerous, and especially among the Spaniards and Irish.

The siege of San Sebastian was renewed. Guns, formerly employed, were re-landed, the trenches occupied again, and a large supply of heavy ordnance and mortars, received opportunely from the home country, were placed in battery. Lord Wellington was reinforced by a company of sappers and miners, and the navy, under Sir George Collier, assisted him with both men and guns. The batteries were consequently enlarged, and a furious sortie by the garrison on the night of the 24th August producing little effect, on the 26th a crushing fire opened from fifty-seven pieces of siege artillery.

On the same night the island of Santa Clara, situated at the entrance of the harbour, and partially enfilading the defences of the castle, was surprised and stormed by a mixed party of sailors and soldiers, and its garrison made prisoners. On the 27th, a second sortie on the whole front of the isthmus failed entirely, and the assailants were instantly driven back. The siege and working artillery had been now augmented to eighty pieces, and on the 30th the breaches were so extensively battered down, that Lord Wellington issued orders that they should be assaulted, and the next morning was named for the attempt.

In the annals of modern warfare, perhaps there is no conflict recorded which was so sanguinary and so desperate as the storming of that well-defended breach. During the blockade, every resource of military ingenuity was tried by the French governor, and the failure of the first assault, with the subsequent raising of the siege, emboldened the garrison, and rendered them the more confident of holding out until Soult could advance and succour them. The time from which the bartering guns had been withdrawn, until they had been again placed in battery, was assiduously employed in constructing new defences and strengthening the old ones. But though the place when reinvested was more formidable than before, the besiegers appeared only the more determined to reduce it.

Storming of San Sebastian

Morning broke gloomily, an intense mist obscured every object, and the work of slaughter was for a time delayed. At nine the sea-breeze cleared away the fog; the sun shone gloriously out, and in two hours the forlorn hope issued from the trenches. The columns succeeded, and every gun from the fortress that could bear, opened on them with shot and shells. The appearance of the breach was perfectly delusive; nothing living could reach the summit; no courage, however desperate, could overcome the difficulties, for they were alike unexpected and insurmountable.

In vain the officers rushed forward, and devotedly were they followed by their men. From entrenched houses behind the breach, the traverses, and the ramparts of the curtain, a withering discharge of musketry was poured on the assailants, while the Mirador and Prince batteries swept the approaches with their guns. To survive this concentrated fire was impossible; the forlorn hope were cut off to a man, and the heads of the columns annihilated. At last the debouches were choked with the dead and wounded, and a further passage to the breach rendered impracticable from the heap of corpses that were piled upon each other.

Then, in that desperate moment, when hope might have been supposed to be over, an expedient unparalleled in the records of war was resorted to. The British batteries opened on the curtain, and the storming parties heard with surprise the roar of cannon in the rear, while, but a few feet above their heads, their iron shower hissed horribly, and swept away the enemy and their defences.

This was the moment for a fresh effort. Another brigade was moved forward, and, favoured by an accidental explosion upon the curtain, which confused the enemy while it encouraged the assailants, the *terre-plain* was mounted, and the French driven from the works. A long and obstinate resistance was continued in the streets, which were in many places barricaded, but by five in the evening opposition had ceased, and the town was in the possession of the British. Seven hundred of the garrison were prisoners, and the remainder were either disabled in the assault or shut up in the castle.

The town presented a dreadful spectacle, both of the work of war and of the wickedness which in war is let loose.

It had caught fire during the assault, owing to the quantity of combustibles of all kinds which were scattered about. The French rolled their shells into it from the castle, and while it was in flames the troops were plundering, and the people of the surrounding country flocking to profit by the spoils of their countrymen. The few inhabitants who were to be seen seemed stupefied with horror; they had suffered so much that they looked with apathy ait all around them, and when the crash of a falling house made the captors run, they scarcely moved. Heaps of dead were lying everywhere—British, Portuguese, and French, one upon another; with such determination had the one side attacked and the other maintained its ground.

Very many of the assailants lay dead on the roofs of the houses which adjoined the breach. The bodies were thrown into the mines and other excavations, and there covered over so as to be out of sight, but so hastily and so slightly, that the air far and near was tainted, and fires were kindled in the breaches to consume those which could not be otherwise disposed of.

The hospital presented a more dreadful scene, for it was a scene of human suffering; friend and enemy had been indiscriminately carried thither, and were there alike neglected.

On the third day after the assault, many of them had received neither surgical assistance nor food of any kind, and it became necessary to remove them on the fifth, as the flames approached the building. Much of this neglect would have been unavoidable, even if that humane and conscientious diligence which can be hoped for from so few, had been found in every individual belonging to the medical department, the number of the wounded being so great; and little help could be received from the other part of the army, because it had been engaged in action on the same day.

The unfortunate town seemed alike devoted by friends and enemies to destruction. The conquerors were roaming through the streets, the castle firing on the houses beneath its guns, in many places fire had broken out, and a storm of thunder, rain, and lightning added to the confusion of a scene which even in warfare finds no parallel.

The assault of San Sebastian cost a large expense of life, there being seven hundred and sixty-one killed, one thousand six hundred and ninety-seven wounded, and forty-five missing, and in that number many valuable officers were included. The head of the engineer department, Sir Richard Fletcher, was killed, and Generals Leith, Oswald, and Robinson were returned in the list of wounded.

Vigorous measures were in preparation for the reduction of the castle of San Sebastian. From the height of its escarp, and the solidity of the masonry, La Mota could not be assaulted with any certainty of success, and a regular investment was requisite to obtain the place.

On the 1st of September, the mortar-batteries commenced throwing shells; and as the castle was indifferently provided with bomb-proof casemates, a considerable loss induced the governor to offer a capitulation, but the terms were not such as could be granted. Batteries with heavy ordnance were erected on the works of the town, and on the 8th opened with such terrible effect, that in two hours the place was unconditionally surrendered. The garrison amounted to eighteen hundred men, of whom nearly a third were disabled.

At noon, the French garrison marched out of the castle gate with the customary honours of war. At its head, with sword drawn, and firm step, appeared General Rey, accompanied by Colonel Songeon, and the officers of his staff; as a token of respect he was saluted as he passed. The old general dropped his sword in return to the civilities of the British officers, and leading the remains of his brave battalions to the glacis, there deposited their arms, with a well-founded confidence of having nobly done his duty, and persevered to the utmost in an energetic and brilliant defence.

On the 10th, the Portuguese were formed in the streets of the ruined city, the British on the ramparts. The day was fine, after a night of heavy rain. About noon the garrison marched out at the Mirador gate. The bands of two or three Portuguese regiments played occasionally, but altogether it was a dismal scene, amid ruins and vestiges of fire and slaughter; a few inhabitants were present, and only a few.

San Sebastian was held to the last with excellent judgment and dauntless gallantry. Indeed, the loss of the besiegers bore melancholy confirmation of the fact, for the reduction of that fortress cost the allies nearly four thousand men.

CHAPTER 20

The Battles of the Pyrenees: Part Second, 1813

Winter had now set in, and a season of unusual severity commenced. The allies were sadly exposed to the weather, and an increasing difficulty was felt every day in procuring necessary supplies. Forage became so scarce, that part of the cavalry had nothing for their horses but grass; while the cattle for the soldiers' rations, driven sometimes from the interior of Spain, perished in immense numbers by the way, or reached the camp so wretchedly reduced in condition as to be little better than carrion. Resources from the sea could not be trusted to; for in blowing weather the coast was scarcely approachable, and even in the sheltered harbour of Passages, the transports could with difficulty ride to their moorings, in consequence of the heavy swell that tumbled in from the Atlantic. The cold became intense, sentries were frozen at their posts, and a picket at Roncesvalles, regularly snowed up, was saved with great difficulty. All this plainly showed that the present position of the allies was not tenable much longer, and that a forward movement into France was unavoidable.

But great difficulties in advancing presented themselves; and, all things considered, success was a matter of uncertainty. Soult's army had been powerfully reinforced by the last conscription; and for three months the French marshal had been indefatigable in fortifying the whole line of his position, and strengthening his defences, wherever the ground would admit an enemy to approach.

The field-works extended from the sea to the river, as the right rested on St. Jean-de-Luz, and the left on the Nivelle. The centre was at Mont La Rhune and the heights of Sarré. The whole position passed in a half-circle through Irogne, Ascain, Sarré, Ainhoue, and Espelette.

Though the centre was commanded by a higher ridge, a narrow valley interposed between them. The entire front was covered with works, and the sierras defended by a chain of redoubts. The centre was particularly strong—in fact, it was a work regularly ditched and palisaded. To turn the position, by advancing Hill's corps through St. Jean Pied-de-Port, was first determined on; but, on consideration, this plan of operations was abandoned, and, strong as the centre was, the allied leader resolved that on it his attack should be directed, while the heights of Ainhoue, which formed its support, should, if possible, be simultaneously carried.

A commander less nerved than Lord Wellington, would have lacked resolution for this bold and masterly operation. Everything was against him, and every chance favoured the enemy. The weather was dreadful, the rain fell in torrents, and while no army could move, the French had the advantage of the delay to complete the defences of a position which was already deemed perfect as art and nature could render it. Nor did their powerful works produce in the enemy a false security. Aware of the man and the troops which threatened them, they were always ready for an attack, and their outpost duty was rigidly attended to. Before day their corps were under arms, and the whole line of defence continued fully garrisoned until night permitted the troops to be withdrawn.

At last the weather moderated. Ainhoue was reconnoitred by Wellington in person, and the plan of the attack arranged. No operation could be more plain or straightforward. The centre was to be carried by columns of divisions, and the right centre turned. To all the corps their respective points of attack were assigned, while to the light division and Longa's Spaniards the storming of La Petite Rhune was confided. The latter were to be supported by Alten's cavalry, three brigades of British artillery, and three mountain guns.

The successful result of the battle was owing in no inconsiderable degree to the able direction of the artillery under Colonel Dickson. Guns were brought to bear on the French fortifications from situations which they considered totally inaccessible to that arm. Mountain guns on swivel carriages, harnessed on the backs of mules purposely trained for that service, ascended the rugged ridges of the mountains, and showered destruction on the entrenchments below. The foot and horse-artillery displayed a facility of movement which must have astonished the French, the artillerymen dragging the guns with ropes up steep precipices, or lowering them down to positions from whence they could with more certain aim pour forth their fatal volleys against the enemy.

The 8th December had been named for the attack, but the roads were so dreadfully cut up, that neither the artillery nor Hill's brigade could get into position, and it was postponed for two days longer, when the 10th dawned, a clear and moonlight morning. Long before day, Lord Wellington, and several of the generals of division and brigade with their respective staffs, had assembled in a small wood, five hundred yards from the redoubt above the village of Sarré, waiting for sufficient light to commence the arranged attack.

Nothing could exceed the courage and rapidity with which the troops rushed on, and overcame every artificial and natural obstacle. The 3rd and 7th advanced in front of the village, Downie's Spanish brigade attacked the right, while the left was turned by Cole's, and the whole of the first line of defences remained in possession of the allies.

On this glorious occasion, the light division was pre-eminently distinguished. By moonlight it moved from the greater La Rhune, and formed in a ravine which separates the bolder from the lesser height. This latter was occupied in force by the enemy, and covered on every assailable point with entrenchments. As morning broke, the British light troops rushed from the hollow which had concealed them. To withstand their assault was impossible; work after work was stormed; forward they went with irresistible bravery, and on the summit of the hill united themselves with Cole's division, and then pushed on against the entrenched heights behind, which formed the strongest part of the position.

Here, a momentary check arrested their progress; the supporting force (Spanish) were too slow, and the ground too rugged for the horse artillery to get over it at speed. The rifles were attacked in turn, and for a moment driven back by a mass of the enemy. But the reserve came up; and again the light troops rushed forward, the French gave way, and the whole of the lower ridge was left in possession of the assailants.

For four hours the combat had raged, and on every point the British were victorious. A more formidable position still remained behind, and Wellington combined his efforts for a vigorous and general attack.

This mountain position extended from Mondarin to Ascain, and a long valley, through which the Nivelle flows, traversed it; where the surface was unequal, the higher points were crowned with redoubts, and the spaces of leveller surface occupied by the French in line or column, as the nature of the ground best admitted. Men inclined to fight never had a field that offered so many advantages; and there were none, save the British leader and the splendid army he commanded, who would have ventured to assault equal numbers posted as the enemy were.

The dispositions were soon complete, the word was given, and in six columns, with a chain of skirmishers in front, the allies advanced to the attack.

To carry a strong work, or assail a body of infantry in close column, placed on the crest of an acclivity that requires the attacking force to halt frequently for breathing-time, requires a desperate and enduring valour which few armies can boast—but such bravery on that occasion characterised the allied divisions. Masses posted on a steep height were forced from it by the bayonet, though hand and foot were often required to enable the assaulting party to reach them. Redoubts were carried at a run, or so rapidly turned by the different brigades that the defenders had scarcely time to escape by the rear. Nothing could resist the dash and intrepidity of the British; and over the whole extent of that formidable position, on no point did the attack fail.

The French were driven from their works, and forced in great confusion on the bridge of the Nivelle. One redoubt, from its superior strength, had been obstinately maintained, but the regiment that occupied it was completely cut off from retreating, and the whole were made prisoners.

In every other point the British attack succeeded. Hill's division carried the heights of Ainhoue, the whole of the redoubts falling to the British and Portuguese under Hamilton; while Stewart drove the enemy from a parallel ridge in the rear, and the divisions, by an united attack, forcing the enemy from their works at Espelette, obliged them to retire towards Cambo, thus gaining the rear of the position originally occupied, and forcing Soult's centre on his right

The French marshal formed in great force on the high grounds over Ascain and St. Pe, and Lord Wellington made instant dispositions to attack him. Three divisions, the third, sixth, and seventh, advanced against the heights—two by the left of the Nivelle, and one, the sixth, by the right bank. As the position was exceedingly strong, the enemy determined to hold it to the last, and maintained a furious cannonade, supported by a heavy fire of musketry. But the steady and imposing advance of the allies could not be repelled, and the French retired hastily.

The right of the position was thus entirely cut through, and though for months the Duke of Dalmatia had been arming every vulnerable point, and his engineers had used their utmost skill in perfecting its defences, the British commander's dispositions were so admirably made and so gallantly carried out, that his numerous and most difficult attacks were crowned with brilliant success, unalloyed by a single failure.

Night ended the battle, the firing ceased, Soult retreated, and, covered by the darkness, withdrew a beaten army, that had numbered fully seventy thousand men. His killed and wounded exceeded three thousand, besides a loss of fifty guns, and twelve hundred prisoners. The allies reckoned their casualties at two thousand four hundred killed and wounded; which, the nature of the ground, the strength of its defences, and the *corps d'armée* that held it, considered, was indeed a loss comparatively light.

CHAPTER 21

The Battles of the Pyrenees: Part Third, 1813

Soult halted his different corps in the entrenched camp of Bayonne, and Wellington cantoned his troops two miles in front of his opponent, in lines extending from the sea to the Nivelle, his right stretching to Cambo and his left resting on the coast. This change in his cantonments was productive of serious advantages. His wearied soldiery obtained rest and many comforts which in their mountain bivouacs were unattainable; and though the enemy possessed unlimited command of a well-supplied district for their foraging parties, and the surface over which Lord Wellington might obtain supplies was necessarily circumscribed, his direct communication with the sea, and a month's rest in tolerable quarters, recruited his exhausted army and produced the best results.

But Wellington merely waited to mature his preparations; and, to extend his line of supply, he determined to seize the strong ground between the Nive and the Adour, and confine Soult to the immediate vicinity of his own camp. Accordingly, on the 9th of December, the left wing of the allies, advancing by the road of St. Jean de Luz, gained the heights domineering the entrenchments of the French. The right forded the Nive above Cambo, while, by a bridge of boats, Clinton crossed at Nostariz, and obliged the enemy, to avoid being cut off, to fall back on Bayonne.

At night, the French having retired to their posts within the fortified position they had occupied, Hope, with the left of the allies, recrossed the river to his former cantonments, having a direct communication open with Sir Rowland Hill, who had taken a position with his division, his right on the Adour, his centre in the village of St.

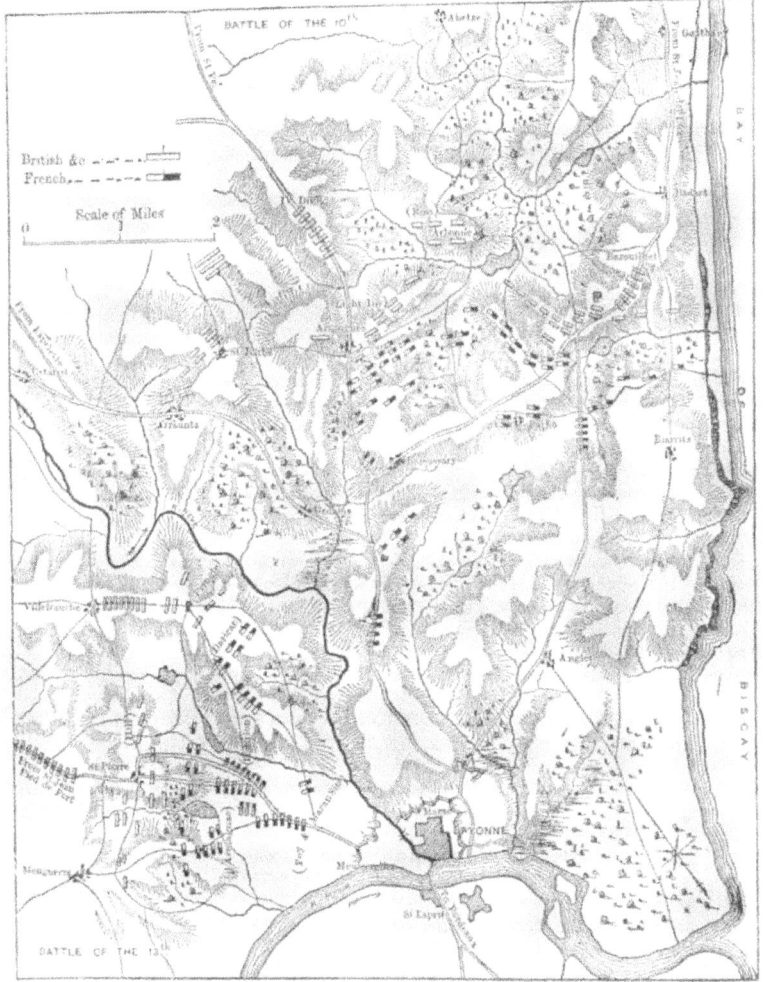

PLAN OF THE BATTLES ON THE NIVE.

Pierre, and his left *appuied* on the heights of Ville Franque. Morillo's division was in observation at Urcuray, and a cavalry corps at Hasparren.

The relative positions of the rival armies were greatly different. Soult possessed immense advantages; his *corps d'armée* were completely bivouacked, with easy communications, every facility for rapid concentration, and the citadel of Bayonne to protect him if he found it necessary to fall back. The allies extended over an irregular line intersected by the Nive, with bad roads, that rendered any rapid reinforcement of a threatened point altogether impracticable.

Hence, Wellington was everywhere open to attack, and Soult could fall on him with overwhelming numbers and force an unequal combat, while but a part of the allies should be opposed to the combined efforts of the enemy. The French marshal was aware of this, and it was not long before he endeavoured to profit by his advantage.

The left of the allies, under Sir John Hope, had the fifth division (Hay's) posted on the heights of Barouillet, with Campbell's Portuguese brigade on a narrow ridge immediately in their front. At Arrangues, the light division was formed on a strong height, at a distance of two miles from the fifth.

The positions were separated by the low grounds between the hills, and the corps were consequently unconnected. Although both were strongly posted, still, in case of an attack, each must trust entirely to his own resources, and repulse the enemy without counting on support from the other.

Early on the 10th of December, Soult appeared on the road of St. Jean de Luz, and in great force marched directly against the allied left. The light and fifth divisions were simultaneously assailed, the former driven back into its entrenchments, and Campbell's brigade forced back upon Hay's at Barouillet. The intermediate ground between the allied positions was now in the possession of the enemy, and thus Soult was enabled to attack the right of the fifth with vigour. Although assailed in front and flank, the allied division gallantly withstood the assault; and when the position was completely penetrated, and the orchard on the right forced and occupied by the French with overwhelming numbers, still the British and Portuguese held the heights, and, while whole sections fell, not an inch of ground was yielded.

Another and a more determined effort was now made by the French marshal, and made in vain, for by a bold and well-timed movement of the 9th British and a Portuguese battalion, wheeling round suddenly and charging the French rear, the enemy were driven back with the loss of a number of prisoners. Fresh troops were fast arriving, the guards came into action, and Lord Wellington reached the battle-ground from the right. But the French had been repulsed in their last attempt so decisively that they did not venture to repeat it; evening closed, the firing gradually died away, and the allied divisions held the same positions from which Soult, with an immense numerical superiority in men and guns, had vainly striven to force them.

The slaughter was great on both sides; and, wearied by long sustained exertion, and weakened by its heavy loss, the fifth division was relieved by the first, who occupied the post their comrades had maintained so gloriously. The fourth and seventh were placed in reserve, and enabled, in case of attack, to assist on either point, should Soult, on the following morning, as was expected, again attempt to make himself master of Barouillet.

Nothing could surpass the reckless gallantry displayed by the British officers throughout this long and sanguinary struggle. Sir John Hope, with his staff, was always seen where the contest was most furious; and the only wonder was that in a combat so close and murderous, one remarkable alike in personal appearance and "daring deed," should have outlived that desperate day.

His escapes indeed were many. He was wounded in the leg, contused in the shoulder, four musket-bullets passed through his hat, and he lost two horses. General Robinson, in command of the second brigade, was badly wounded, and Wellington himself was constantly exposed to fire. Unable to determine where the grand effort of his adversary would be directed, he passed repeatedly from one point of the position to the other, and that life, so valuable to all beside, seemed "of light estimation" to himself alone.

The next sun rose to witness a renewal of the contest. In their attack upon the light divisions at Arrangues, the French, driven from the defended posts the *château* and churchyard afforded, retired to the plateau of Bassusarry, and there established themselves for the night. During the forenoon some slight affairs between the pickets occurred; but at noon, the fusillade having ceased, the allies collected wood, lighted fires, and cooked their dinners. At two, a considerable stir was visible in the enemy's line, and their pioneers were seen cutting down the fence for the passage of artillery.

Soult's first demonstration of attack was made against Arrangues; but that was only to mask his real object. Presently his *tirailleurs* swarmed out in front of Barouillet, attacked the British outposts, drove the pickets back, and moving in strong columns by the Bayonne road, furiously assailed the heights of the position. The wood-cutters, surprised by the sudden onset of the French, hurried back to resume their arms and join their regiments; while the enemy, mistaking the cause of this rush to their alarm posts, supposed a panic had seized the troops, and pressed forward with increased impetuosity. But the same results attended their attempt upon the first as on the fifth division; and the French were driven back with heavy loss. In the contests of two days not an inch of ground was yielded, and the left wing of the allies remained firm in its position, when night brought the combat to a close.

During the 12th, Soult still continued in front of the heights of Barouillet, and preserved throughout the day a threatening attitude. No serious attack, however, was made; some sharp skirmishing occurred between the pickets, and darkness ended these occasional affairs.

The grand object of the French marshal in his sustained attacks upon the allied left, was to force the position and penetrate to St. Jean de Luz. Although so severely handled in his attempts upon the 10th and 11th, the bustle visible along his line, and the activity of the officers of his staff during the morning of the 12th, showed that he still meditated a fresh effort. The imposing appearance of the allied troops on the heights of Barouillet induced him to change his intention; and he made arrangements to throw his whole disposable force suddenly upon the right wing of the British, and attack Sir Rowland Hill with overwhelming numbers;.

This probable attack had been foreseen by Lord Wellington, and, with his accustomed caution, means had been adopted to render it unsuccessful. In the event of assistance being required, the sixth division was placed at Hill's disposal; and early on the morning of the 13th, the third and fourth divisions moved towards the right of the allied lines, and were held in readiness to pass the river should circumstances demand it. As Lord Wellington had anticipated, Soult marched his main body through Bayonne during the night of the 12th, and at daylight, pushing forward thirty thousand men in columns of great strength, attacked furiously the right wing of the allies.

Hill had only fourteen thousand British and Portuguese to repel the French marshal's assault, but the ground he occupied was capable of being vigorously defended. On the right, General Byng's brigade was formed in front of the Vieux Monguerre, occupying a ridge, with the Adour upon the right, and the left flanked by several mill dams. The brigades of Generals Barnes and Ashworth were posted on a range of heights opposite the village of St. Pierre, while two Portuguese brigades were formed in reserve immediately behind Ville Franque. The general form of the line nearly described a crescent, and against its concave side the efforts of the French marshal were principally directed. The position extended from the Adour to the Nive, occupying a space, from right to left, of four miles.

The outposts stationed on the road from Bayonne to St. Jean Pied de Port were driven back by the enemy's *tirailleurs*, followed by the main body of the French, who mounted the sloping ground in front of the British position, and supported by another division, which moved by a hollow way between the left centre and Pringle's brigade, they came forward in massive columns. Sir Rowland Hill, at once perceived that Soult's design was to force his centre, and carry the heights of St. Pierre.

To strengthen that part of the position, the brigade of General Byng was promptly moved to the right of the centre, leaving the third (Buffs) regiment and some light companies at Vieux Monguerre, while a Portuguese brigade was marched from behind Ville Franque to support the left. The sixth division was apprised of the threatened attack, and an *aide-de-camp* was despatched to order its immediate march upon the centre.

The French came on with all the confidence of superior strength, and a full determination to break through the British position, and thus achieve upon the right that object which they had essayed upon the left, and twice in vain. Exposed to a tremendous fire of grape from the British guns, and a withering fusillade from the light infantry, they pressed steadily on, and, by strength of numbers, succeeded in gaining ground in front of the heights. But further they never could attain, as the supporting brigades joined on either flank, and every continued essay to force the centre was repulsed.

A long and bloody combat, when renewed, produced no happier result, for the allies obstinately held their position. The Buffs and light companies, who had been forced by an overwhelming superiority to retire for a time from Vieux Monguerre, re-formed, charged into the village, and won it back at the point of the bayonet, when, after exhausting his whole strength in hopeless efforts to break the British line, Soult abandoned the attack, and reluctantly gave the order to fall back.

Not satisfied with repelling the enemy's attack, Hill in turn became the assailant, and boldly pursued the broken columns as they retired from the front of the position. On a high ground in advance of his entrenched lines, Soult drew up in force, and determined to fall back no further. The hill was instantly assaulted by Byng's brigade, led on by the general in person. Unchecked by a storm of grape and a heavy fire of musketry, the British, reinforced by a Portuguese brigade, carried the height, and the French were beaten from a strong position with a serious loss in men, and the capture of two pieces of cannon.

The third and sixth divisions came up as quickly as distance and difficult roads would permit, but the contest was ended; and Hill, unassisted by any supporting troops, had, with his own corps, achieved a complete and glorious victory.

This glorious battle was fought and won by Sir Rowland Hill with his own corps, alone and unassisted. Lord Wellington could not reach the field till the victory was achieved, and as he rode up to his successful general, he shook him heartily by the hand, with the frank remark, "Hill, the day's your own." He was exceedingly delighted with Sir Rowland's calm and beautiful conduct of this action, and with the intrepid and resolute behaviour of the troops.

Every effort, continued with unabated vigour for five hours, and with decided advantages on his side, had signally failed, and the French commander was forced again to retire within his fortified lines between the Nive and the Adour, while the allies pushed their advanced posts to the verge of the valley immediately in front of St. Pierre.

In these continued actions the loss on both sides was immense. In the casualties of the 9th, 10th, 11th, 12th, and 13th of December, the total, including four generals, amounted to five thousand and sixty-one *hors de combat*.

The French loss was infinitely greater; it is but a moderate estimate to place it at six thousand men. Indeed, no contests, sanguinary as most of them had been during the Peninsular campaigns, were attended with greater loss of life, and those well accustomed to view a battlefield expressed astonishment at the slaughter the limited spaces on which the repeated struggles had occurred exhibited at the close of every succeeding engagement.

Soult, defeated in the presence of thousands of his countrymen, and with every advantage locality could confer, had no apology to offer for the failure of his attacks, and if any additional mortification were necessary, the defection of the regiments of Nassau-Usingen and

Frankfort would have completed it.

A Frankfort officer now made his way to the outposts of our fourth division in the centre of the allies, and announced the intended defection, requiring a general officer's word of honour that they should be well received and sent to Germany. No general being on the spot, Colonel Bradford gave his word; means were immediately taken to apprise the battalions, and they came over in a body, thirteen hundred men, the French not discovering their intention till just when it was too late to frustrate it.

The winter had now set in with severity, and ended all military movements for a season.

Batty says:

> During this period of mutual repose, the French officers and ours soon became intimate; we used to meet at a narrow part of the river, and talk over the campaign. They would never believe, or pretended not to believe, the reverse of Napoleon in Germany; and when we received the news of the Orange Boven affair in Holland, they said that it was impossible to convince them. One of our officers took *The Star* newspaper, rolled a stone up in it, and attempted to throw it across the river; unfortunately, the stone went through it, and it fell into the water; the French officer very quietly said, in tolerably good English, 'Your good news is very soon damped.'
>
> During the campaign we had often experienced the most gentlemanly conduct from the French officers. A day or two before the battle, when we were upon our alarm-post, at break of day, a fine hare was seen playing in a cornfield between the outposts; a brace of greyhounds were very soon unslipped, when, after an exciting course, poor puss was killed within the French lines. The officer to which the dogs belonged, bowing to the French officer, called off the dogs, but the Frenchman politely sent the hare, with a message and his compliments, saying that we required it more than they did.

The roads were impassable from constant rain, and the low grounds heavily flooded. The French took up cantonments on the right bank of the Adour; while the allies occupied the country between the left of that river and the sea. Every means were employed to render the troops comfortable in their winter quarters, and, to guard against surprises, telegraphs were erected in communication with every post, which, by a simple combination of flags, transmitted intelligence along the line of the cantonments, and apprised the detached officers of the earliest movement of the enemy. Abundant supplies, and the advantage of an open communication with Britain, enabled the army to recruit its strength; and, with occasional interruptions of its quiet, the year 1813 passed away, and another, "big with the fate of empires," was ushered in.

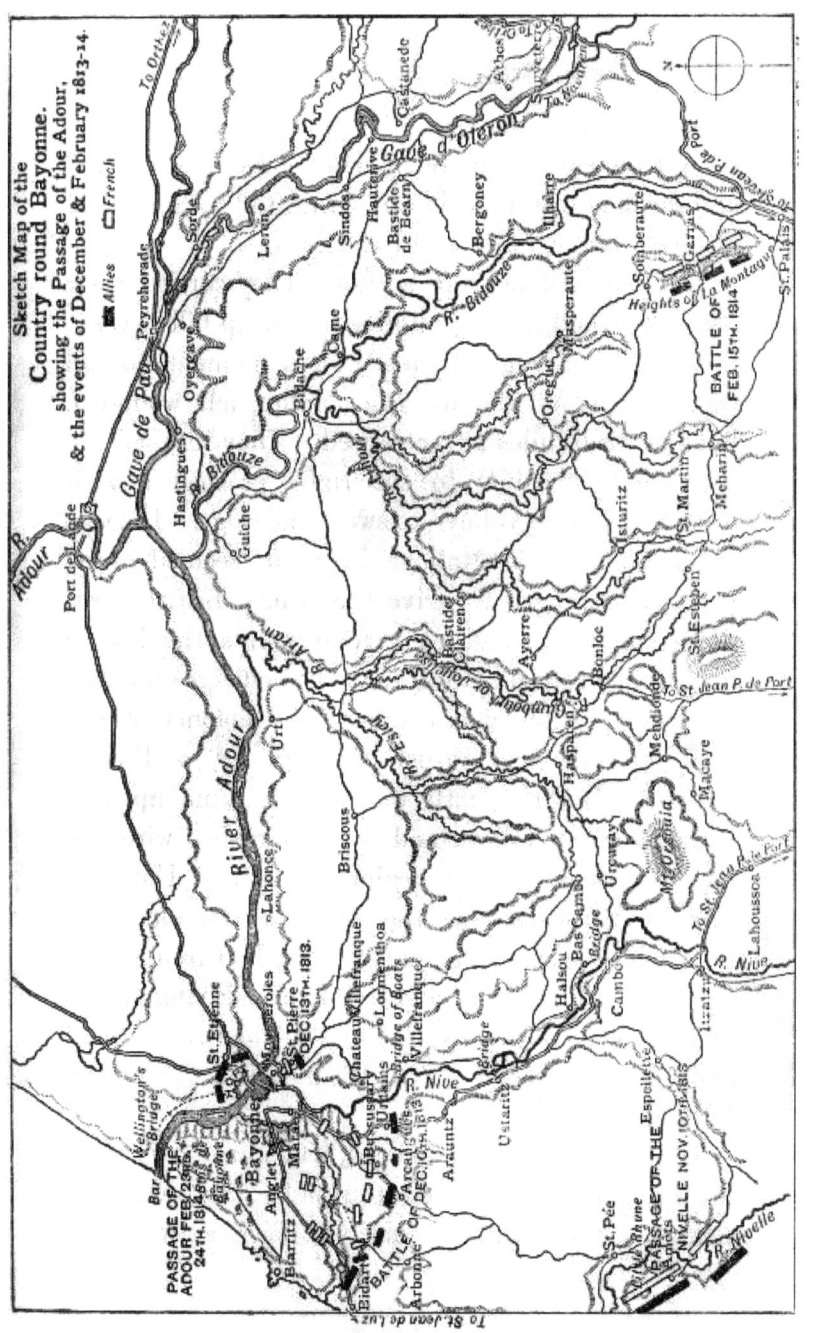

CHAPTER 22

The Battles of the Pyrenees: Part Fourth, 1814

The entrenchments into which Soult, on the failure of his attempts upon the allied positions had withdrawn his troops, covered the approach to Bayonne on the side opposite to Anglet.

Six weeks passed on. The weather was too inclement to allow movements to be made on either side, and the French marshal was occupied in defending his extensive lines, and the allied general in preparing secretly for passing the Adour.

In February the weather changed, the cross roads became practicable, and Lord Wellington with his characteristic promptness, commenced preparatory movements for the execution of his grand conception.

To distract the attention of Soult from the defence of the Adour, Wellington threatened the French left on the Bidouse.

The road, however, communicating with the bridge of St. Palais was uncovered, and though evening had come on, and the second division, with a Spanish corps under Morillo, were alone in hand, Lord Wellington determined to force the position. The Spaniards were desired to march rapidly on St. Palais, while, with Stewart's division, the heights should be carried. The attack was gallantly made, the enemy offered a brave resistance, but the position was stormed in fine style, and held against every effort the French could make for its recovery.

The contest continued until darkness had shrouded distant objects, while the battalions still fought with such furious obstinacy, that volleys were interchanged within pistol range, and the bayonet frequently resorted to. Finding it impossible to force those enduring troops from the ground they seemed determined upon keeping, Harispe, before

Morillo could seize the bridge, succeeded in retiring his beaten corps. Falling back upon the Gave de Mauleon, he destroyed the bridge of Navarette, but the river was forded by the British, Harispe's position forced, and his division driven behind Gave d'Oleron.

Soult instantly destroyed the communications, and rendered the bridges over the Adour impassable. The centre of the allies being now in force on the Bidouse, and concentrating on Sauveterre, the French marshal retired from Bayonne, leaving a powerful garrison behind him for the protection of that important city.

The citadel of Bayonne is a truly formidable work, standing on a commanding hill upon the right bank of the Adour, and greatly elevated above all the other defences of the city, nearly fronting the mouth of the Nive. It is almost a perfect square, with strongly-built *oreillon* bastions at the four angles. A double range of barracks and magazines enclose a quadrangular space in the centre called the *place d'armes*, the sides of which are parallel with the curtains of the citadel. The north-east, north-west, and south-west bastions are surmounted by cavaliers which appear to be well armed with cannon mounted *en barbette*.

All necessary preparations for the passage of the Adour had been completed, and from the co-operation of the British navy much assistance was expected. That hope was fully realised; and the noble exertions of the British sailors on the eastern coast of Spain, at St. Sebastian, and at Passages, were crowned by the intrepidity with which the bar of the Adour was crossed. Undaunted by the failure of the leading vessels, which perished in the surf, with death before their eyes, and their comrades swamping in the waters, on came the succeeding *chasse-marées*.

At last the true channel was discovered. Vessel succeeded vessel, and before night a perfect bridge was established over the Adour, able from its solidity to resist a river current, and protected from any effort of the enemy by a line of booms and spars, which stretched across the river as a security against fire ships, or any other means which the French might employ for its destruction.

Before the flotilla had entered the Adour, or the pontoons had arrived from Bedart, the guards attempted a passage of the river by means of the small boats and a temporary raft formed of a few pontoons, and worked as a flying bridge, by means of a hawser extended from the opposite bank. As the strength of the tide interrupted this precarious mode of passage, when only six companies, with two of the

Battle of Orthez, February 27th, 1814

60th Rifles, and a party of the rocket corps, had crossed, the position of this small body, isolated as it was, and open to the attack of overwhelming numbers, was dangerous in the extreme. Colonel Stopford, however, made the best dispositions in his power for defence, and formed with one flank upon the river, and the other *appuied* upon a morass, while the heavy guns that had been placed in battery on the other shore, swept the ground in front of the position with their fire.

As had been truly apprehended, an attack was made. The French advanced with fifteen hundred men, and the Guards and Rifles received them steadily, the rocket corps, on either flank, opening with this novel and destructive projectile. A few discharges completely arrested the enemy's advance, and they hastily retired from the attack; while at the turning of the tide, reinforcement were ferried over, and the position secured until the following evening, when the whole of the first division, with two guns and a few troops of dragoons, succeeded in effecting a passage.

Bayonne, in the meantime, was closely invested, and the garrison forced back from the villages in front of their lines, by Sir John Hope. Lord Wellington, having secured the attention of Soult by a formidable demonstration on his front, enabled Sir Rowland Hill to pass the Gave d'Oleron unopposed, and thus turn the left flank of the French marshal. Soult instantly retired and took a position behind the Pau, establishing his headquarters at Orthez. Picton, with the third and light divisions, had followed Hill; Clinton, with the sixth, had crossed between Laas and Montford; and Beresford observed the enemy at Peyrehorade closely, and kept them within their entrenchments.

Lord Wellington had decided on an immediate attack. The French were very strongly posted; their left wing, commanded by Clausel, rested on the Gave, and occupied the town of Orthez; the centre, under d'Erlon, was formed on the heights in the rear; while the right wing extended behind St. Boes, and held that village. Harispe's division was placed as a reserve in the rear, and crossed the great roads leading to Bordeaux and Toulouse.

On the 27th February, Wellington commenced his operations. The allied left wing, composed of the fourth and seventh divisions and Vivian's brigade, under Marshal Beresford, attacked the enemy's right at St. Boes; while the third and sixth divisions, under Sir Rowland Hill, with Lord Edward Somerset's light cavalry, were directed against Soult's left and centre. The British movements were ably executed.

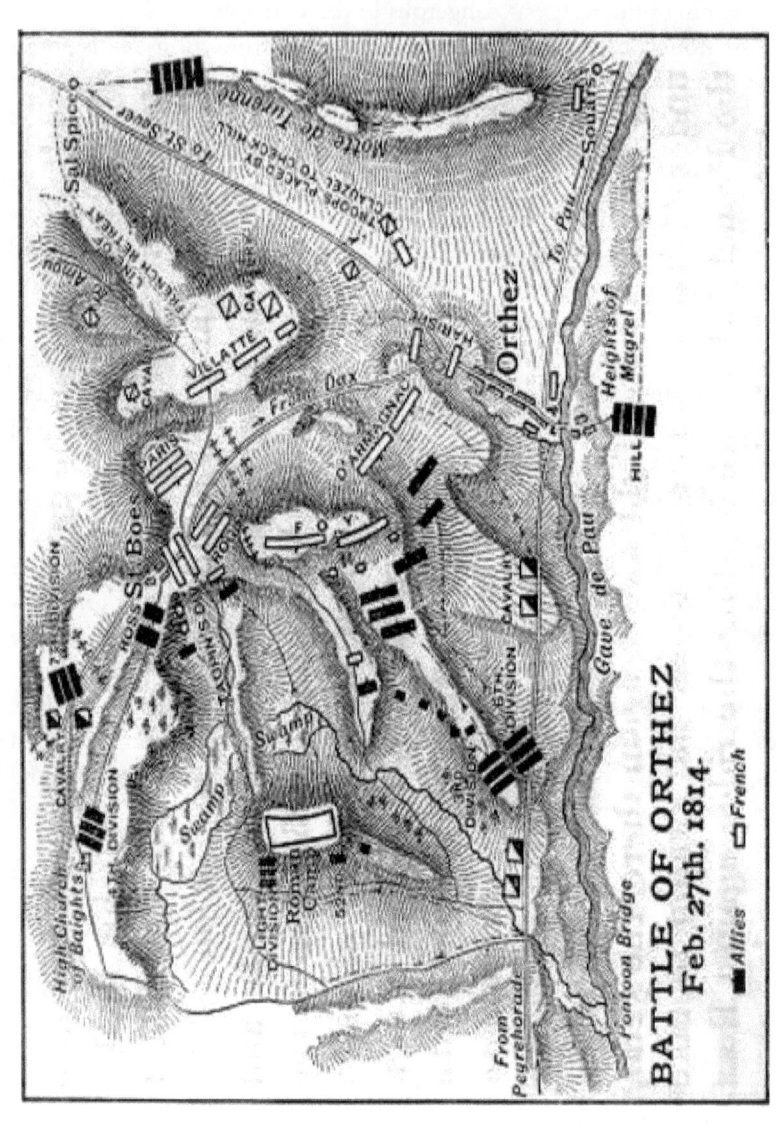
BATTLE OF ORTHEZ
Feb. 27th, 1814.

Hill crossed the river in front of the French left, and turned their flank—the enemy holding their ground with great obstinacy, while the allied attack was as remarkable for its impetuosity.

A final and protracted struggle ensued, but the French unable to sustain the combined assault of the allies, commenced retreating by divisions, and contesting every inch of ground as they abandoned it. Hill's parallel march was speedily discovered, and as that movement threatened their rear, the order of the retreat was accelerated, and gradually assumed the character of a flight. The British pressed rapidly forward, the French as quickly fell back; both strove to gain Sault de Navailles, and though charged by the British cavalry, the enemy crossed the Luy de Bearne before Hill could succeed in coming up.

The defeat of the 27th was decisive. The French loss in killed and wounded was immense. Six guns and a number of prisoners were taken; the troops threw away their arms, many deserted altogether, and few defeats were marked by more injurious results to the vanquished, than those attendant upon that of Orthez.

The allied loss amounted to two hundred and seventy-seven killed, one thousand nine hundred and twenty-three wounded, and seventy missing.

One circumstance occurred during this obstinate contest that displayed the readiness of Lord Wellington's decisions, and the rapidity with which he adopted measures to meet any incidental exigency.

A Portuguese battalion in advancing had been so roughly received that it broke and fell back upon a brigade of the light division, who succeeded in covering its retreat. The nature of the ground on which the right of the enemy was posted, from its narrow front, confining the attack to a line of but two battalions; while a heavy battery of guns and a converging fire of musketry swept its approach, and rendered the boldest efforts of the assailants unavailing in carrying the height.

Wellington perceived the difficulty, and in a moment changed his method of attack. Walker, with the seventh division, and Barnard, with a light brigade, were pushed up the left of the height to attack the right of the French at its point of junction with the centre; and Picton and Clinton were directed to advance at once, and not us they had been originally ordered, await the result of Beresford's attempt upon the hill. The whole face of the battle was thus suddenly changed, the heights were speedily won, and the enemy, after a fierce resistance, driven fairly from their ground, and forced from a most formidable position.

Battle of Orthez, February 27th, 1814

That night the French retired to Hagetman, and, joined by the garrison of Dax, fell back on St. Sever, and afterwards on Agen—Beresford advancing by Mont de Marsan, and Hill in the direction of Aire. Heavy rains favoured the French retreat, by impeding the advance of the allies, and it was the 2nd of March before Hill overtook them in front of Aire.

Although posted on formidable ground, Sir Rowland instantly and successfully brought them to action. The second division, with De Costa's Portuguese, advanced to the attack; the former by the road to Aire, and the latter by the heights upon the left of the enemy. The movement of Stewart's division was most brilliant; and though the Portuguese behaved gallantly and won the ridge, they were attacked furiously, and unable to hold the ground, deforced, and driven in great confusion from the height.

The French followed with a strong column, and the consequences threatened to be disastrous, but the success of the second division permitted Sir Rowland to detach Byng's brigade to the assistance of De Costa; and in place of assailing a broken corps, the enemy's columns were confronted by one in equal order, and already buoyant with success. The result was what might have been expected; the French were charged and beaten from the field, the town and the position abandoned, the Adour hastily crossed, a number of prisoners made, and a regiment cut off and obliged to retire to Pau.

Soult pursued the line of the right bank of the Adour, and concentrated at Plaisance and Maubourget, to await Lord Wellington's attack; but finding the road to Bordeaux uncovered, the allied general marched his left wing directly on that city. On Beresford's approach, the garrison evacuated the place, crossing over to the right bank of the Garonne; and the authorities and inhabitants generally assumed the white cockade, and declared themselves in favour of the Bourbons.

CHAPTER 23

The Battle of Toulouse, 1814

The celebrated conference at Chatillon terminated on the 19th of March, and the allied Sovereigns determined to march direct upon the capital, of which they obtained possession on the 31st. The intelligence of this momentous event had not reached the south of France, and Lord Wellington was busy making immense preparations to enable him to invest and reduce Bayonne. Fascines and gabions were obtained in abundance; a large supply of siege artillery, with shot and shells, was landed at Passages from the home country; scaling-ladders were constructed in the woods, the site of the batteries marked out, and all was ready for an investment.

Meanwhile, to guard against a menaced attack on his rear, the French marshal retired under cover of night, and fell back upon Toulouse, destroying the bridges as he passed them, where the British followed him.

The unavoidable difficulty in crossing flooded rivers, and moving pontoons over roads nearly impassable from heavy rains, however greatly delayed the allied march. Soult reached Toulouse in four days, while Wellington, by great exertion, was only enabled to arrive before it in seven.

Toulouse stands on the right bank of the Garonne, which separates it from a large suburb called Saint Cyprien. The eastern and northern sides of the city are enclosed by the canal of Languedoc, which joins the Garonne a mile below the town. On the east of the city is the suburb of Saint Etienne; on the south that of Saint Michael, and on that side the great road from Carcassone and Montpellier enters the town. The population was estimated at fifty thousand souls, and it was generally understood that the inhabitants of Toulouse were secretly attached to the Bourbons.

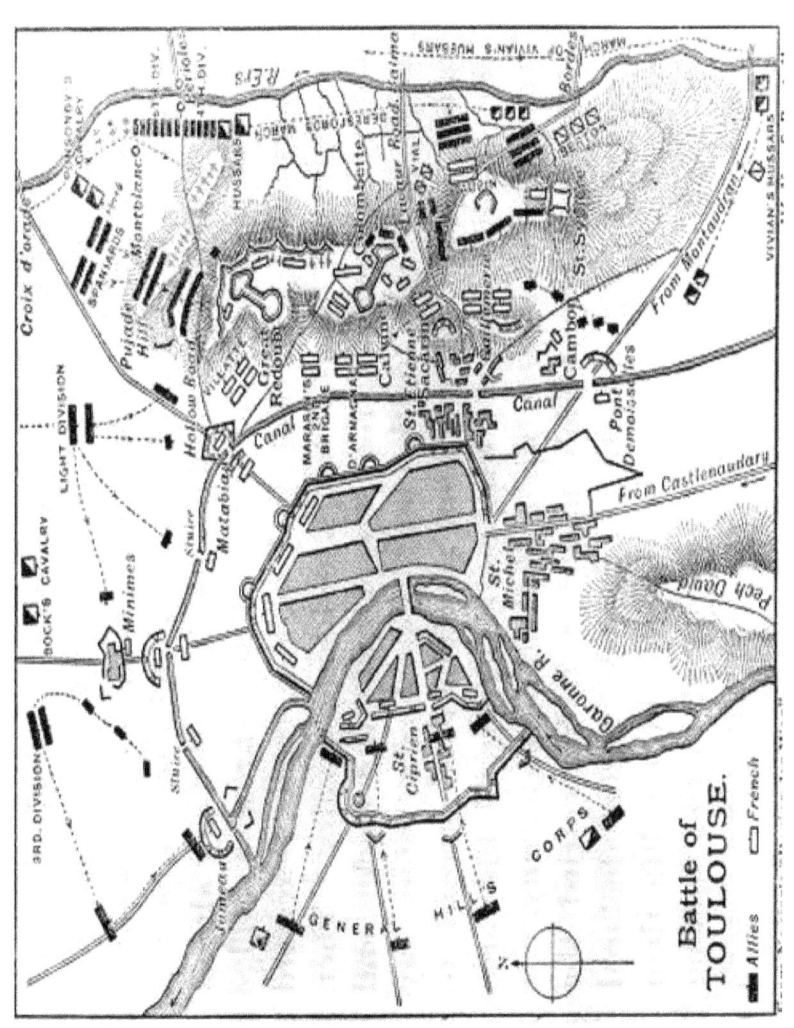

The city is walled and connected by ancient towers—but these antiquated defences would avail little against the means employed in modern warfare. Soult, therefore, entrenched the faubourg of Saint Cyprien, constructed *têtes du pont* at all the bridges of the canal, threw up redoubts and breastworks, and destroyed the bridges across the Ers. The southern side he considered so secure as to require no additional defences, trusting for its protection to the width and rapidity of the Garonne.

The first attempt of the allied leader to throw a pontoon bridge across the river, was rendered impracticable by the sudden rising of its waters. Higher up, however, the passage was effected, but the roads were quite impassable, and Lord Wellington determined to lay the pontoons below the city, which was accordingly done, and Beresford with the fourth and sixth divisions, was safely placed upon the right bank.

This temporary success might have been followed by disastrous consequences. The Garonne suddenly increased; a flood came pouring down; the swollen river momentarily rose higher, and to save the pontoons from being swept away, the bridge was removed, and the divisions left unsupported, with an overpowering force in front, and an angry river in their rear. Soult neglected this admirable opportunity of attacking them; and on the second day the flood had sufficiently abated to allow the pontoons to be laid down again, when Frere's Spanish corps passed over, and reinforced the isolated divisions. The bridge was now removed above the city, to facilitate Hill's communications, who, with the second division, was posted in front of the faubourg of Saint Cyprien. The passage of the third and light divisions was effected safely, and Picton and Baron Alten took up ground with their respective corps in front of the canal, and invested the northern face of Toulouse.

Early on the morning of the 10th March, the fortified heights on the eastern front of the city were attacked. Soult had placed all his disposable troops in this position, and thus defended, nothing but determined gallantry on the part of the assailants could expect success.

The bridge of Croix d'Orade, previously secured by a bold attack of the 18th Hussars, enabled Beresford and Frere to move up the left bank of the Garonne, and occupy ground in front of the heights preparatory to the grand attack. The sixth division was in the centre, with the Spaniards on the right, and the fourth British on the left. The cavalry of Sir Stapleton Cotton and Lord Edward Somerset were formed

Fighting in the suburbs

in support of the left and centre; and Arentchild, now in command of Vivian's brigade, was attached to the left flank, while Ponsonby protected the right.

The light division occupied the vacant ground between the River Garonne and the road to Croix d'Orade; its left abutting on the division under Frere; and the third, its right resting on the river, communicated with Hill's corps upon the left by means of the pontoon bridge. These divisions—those of Hill, Picton, and Alten—were ordered to attack the enemy's entrenchments in front of their respective corps, simultaneously with the grand assault upon the heights.

The fourth and sixth divisions moved obliquely against the enemy's right, carried the heights, and seized a redoubt on the flank of the position; while the fourth Spanish corps, directed against the ridge above the road to Croix d'Orade, advanced with confidence, and succeeded in mounting the brow of the hill. But the heavy fire of the French batteries arrested their onward movement. They recoiled, became confused, and sought shelter from the fury of the cannonade in a hollow way in front of the enemy's position. The French, perceiving their disorder, advanced and vigorously charged. Frere vainly endeavoured to rally his broken troops and lead them on again; they were driven back confusedly on the Ers, and their *déroute* appeared inevitable.

Lord Wellington saw and remedied this reverse. Personally, he rallied a Spanish regiment, and bringing up a part of the light division, arrested the French pursuit, and allowed the broken regiments time to be re-organised. The bridge across the Ers was saved; Frere reformed his battalions, and the fugitives rejoined their colours.

Beresford immediately resumed the attack, two redoubts were carried, and the sixth division dislodged the enemy, and occupied the centre of their position. The contest here was exceedingly severe; Pack, in leading the attack, was wounded, and in an attempt to recover the heights by the French, Taupin, who commanded the division, was killed. Every succeeding effort failed, and the British held the ground their gallantry had won.

Picton had most imprudently changed a false into a real attack upon the bridge over the canal of Languedoc nearest its entrance into the Garonne, but the *tête du pont* was too strong to be forced, and he fell back with considerable loss. On the left, Sir Rowland Hill menaced the faubourg of Saint Cyprien, and succeeded in fully occupying the attention of its garrison, thus preventing them from rendering any assistance when Soult was most severely pressed.

In the meantime, Beresford, having obtained his artillery, resumed offensive movements, and advanced along the ridge with the divisions of Cole and Clinton. Soult anticipated the attack, and threw himself in front and flank in great force upon the sixth division; but the effort failed. The French marshal was driven from the hill, the redoubts abandoned, the canal passed, and, beaten on every point, he sought refuge within the walls of Toulouse.

Few victories cost more blood than this long and hard-contested battle. The allied casualties, including two thousand Spaniards, nearly extended to seven thousand men. Several regiments lost half their number, and two, the 45th and 61st, their colonels. It was impossible to ascertain the extent to which the French suffered. Their loss was no doubt commensurate with that of the victors. Of their superior officers alone, two generals were killed, and three wounded and made prisoners.

On the night of the succeeding day, Soult, alarmed by Wellington's movements on the road to Carcassone, retired from the city, which next morning was taken possession of by the allies, although the French unblushingly assert that they gained a victory.

There was seldom a bloodier, and never a more useless, battle fought than that of the 10th of March, for on the evening of the 12th a British and French field officer, Colonels Cooke and St. Simon, arrived at the allied headquarters, with intelligence that, on the 3rd, hostilities had ceased, and the war was virtually terminated. A courier, despatched from the capital with this important communication, had been unfortunately interrupted in his journey; and in ignorance of passing events, the contending armies wasted their best energies, and lost many of their bravest on both sides, in a bootless and unnecessary encounter.

Soult, on having the abdication of Napoleon formally notified to him on the night of the 13th, refused to send in his adherence to the Bourbons, merely offering a suspension of hostilities, to which Lord Wellington most properly objecting, instantly recommenced his pursuit of the French marshal's beaten divisions.

The bold and decisive measures of the allied leader doubtless hastened the Duke of Dalmatia in making his decision, and, on the arrival of a second official communication, Soult notified his adherence, and hostilities ceased. Suchet had already shewn him the example, and Toulouse displayed the white flag. A line of demarcation was made by commissioners between the rival armies, and a regular convention signed by the respective commanders.

On the 27th, Thouvenot was instructed by Soult to surcease hostilities, and acknowledged the Bourbons—the lilies floated over the citadel—and saluted by three hundred rounds of artillery, Napoleon's abdication, and the restoration of the Bourbons, were formally announced.

With political events we have no business, and it is sufficient to cursorily observe, that arrangements were effected for Napoleon's retirement from public life to the "lonely isle," where he might still, in fancy, "call himself a king." To this secluded spot, many of his old and devoted followers accompanied him. Peace was generally proclaimed over Europe; tranquillity restored in France; the "Grand Nation," to all appearance, contented itself with the change of government; the allied sovereigns retired with their respective corps, each to his own dominions; and the victorious army of Wellington quitted the French soil, on which it had consummated its glory; and received, on landing on the shores of Britain, that enthusiastic welcome which its "high deeds" and boundless gallantry deserved from a grateful country.

CHAPTER 24

The Battle of Quatre Bras, 1815

A few months passed away; Europe was apparently at rest; its military attitude was gradually softening down, and all the belligerent Powers, weary of a state of warfare that, with slight intermission, had lasted for a quarter of a century, enjoyed the repose which the overthrow of Napoleon's power had produced. But this state of quietude was delusory; it was the treacherous calm that precedes a tempest. Untamed by adversity, that ambitious spirit was gathering strength for another effort; France was ready to receive him; past victories would thus be rendered useless, Europe convulsed again, and none could foresee what strange events the descent of Napoleon might produce.

No recorded career parallels that of Napoleon Buonaparte; and in the history of kings and conquerors, the strangest story was his own. He seemed the shuttlecock of Fortune—and she placed him "on a pinnacle of pride merely to mark her own mutability." Hurled from the sovereignty of half the world, his star had lost its ascendancy, apparently to rise no more, when, by the happiest accident, his voyage from Elba was uninterrupted, his landing unopposed, an enthusiastic welcome everywhere was given to the intruder, legions congregated at his bidding, the empire was offered and accepted, and the first intelligence of his descent was closely followed by a formal acknowledgment of his restoration to the sovereignty of France.

Napoleon landed in the Var on the 1st of March, and on the 19th he slept in the palace of Fontainbleau. Louis had abandoned the capital, and in a few hours the dynasty of the Bourbons seemed forgotten. None opposed the return of the exile; his decrees were absolute; his wishes were anticipated. The splendour of military parade delighted the soldiery, while the theatric glitter of a *champ de Mai* was admirably adapted to catch the fancies, and win the momentary attachment of a gay and thoughtless people. The whole pageant, in scenic effect, was suited for those whom it was designed to lure, and on the 17th of April, Napoleon was formally restored to that empire, from which the same "sweet voices" had, but a few months before, so formally deposed him.

Parisian adulation, and the military devotion he received from the moment his foot touched the shore at Cannes, did not blind him to "coming events." A vain effort to make terms with the allied Powers was scornfully rejected. At Vienna, his overtures were treated with disdain, and his letter to the British regent was returned with the seal unbroken. He saw from all these premonitory occurrences, that a storm was about to burst, and lost no time in preparing for a determined resistance. A powerful army alone could avert the danger; and, with his customary tact, Napoleon made prodigious efforts to restore the military strength of the empire, which the Russian, German, and Peninsular campaigns had during the last years so miserably weakened.

French vanity was successfully appealed to, the memory of past victories recalled, and martial glory, that powerful touchstone of national feeling, successfully employed to win the people to his standard. The younger of the male population were called out by *ordonnances*, and the retired veterans collected once more around those eagles, which, in prouder days, had entered half the European capitals in triumph.

The military power of France was organised anew. Commissioners, specially employed, enforced the operations of Napoleon's decrees in every department of the kingdom. The Imperial Guard was re-established, the cavalry increased and remounted, that powerful arm, the artillery, by which half the victories of the French Army had been achieved, was enlarged and improved, and, in a time inconceivably short, a most splendid *corps d'armée* perfect in every department, was ready for the field.

While Napoleon was thus engaged, Wellington arrived at Brussels on the 5th of April, to take command of the British Army. There, the troops of the Prince of the Netherlands, with those of Nassau and Brunswick, were placed under his orders, the whole forming the Anglo-Belgic army.

The Prussian *corps d'armée* were cantoned in and about Namur and Charleroi—while Ostend, Antwerp, Tournay, Ypres, Mons, and Ghent, were occupied by the allies. The position of the Anglo-Belgic Army was extended and detached, for the preceding harvest in the Low Countries had been unusually deficient, and, of course, the British

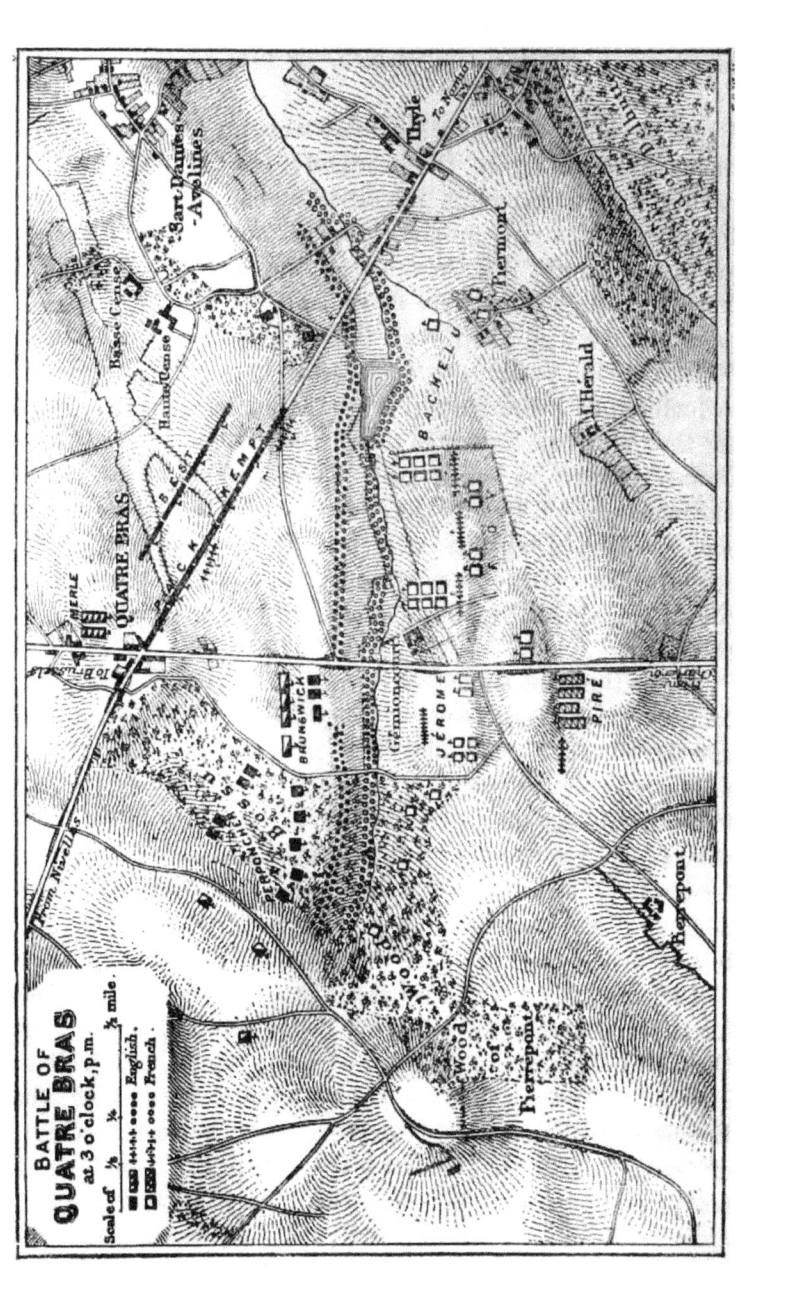

and Belgic cantonments covered an additional surface to obtain the requisite supplies.

The allied corps in June were thus disposed. Lord Hill, with the right wing, occupied Ath. The left, under the Prince of Orange, was posted at Braine-le-Comte and Nivelles. The cavalry under the Marquis of Anglesea, were established round Grammont; and the reserve and headquarters, under the duke, were quartered in Brussels.

Belgium, for centuries, had been the seat of war, and every plain, every fortress, had its tale of martial achievement to narrate. Within its iron frontier there were few places which had not witnessed some affair of arms; the whole country was rife with military reminiscences, and it was destined to prove the scene where the greatest event in modern warfare should be transacted.

As a country, Belgium was admirably adapted for martial operations—the plains, in many places extensive, terminated in undulated ridges or bolder heights; while the surface generally admitted the movements of masses of infantry. Canals, rivers, morasses, and villages, presented favourable positions to abide a battle, and difficult ones for an advancing army to force, while the fortresses everywhere afforded facilities for retiring upon, and presented serious obstacles to those who must mask or carry them when advancing.

To a commander circumstanced like Wellington, great perplexity as to the distribution of his army must arise, for the mode and point of Napoleon's attack were alike involved in mystery. He might decide on adopting a defensive war, and permit the allies to become the assailants. This course, however, was not a probable one; but where he would precipitate himself was the difficulty.

The dangerous proximity of Brussels to the point where Napoleon's *corps d'armée* were concentrating, naturally produced an anxious inquietude among the inhabitants and visitors. The city was filled every hour with idle rumours, but time alone could develope Napoleon's plans.

The first intelligence of a threatening movement on the part of the French emperor was forwarded to the Duke of Wellington, when Blucher learned that Zeithen's corps was attacked. The despatch reached Brussels at half-past four, but, as it merely intimated that the Prussian outposts had been driven back, the information was not of sufficient) importance to induce the British commander to make any change in the cantonments of the allied army.

A second despatch reached the duke at midnight, and its intelligence was more decisive than the former. Napoleon was across the Sambro, and in full march on Charleroi and Fleurus. Orders were instantly issued for the more detached corps to break up from their cantonments and advance upon Nivelles, while the troops in Brussels should march direct by the forest of Soignies, on Charleroi. Thus there would be a simultaneous reunion of the brigades as they approached the scene of action, while their communication with the Prussian right should be carefully secured.

Blucher's second despatch was delivered to the British general in the ballroom of the Duchess of Richmond. That circumstance most probably gave rise to the groundless report that Wellington and the Prussian marshal were surprised; but nothing could be more absurd than this supposition. Both commanders were in close and constant communication, and their plans for mutual co-operation were amply matured.

Where the intended attack—if Napoleon would indeed venture to become aggressor—should be made, was an uncertainty, and it had been arranged that if Blucher were assailed, Wellington should move to his assistance, or, in the event of the British being the first object with Napoleon, then the Prussian marshal should sustain the duke with a corps, or with his whole army, were that found necessary. Nothing could be more perfect than the cordial understanding between the allied commanders, and the result proved how faithfully these mutual promises of support were realised.

Two hours after midnight the gaiety of "fair Brussels" closed, the drums beat to arms, and all was hurry and preparation, Momentarily the din increased, "and louder yet the clamour grew" as the Highland pibroch answered the bugle-call of the light infantry. The soldiery, startled from their sleep, poured out from the now deserted dwellings; and the once peaceful city exhibited a general alarm.

The sun rose on a scene of confusion and excitement. The military assembled in the Place Royale; and the difference of individual character might be traced in the respective bearings of the various soldiery. Some were taking a tender, many a last, leave of wives and children; others, stretched upon the pavement, were listlessly waiting for their comrades to come up, while not a few strove to snatch a few moments of repose, and appeared half insensible to the din of war around them. Waggons were loading and artillery harnessing; orderlies and *aides-de-camp* rode rapidly through the streets; and in the gloom of early morning the pavement sparkled beneath the iron feet of the cavalry, as they hurried along the causeway to join their respective squadrons, which were now collecting in the Park.

The appearance of the British brigades as they filed from the Park and took the road to Soignies, was most imposing. The martial air of the Highland regiments, the bagpipes playing at their head, their tartans fluttering in the breeze, and the early sunbeams flashing from their glittering arms, excited the admiration of the *burghers* who had assembled to see them march. During the winter and spring, while they had garrisoned Brussels, their excellent conduct and gentle demeanour had endeared them to the inhabitants; and:

"They were so domesticated in the houses where they were quartered, that it was no uncommon thing to see the Highland soldier taking care of the children, or keeping the shop of his host."

Regiment after regiment marched—the organisation of all most perfect; the Rifles, Royals, 28th, each exhibiting some martial peculiarity, on which the eye of Picton appeared to dwell with pride and pleasure as they filed off before him. To an intelligent spectator a national distinction was clearly marked. The bearing of the Scotch bespoke a grave and firm determination, while the light step and merry glance of the Irish militiaman told that war was the game he loved, and a first field had no terrors for him.

Eight o'clock pealed from the steeple clocks; all was quiet—the brigades, with their artillery and equipages, were gone—the crash of music was heard no longer—the bustle of preparation had ceased—and an ominous and heart-sinking silence succeeded the noise and hurry that ever attends a departure for the field of battle.

Napoleon's plan of penetrating into Belgium was now so clearly ascertained, that Wellington determined to concentrate on the extreme point of his line of occupation. His march was accordingly directed on Quatre Bras, a small hamlet situated at the intersection of the road to Charleroi, by that leading from Namur to Nivelles.

This village, which was fated to obtain a glorious but sanguinary celebrity, consists of a few mean houses, having a thick and extensive wood immediately on the right called Le Bois de Bossu. All around the wood and hamlet, rye-fields of enormous growth, and quite ready for the sickle, were extended.

After a distressing march of twenty miles in sultry weather, and over a country destitute of water, the British brigades reached the scene of action at two o'clock. They found the Prince of Orange with a division of his army endeavouring to hold the French in check, and maintain a position of whose great importance he was so well aware. The prince, unable to withstand the physical superiority of Ney's corps, had gradually lost ground, the Hanoverians had been driven back, and the Bois de Bossu was won and occupied by the enemy.

To recover this most important wood, from which the French could debouche upon the road to Brussels, was the duke's first object. The 95th were ordered to attack the tirailleurs who held it; the order was gallantly executed, and after a bloody and sustained resistance, the French were forced to retire.

On the left, the Royals and 28th were hotly engaged, and on the right the 44th and Highland regiments were simultaneously assailed. The battle now became general. Before the British could deploy, the French cavalry charged furiously, the tall rye masking their advance and favouring the attack. Generally these charges were unsuccessful, and the perfect discipline and steady courage of the British enabled them to repel the enemy. Lancers and *cuirassiers* were driven back with desperate slaughter—while whole squadrons, shattered in their retreat, and leaving the ground covered with, their dead and dying, proved with what fatal precision the British squares sustained their fusillade.

The efforts of the French to break the squares, however, were fierce and frequent. Their batteries poured upon these unflinching soldiers a storm of grape, and when an opening was made by the cannon, the lancers were ready to rush upon the devoted infantry. But nothing could daunt the lion-hearted British—nothing could shake their steadiness. The dead were coolly removed, and the living occupied their places. Though numbers fell, and the square momentarily diminished, it still presented a serried line of glittering bayonets, through which lancer and *cuirassier* endeavoured to penetrate, but in vain.

One regiment, after sustaining a furious cannonade, was suddenly, and on three different sides, assailed by cavalry. Two faces of the square were charged by the lancers, while the *cuirassiers* galloped down upon another. It was a trying moment. There was a death-like silence; and one voice alone, clear and calm, was heard. It was their colonel's, who called upon them to be "Steady!"

On came the enemy; the earth shook beneath the horsemen's feet, while on every side of the devoted band, the corn bending beneath the rush of cavalry disclosed their numerous assailants. The lance blades nearly met the bayonets of the kneeling front rank, the *cuirassiers* were within a few paces, yet not a trigger was drawn. But, when the word "Fire!" thundered from the colonel's lips, each side poured out its deadly volley, and in a moment the leading files of the French lay before the square, as if hurled by a thunderbolt to the earth. The assailants, broken and dispersed, galloped off for shelter to the tall rye, while a constant stream of musketry from the British square, carried death into their retreating squadrons.

But, unhappily, these furious and continued charges were not always inefficient. On the right, and in the act of forming square, the 42nd were attacked by the lancers. The sudden rush, and the difficulty of forming in corn reaching to the shoulder, gave a temporary success to the assailants. Two companies, excluded from the square, were ridden over and cut down. The colonel was killed, half the regiment disabled, but the remainder formed and repulsed the charge, while those detached in the *mêlée* fought back to back with desperate coolness, until the withering fusillade of their companions dispersed the cavalry, and enabled them to rejoin their ranks.

The remaining regiments of the Highland brigade were hotly pressed by the enemy; they had not a moment's respite; for no sooner were the lancers and *cuirassiers* driven back, than the French batteries opened with a torrent of grape upon the harassed squares, which threatened to overwhelm them. Numbers of officers and men were already stretched upon the field, while the French, reinforced by fresh columns, redoubled their exertions, while the brave and devoted handful of British troops seemed destined to cover with their bodies that ground their gallantry scorned to surrender. Wellington, as he witnessed the slaughter of his best troops, is said to have been deeply affected; and repeated references to his watch, showed how anxiously he waited for reinforcements.

The Bois de Bossu had continued to be the scene of a severe and fluctuating combat. The 95th had driven the French out, but under a heavy cannonade, and supported by a cavalry movement, the rifles were overpowered by numbers and forced to retire, fighting inch by inch, and contesting every tree. Ney established himself at last within the wood, and ordered up a considerable addition to the light troops, who had already occupied this important point of the position.

The contest was at its height. The incessant assaults of the enemy were wasting the British regiments, but, with the exception of the Bois de Bossu, not an inch of ground was lost The men were falling in hundreds, death was busy everywhere, but not a cheek blanched, and not a foot receded! The courage of these undaunted soldiers needed no incitement, but, on the contrary, the efforts of their officers were

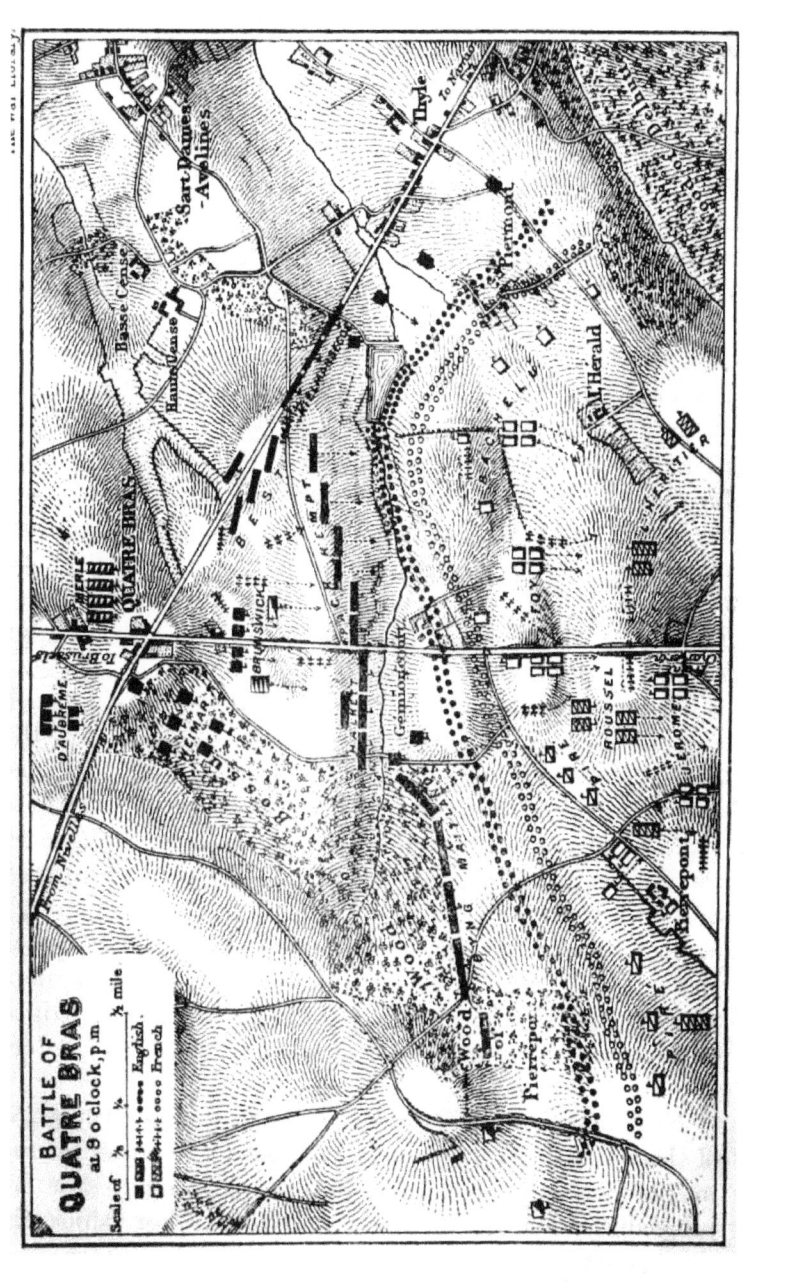

constantly required to restrain the burning ardour that would, if unrepressed, have led to ruinous result. Maddened to see their ranks thinned by renewed assaults which they were merely suffered to repel, they panted for the hour of action. The hot blood of Erin was boiling for revenge, and even the cool endurance of the Scotch began to yield, and a murmur was sometimes heard of, "Why are we not led forward?"

And yet, though forward movements were denied them, the assailants paid dearly for this waste of British blood. For a long hour the 92nd had been exposed to a destructive fire from the French artillery that occasioned a fearful loss. A regiment of Brunswick cavalry had attempted to repel a charge of *cuirassiers*, and repulsed with loss, were driven back upon the Highlanders in great disorder. The hussars galloped down a road on which part of the regiment was obliqued—the remainder lining the ditch in front.

The rear of the Brunswickers intermingled with the headmost of the French horsemen, and for a while the 92nd could not relieve them with their musketry. At last the pursuers and pursued rode rapidly past the right flank of the Highlanders, and permitted them to deliver their volley. The word "Fire!" was scarcely given, when the close and converged discharge of both wings fell with terrible effect upon the advanced squadron. The *cuirassiers* were literally cut down by that withering discharge, and the road choked up with men and horses rolling in dying agony, while the shattered remnant of what but a few moments before had been a splendid regiment, retreated in desperate confusion to avoid a repetition of that murderous fusillade.

At this period of the battle, the guards, after a march of seven-and-twenty miles, arrived from Enghein, from whence they had moved at three in the morning. Exhausted by heat and fatigue, they halted at Nivelles, lighted fires, and prepared to cook their dinners. But the increasing roar of cannon announced that the duke was seriously engaged, and a staff officer brought orders to hurry on. The bivouac was instantly broken up, the kettles packed, the rations abandoned, and the wearied troops cheerfully resumed their march.

The path to the field of battle could not be mistaken; the roar of cannon was succeeded by the roll of musketry, which at every step became more clearly audible; fund waggons, heaped with wounded British and Brunswickers interspersed, told that the work of death was going on.

The Guards, indeed, came up at a fortunate crisis. The Bois de

Bossu was won, and the *tirailleurs* of the enemy, debouching from its cover, were about to deploy upon the roads that it commanded, and would thus intercept the duke's communication with the Prussians. The fifth division, sadly reduced, could hardly hold their ground, any offensive movement was impracticable, and the French *tirailleurs* were actually issuing from the wood, but on perceiving the advancing columns, they halted.

The first brigade of Guards, having loaded and fixed bayonets, were ordered to advance, and, wearied as they were with a fifteen hours' march, they cheered, and pushed forward. In vain the thick trees impeded them, and although every bush and coppice was held and disputed by the enemy, the *tirailleurs* were driven in on every side. Taking advantage of a rivulet which crossed the wood, the enemy attempted to form and arrest the progress of the Guards, That stand was momentary; they were forced from their position, and the wood once more was carried by the British.

Their success was, however, limited to its occupation; the broken ground and close timber prevented the battalion from forming; and when it emerged, and of course in considerable disorder, from its cover, the masses of cavalry drawn up in the open ground charged and forced it back. At last, after many daring attempts to debouch and form, the first brigade fell back upon the third battalion, which, by flanking the wood, had been enabled to form square, and repulse the cavalry, and there the brigade halted. Evening was now closing in, the attacks of the enemy became fewer and feebler, a brigade of heavy cavalry with horse artillery came up, and, worn out by the sanguinary struggle of six long hours, the assailants ceased their attack, and the fifth and third divisions took a position for the night upon the ground their unbounded heroism had held through this long and bloody day.

Thus terminated the fight of Quatre Bras, and a more glorious victory was never won by British bravery. Night closed the battle, and when the limited number of the allied troops actually engaged is considered, this sanguinary conflict will stand almost without a parallel.

At the opening of the action at half-past two, the duke's force could not have exceeded sixteen thousand, his whole army consisting of some Brunswick hussars, supported by a few Belgian and Hanoverian guns, and the great distance of their cantonments from the field of battle prevented the British cavalry and horse artillery arriving until late in the evening. Vivian's brigade (1st Hanoverian, and 10th and 18th hussars) came up at seven o'clock, but the rest only reached Qua-

tre Bras at the close of the action, having made a forced march from behind the Dender, over bad roads for more than forty miles. Ney, by his own account, commenced the battle with the second corps and Excelman's cavalry, the former numbering thirty thousand strong in artillery, and its cavalry, that of the second corps included, amounting to three thousand six hundred.

The French marshal complains that the first corps, originally assigned to him, and which he had left at Frasnes in reserve, had been withdrawn by Napoleon without any intimation, and never employed during the entire day, and thus, as Ney writes to Fouche:

> Twenty-five or thirty thousand men were, I may say, paralysed, and idly paraded during the battle, from the right to the left, and the left to the right, without firing a shot.

All this admitted, surely his means were amply sufficient to have warranted a certain victory. In numbers his cavalry were infinitely superior, his artillery was equally powerful, while in those important arms, Wellington was miserably weak, and all he had to oppose to his stronger antagonist were the splendid discipline and indomitable courage of British infantry.

The loss sustained by the British and their allies in this glorious and hard-contested battle amounted to three thousand seven hundred and fifty, *hors de combat*. Of course, the British suffered most severely, having three hundred and twenty men killed, and two thousand one hundred and fifty-five wounded. The Duke of Brunswick fell in the act of rallying his troops, and an, immense number of British officers were found among the slain and wounded.

During an advanced movement, the 92nd, while repulsing an attack of both cavalry and infantry, met a French column, retreating to the wood, which halted and turned its fire on the Highlanders, already assailed by a superior force. Notwithstanding, the regiment bravely held its ground until relieved by a regiment of the Guards, when it retired to its original position. In this brief and sanguinary conflict, its loss amounted to twenty-eight officers, and nearly three hundred men.

The casualties, when compared with the number of the combatants, will appear enormous. Most of the battalions lost their commanding officers, and the rapid succession of subordinate officers on whom the command devolved, told how fast the work of death went on. Trifling wounds were disregarded, and men severely hurt refused to retire to the rear, or rejoined their colours after a temporary dressing. Picton's was a remarkable instance of this disregard of suffering; he was severely wounded at Quatre Bras, and the fact was only ascertained after his glorious fall at Waterloo.

The French loss, according to their own returns, was "very considerable, amounting to four thousand two hundred killed or wounded"; and Ney in his report says:

> I was obliged to renounce my hopes of victory; and in spite of all my efforts, in spite of the intrepidity and devotion of my troops, my utmost efforts could only maintain me in my position till the close of the day.

Ney fell back upon the road to Frasnes. The moon rose angrily, still a few cannon-shot were heard after the day had departed; but gradually they ceased. The fires were lighted, and such miserable provisions as could be procured were furnished to the harassed soldiery; and while strong pickets were posted in the front and flanks, the remnant of the British, with their brave allies, piled their arms and stretched themselves on the field.

While the British held their battleground, the Prussians had been obliged to retire in the night from Ligny. This, however, was not ascertained until morning, as the *aide-de-camp* despatched with the intelligence to Quatre Bras had unfortunately been killed on the road. Corps after corps arrived during the night, placing the Duke of Wellington in a position to have become assailant next morning had Blucher succeeded in maintaining his position, and repulsed Napoleon's attack.

The night passed, the wounded were removed, the dead partially buried; disabled guns were repaired, ammunition served out, and all was ready for "a contest, on the morrow."

The intelligence of the Prussian retreat, of course, produced a correspondent movement, and the Duke of Wellington, to maintain his communications with Marshal Blucher, decided on falling back upon a position in front of the village of Waterloo, which had been already surveyed, and selected by the allied leader as the spot on which he should make a stand.

CHAPTER 25

The Battle of Waterloo, 1815

Napoleon had reached Frasnes at nine o'clock on the morning of the 17th, and determined on attacking the allied commander. Still uncertain as to the route by which Blucher was retiring, he detached Grouchy in pursuit with the third and fourth corps, and the cavalry of Excelmans and Pajol, with directions to overtake the Prussian marshal, if possible, and in that case bring him, to action.

While Buonaparte delayed his attack until his reserve and the sixth corps came up, his abler antagonist was preparing to retire. This operation in open day was difficult, as the Dyle was in the rear of the allies, and the long and narrow bridge at the village of Genappe the only means by which the *corps d'armée* could effect its passage. Wellington disposed some horse-artillery and dismounted dragoons upon the heights, and leaving a strong rear-guard in front of Quatre Bras, he succeeded in making his retreat, until, when discovered, it was too late to offer any serious interruption to the regressive movement of the allies.

While the rear of the columns were still defiling through the narrow streets of Genappe, Napoleon's advanced cavalry overtook and attacked the rear-guard, and a sharp affair ensued. The 7th Hussars, assisted by some squadrons of the 11th and 23rd Light Dragoons, charged the French horsemen boldly, but they were repulsed; and a second effort was bravely but ineffectually attempted. The Life Guards were instantly ordered up, and led in person to the charge by Lord Anglesea, who was in command of the British rear-guard. Their attack was decisive; the enemy were severely checked, and driven in great disorder back upon their supports. No other attempt was made by the French cavalry to embarrass the retreat of the allied columns, and except by an occasional cannonade, too distant to produce any serious

Life Guards at Waterloo

effect, the remainder of the march on Waterloo was undisturbed by the French advance.

The allies reached the position early in the evening, and orders were issued for the divisions to halt and prepare their bivouacs. The ground for each brigade had been already marked out; the troops piled their arms, the cavalry picketed their horses, the guns were parked, fires were lighted along the lines, and all prepared the best mode of sheltering themselves from the inclemency of the weather, which scanty means could afford them in an exposed position like that of Waterloo.

All through the day rain had occasionally fallen, but as night came on the weather became more tempestuous. The wind rose, and torrents of rain, with peals of thunder and frequent lightning, rendered the dreary night before the battle anything but a season of repose.

While the troops bivouacked on the field, the Duke of Wellington with the general officers and their respective staffs occupied the village of Waterloo. On the doors of the several cottages the names of the principal officers were chalked "and frail and perishing as was the record, it was found there long after many of those whom it designated had ceased to exist!"

The ground on which the allied commander had decided to accept battle was chosen with excellent judgment. In front of the position, the surface declined for nearly a quarter of a mile, and rose again for an equal distance, until it terminated in a ridge of easy access, along which the French had posted a number of their brigades, the intermediate space between the armies being covered by a rich crop of rye nearly ready for the sickle. In the rear, the forest of Soignies, intersected by the great roads from Charleroi to Brussels, extended; and nearly at the entrance to the wood, the little village of Waterloo was situated.

The right of the British was stretched over to Merke Braine, and the left *appuied* upon a height above Ter le Haye. The whole line was formed on a gentle acclivity, the flanks partially defended by a small ravine with broken ground. The farmhouse of La Haye Sainte, in front of the left centre, was defended by a Hanoverian battalion, and the chateau of Hougomont, in advance of the right centre, held by a part of the Guards and a few companies of Nassau riflemen. This was the strongest point of the whole position; and the duke had strengthened it considerably, by erecting barricades and perforating the walls with loopholes, to permit the musketry of its defenders to be effectively

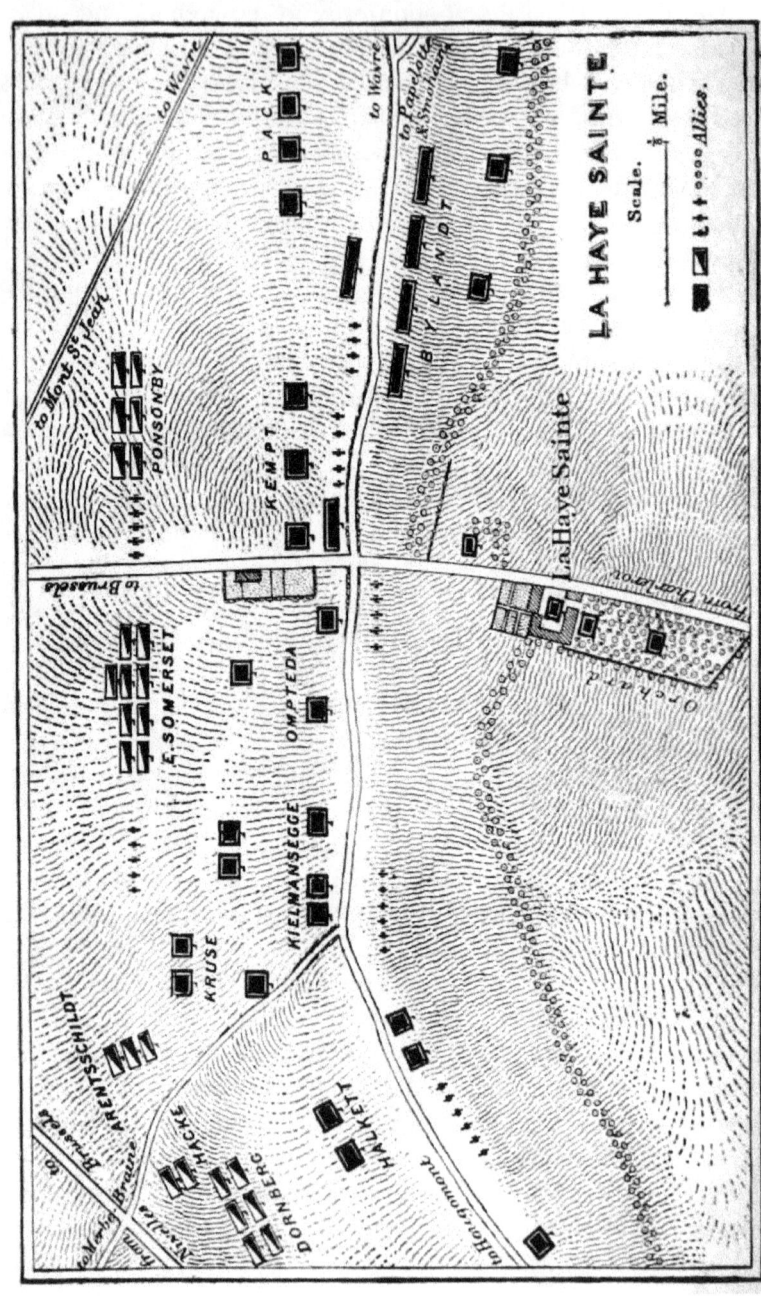

employed.

Wellington's first line, comprising some of his best regiments, was drawn up behind these posts; the second was still further in the rear, and, from occupying a hollow, was sheltered from the fire of the French artillery. The third was formed of the cavalry; and they were more retired still, extending to Ter le Haye. The extreme right of the British obliqued to Merke Braine, and covered the road to Nivelles, while the left kept the communication with the Prussians open by the Ohain road, which runs through the passes of Saint Lambert. As it was not improbable that Napoleon might endeavour to reach Brussels by marching circuitously round the British right, a corps of observation, composed of the greater portion of the fourth division, under Sir Charles Colville, was detached to Halle; and consequently those troops, during the long and bloody contest of the 18th, were at a distance from the field, and remained *non combattant*.

The allied dispositions were completed soon after daylight, although it was nearly noon before the engagement seriously commenced. The division of Guards, under General Cooke, was posted on a rise immediately adjoining the *château* of Hougomont, its right leaning on the road to Nivelles; the division of Baron Alten had its left flank on the road of Charleroi, and was drawn up behind the house of La Haye Sainte. The Brunswick troops were partly in line with the Guards and partly held in reserve; and the Nassau troops were generally attached to Alten's division. Some of the corps in line, and a battalion acting *en tirailleur*, occupied the wood of Hougomont. This *corps d'armée* was commanded by the Prince of Orange.

The British divisions of Clinton and Colville, two Hanoverian brigades, and a Dutch corps under the command of Lord Hill, were placed *en potence*, in front of the right.

On the left, the division of Picton, a British brigade under Sir John Lambert, a Hanoverian corps, and some troops of the Netherlands, extended along the hedge and lane which traverses the rising ground between the road to Charleroi and Ter le Haye. This village, with the farm of Papilotte, contiguous to the wood of Frichemont, was garrisoned by a post of the Nassau contingent, commanded by the hereditary Prince of Weimar. The cavalry were under the direction of the Earl of Uxbridge, and the artillery were commanded by Sir George Wood.

No part of the allied position was remarkable for natural strength; but where the ground displayed any advantages, they had been care-

GROUND-PLAN OF THE FARM OF LA HAYE SAINTE.

(Not drawn to scale.)

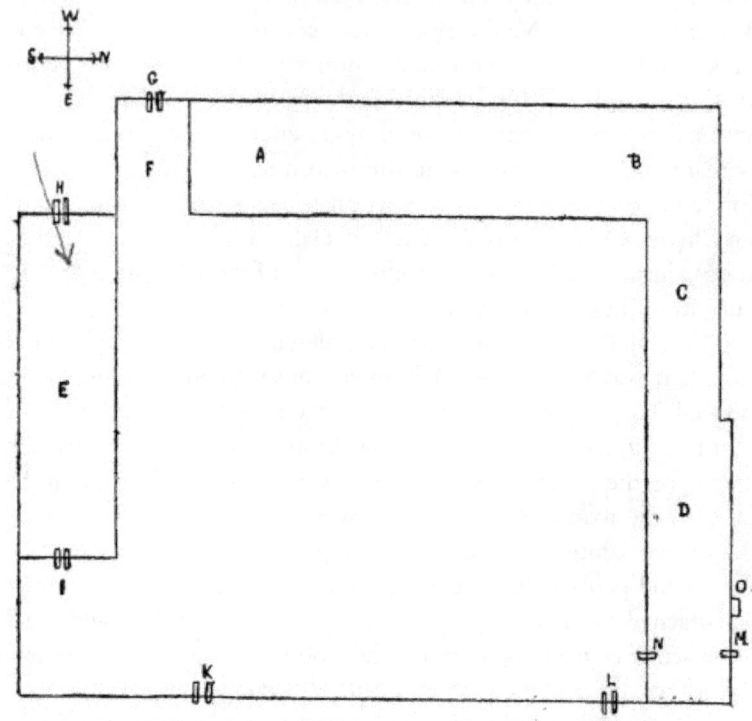

→ THE GREAT ROAD—CHARLEROI TO THE ALLIED POSITION. →

A, B, C, D, Dwelling-house, stables, and cow-house, of which D is the dwelling-house.
E, A barn.
F, A passage.
G, A great gate.
H, A great gate.
I, A door.
K, A great gate.
L, M, N, Doors.
O, A well, being a square building, with loopholes flanking the door and wall.

The interior measure of the yard, from the building C, D to the building E, is 40 yards, and 45 yards from the building A, B to the wall K, L.

The buildings are very strongly roofed and built. The passage F has the same roofing as the houses.

fully made available for defence. The whole surface of the field of Waterloo was perfectly open, and the acclivities of easy ascent. Infantry movements could be easily effected, artillery might advance and retire, and cavalry could charge. On every point the British position was assailable; and the island soldier had no reliance but in "God and his Grace" for all else depended on his own stout heart and vigorous arm.

CHAPTER 26

The Battle of Waterloo (continued), 1815

Napoleon passed the night of the 17th in a farmhouse which was abandoned by the owner, named Bouquean, an old man of eighty, who had retired to Planchenoit. It is situated on the high road from Charleroi to Brussels. It is half a league from the *château* of Hougomont and La Haye Sainte, and a quarter of a league from La Belle Alliance and Planchenoit. Supper was hastily served up in part of the utensils of the farmer that remained. Buonaparte slept in the first chamber of this house; a bed with blue silk hangings and gold fringe was put up for him in the middle of this room. His brother Jerome, the Duke of Bassano, and several generals, lodged in the other chambers. All the adjacent buildings, gardens, meadows, and enclosures, were crowded with military and horses.

Morning broke: the rain still continued, but with less severity than during the preceding night; the wind fell, but the day lowered, and the dawn of the 18th was gloomy and foreboding. The British soldiers recovered from the chill cast over them by the inclemency of the weather, and, from the ridge of their position, calmly observed the enemy's masses coming up in long succession, and forming their numerous columns on the heights in front of La Belle Alliance.

The bearing of the French was very opposite to the steady and cool determination of the British soldiery. With the former, all was exultation and arrogant display; while, with characteristic vanity, they boasted of an imaginary success at Quatre Bras, and claimed a decisive victory at Ligny!

Although in point of fact beaten by the British on the 16th, Napoleon tortured the retrograde movement of the Duke on Waterloo

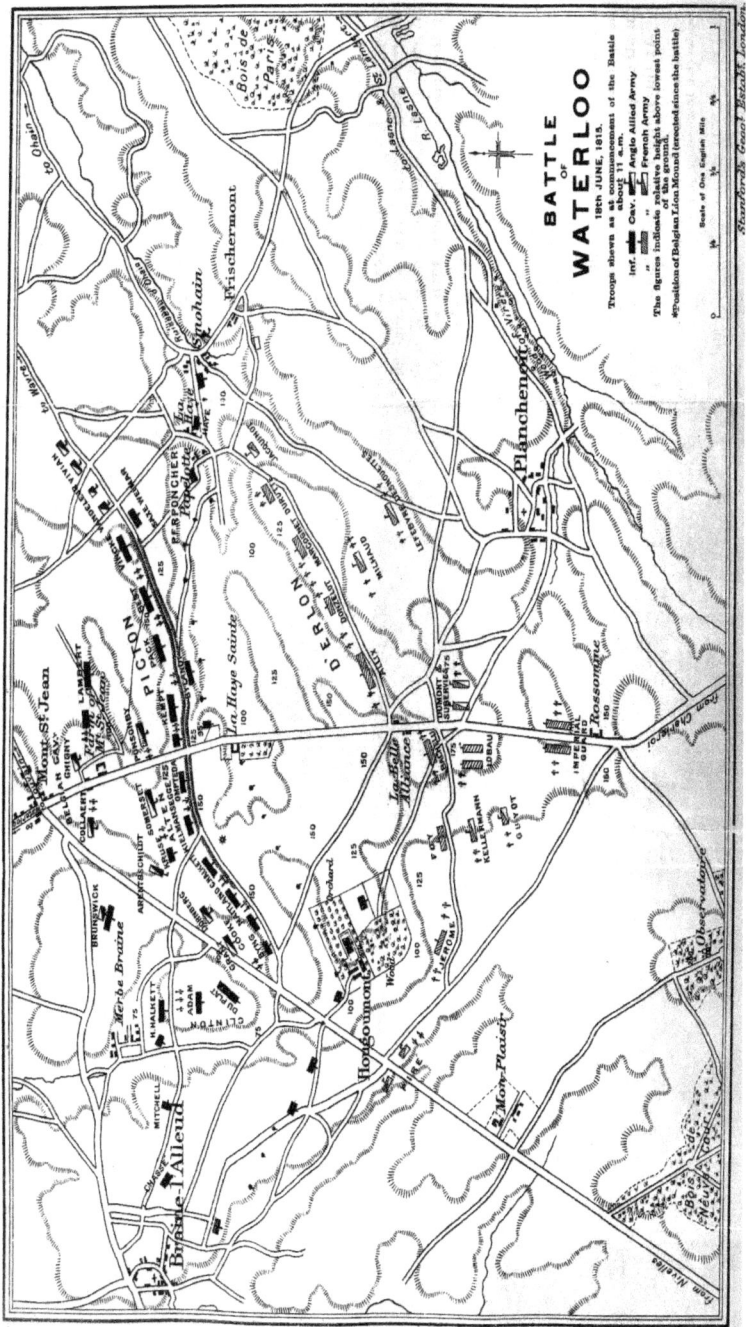

into a defeat, and the winning a field from Blucher, attended with no advantage beyond the capture of a few disabled guns, afforded a pretext to declare in his dispatches that the Prussian Army was routed and disorganised, without a prospect of being rallied.

The morning passed in mutual dispositions for battle, and the French attack commenced soon after eleven o'clock. The first corps, under Count D'Erlon, was in position opposite La Haye Sainte, its right extending towards Frichemont, and its left leaning on the road to Brussels. The second corps, uniting its right with D'Erlon's left, extended to Hougomont, with the wood in its front.

The cavalry reserve (the *cuirassiers*) were immediately in the rear of these corps; and the Imperial Guard, forming the grand reserve, were posited on the heights of La Belle Alliance. Count Lobau, with the sixth corps, and D'Aumont's cavalry, were placed in the rear of the extreme right, to check the Prussians, should they advance from Wavre, and approach by the defiles of Saint Lambert. Napoleon's arrangements were completed about half-past eleven, and immediately the order to attack was given.

The place from which Buonaparte viewed the field, was a gentle rising ground beside the farmhouse of La Belle Alliance. There he remained for a considerable part of the day, dismounted, pacing to and fro with his hands behind him, receiving communications from his *aides-de-camp*, and issuing orders to his officers. As the battle became more doubtful, he approached nearer the scene of action, and betrayed increased impatience to his staff by violent gesticulation, and using immense quantities of snuff. At three o'clock he was on horseback in front of La Belle Alliance; and in the evening, just before he made his last attempt with the Guard, he had reached a hollow close to La Haye Sainte.

Wellington, at the opening of the engagement, stood upon a ridge immediately behind La Haye, but as the conflict thickened, where difficulties arose and danger threatened, there the duke was found. He traversed the field exposed to a storm of balls, and passed from point to point uninjured; and on more than one occasion, when the French cavalry charged the British squares, the duke was there for shelter.

A slight skirmishing between the French *tirailleurs* and British light troops had continued throughout the morning, but the advance of a division of the second corps, under Jerome Buonaparte, against the post of Hougomont, was the signal for the British artillery to open, and was, in fact, the commencement of the Battle of Waterloo. The

THE CHATEAU OF HOUGOMONT.

Taken chiefly from Kennedy's 'Notes on the Battle of Waterloo.'

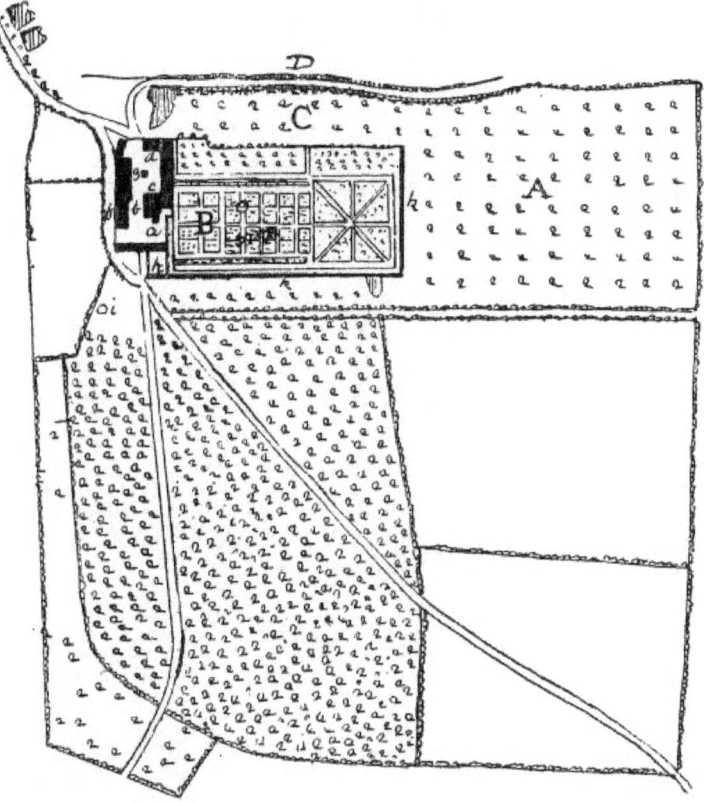

A, Great orchard. B, Kitchen-garden. C, Small orchard. D, Hollow road *a*, Chapel. *b*, Chateau. *c*, Farm buildings. *d*, Cowshed. *e*, Gardener's house. *f* and *g*, Barns. *h*, Small garden. *i*, Haystack. k_1, k_2, Wall loopholed by British troops.

first gun fired on the 18th was directed by Sir George Wood upon Jerome's advancing column; the last was a French howitzer, at eight o'clock in the evening, turned by a British officer against the routed remains of that splendid array with, which Napoleon had begun the battle.

Hougomont was the key of the duke's position, a post naturally of considerable strength, and care had been taken to increase it, It was garrisoned by the light companies of the Coldstream and 1st and 3rd Guards; while a detachment from General Byng's brigade was formed on an eminence behind, to support the troops defending the house and the wood on its left. Three hundred Nassau riflemen were stationed in the wood and garden; but the first attack of the enemy dispersed them.

To carry Hougomont, the efforts of the second corps were principally directed throughout the day. This fine corps, thirty thousand strong, comprised three divisions, and each of these, in quick succession, attacked the well-defended farmhouse. The advance of the assailants was covered by a tremendous cross-fire of nearly one hundred pieces, while the British guns in battery on the heights above, returned the cannonade, and made fearful havoc in the dense columns of the enemy as they advanced or retired from the attack. Although the French frequently occupied the wood, it afforded them indifferent shelter from the musketry of the troops defending the house and garden; for the trees were but slight, and planted far asunder. Foy's division passed entirely through and gained the heights in the rear; but it was driven back with immense loss by part of the Coldstream and 3rd Guards.

At last, despairing of success, the French artillery opened with shells upon the house; the old tower of Hougomont was quickly in a blaze; the fire reached the chapel, and many of the wounded, both assailants and defenders, perished miserably there. But still, though the flames raged above, shells burst around, and shot ploughed through the shattered walls and windows, the Guards nobly held the place, and Hougomont remained untaken.

The attack against the position of Hougomont lasted, on the whole, from twenty-five minutes before twelve until a little past seven at night. Within half an hour one thousand five hundred men were killed in the small orchard at Hougomont, not exceeding four acres. The loss of the enemy was enormous. The division of General Foy alone lost about three thousand; and the total loss of the enemy in

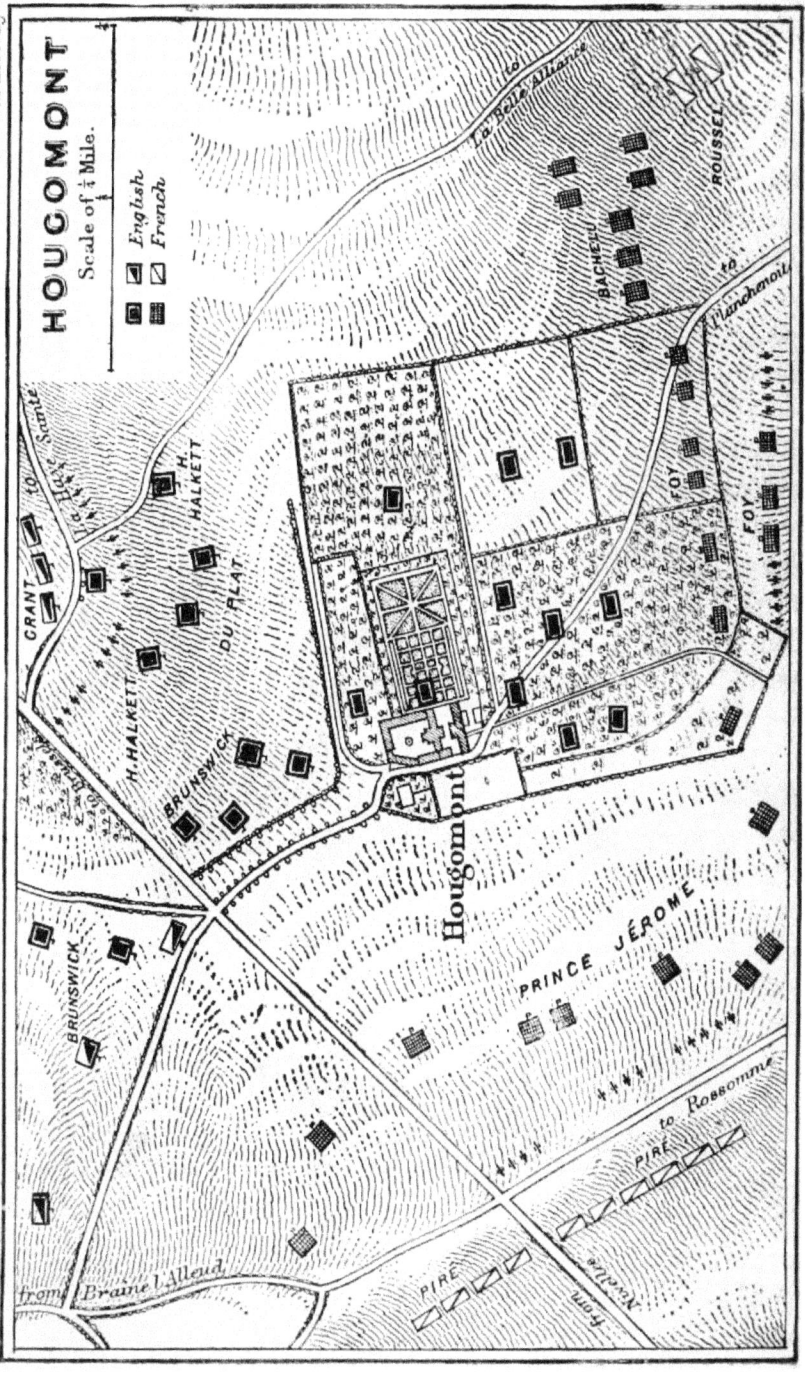

South Gate Hougomont

the attack of this position is estimated at ten thousand in killed and wounded. Above six thousand men of both armies perished in the farm of Hougomont; six hundred British were killed in the wood; twenty-five in the garden; one thousand one hundred in the orchard and meadow; four hundred men near the farmer's garden; two thousand of both parties behind the great orchard. The bodies of three hundred British were buried opposite the gate of the *château*; and those of six hundred French were buried at the same place.

The advance of Jerome on the right was followed by a general onset upon the British line, three hundred pieces of artillery opening their cannonade, and the French columns in different points advancing to the attack. Charges of cavalry and infantry, sometimes separately and sometimes with united force, were made in vain. The British regiments were disposed individually in squares, with triple files, each placed sufficiently apart to allow it to deploy when requisite. The squares were mostly parallel, but a few were judiciously thrown back; and this disposition, when the French cavalry had passed the advanced regiments, exposed them to a flanking fire from the squares behind. The British cavalry were in the rear of the infantry, and the artillery in battery over the line. The fight of Waterloo may be easily comprehended by simply stating, that for ten hours it was a continued succession of attacks of the French columns on the squares; the British artillery playing upon them as they advanced, and the cavalry charging when they receded.

But no situation could be more trying to the unyielding courage of the British Army than this disposition in squares at Waterloo. There is an excited feeling in an attacking body that stimulates the coldest and blunts the thoughts of danger. The tumultuous enthusiasm of the assault spreads from man to man, and duller spirits catch a gallant frenzy from the brave around them.

But the enduring and devoted courage which pervaded the British squares when, hour after hour, mowed down by a murderous artillery, and wearied by furious and frequent onsets of lancers and *cuirassiers*; when the constant order, "Close up! close up!" marked the quick succession of slaughter that thinned their diminished ranks; and when the day wore later, when the remnants of two and even three regiments were necessary to complete the square which one of them had formed in the morning—to support this with firmness, and "feed death," inactive and unmoved, exhibited that calm and desperate bravery which elicited the admiration of Napoleon himself.

At times the temper of the troops had nearly failed; and, particularly among the Irish regiments, the reiterated question of—"When shall we get at them?" showed how ardent the wish was to avoid inactive slaughter, and, plunging into the columns of the assailants, to avenge the death of their companions. But the "Be cool, my boys!" from their officers was sufficient to restrain their impatience, and, cumbering the ground with their dead, they waited with desperate intrepidity for the hour to arrive when victory and vengeance should be their own!

While the second corps was engaged at Hougomont, the first was directed by Napoleon to penetrate the left centre. Had this attempt succeeded, the British must have been defeated, as it would have been severed and surrounded. Picton's division was now severely engaged. Its position stretched from La Haye Sainte to Ter la Haye; in front there was an irregular hedge; but being broken and pervious to cavalry, it afforded but partial protection. The Belgian infantry, who were extended in front of the fifth division, gave way as the leading columns of D'Erlon's corps approached, the French came boldly to the fence, and Picton, with Kempt's brigade, as gallantly advanced to meet them.

A tremendous combat ensued. The French and British closed; for the *cuirassiers,* had been already received in square, and repulsed with immense loss. Instantly Picton deployed the division into line; and pressing forward to the hedge, received and returned the volley of D'Erlon's infantry, and then crossing the fence, drove back the enemy at the point of the bayonet. The French retreated in close column, while the fifth mowed them down with musketry, and slaughtered them in heaps with their bayonets.

Lord Anglesea seized on the moment, and charging with the Royals, Greys, and Enniskilleners, burst through everything that opposed him. Vainly the mailed *cuirassier* and formidable lancer attempted to withstand this splendid body of heavy cavalry; they were overwhelmed, and the French infantry, already broken and disorganised by the gallant fifth, fell in hundreds beneath the swords of the British dragoons. The eagles of the 45th and 105th regiments, and upwards of two thousand prisoners, were the trophies of this brilliant charge.

But, alas! like most military triumphs, this had its misfortune to alloy it. Picton fell! But where could the famed commander of the old "Fighting Third" meet with death so gloriously? He was at the head of the division as it pressed forward with the bayonet; he saw the best troops of Napoleon repulsed; the ball struck him, and he fell from his horse; he heard the Highland lament answered by the deep execration

The charge of the Scots Greys

of Erin; and while the Scotch slogan was returned by the Irish hurrah, his fading sight saw his excited division rush on with irresistible fury. The French column was annihilated, and two thousand dead enemies told how desperately he had been avenged. This was, probably, the bloodiest struggle of the day. When the attack commenced—and it lasted not an hour—the fifth division exceeded five thousand men; and when it ended it scarcely reckoned eighteen hundred bayonets!

While Picton's division and the heavy cavalry had repulsed D'Erlon's effort against the left, the battle was raging at La Haye Sainte, a, post in front of the left centre. This was a rude farmhouse and farm, defended by five hundred German riflemen; and here the attack was fierce and constant, and the defence gallant and protracted.

While a number of guns played on it with shot and shells, it was assailed by a strong column of infantry. Thrice they were repulsed; but the barn caught fire, and the number of the garrison decreasing, it was found impossible, from its exposed situation, to supply the loss and throw in reinforcements. Still worse, the ammunition of the rifle corps failed, and, reduced to a few cartridges, their fire had almost ceased.

Encouraged by this casualty, the French, at the fourth attempt, turned the position. Though the doors were burst in, still the gallant Germans held the house with their bayonets; but, having ascended the walls and roof, the French fired on them from above, and, now reduced to a handful, the post was carried. No quarter was given, and the remnant of the brave riflemen were bayoneted on the spot.

This was, however, the only point where, during this long and sanguinary conflict, Buonaparte succeeded. He became master of a dilapidated dwelling, its roof destroyed by shells, and its walls perforated by a thousand shot-holes; and when obtained, an incessant torrent of grape and shrapnels from the British artillery on the heights above, rendered its acquisition useless for future operations, and made his persistence in maintaining it, a wanton and unnecessary sacrifice of human life.

There was a terrible sameness in the battle of the 18th of June, which distinguished it in the history of modern slaughter. Although designated by Napoleon "a day of false manoeuvres," in reality there was less display of military tactics at Waterloo than in any general action we have on record. Buonaparte's favourite plan, to turn a wing, or separate a corps, was the constant effort of the French leader. Both were tried at Hougomont to turn the right, and at La Haye Sainte to break through the left centre.

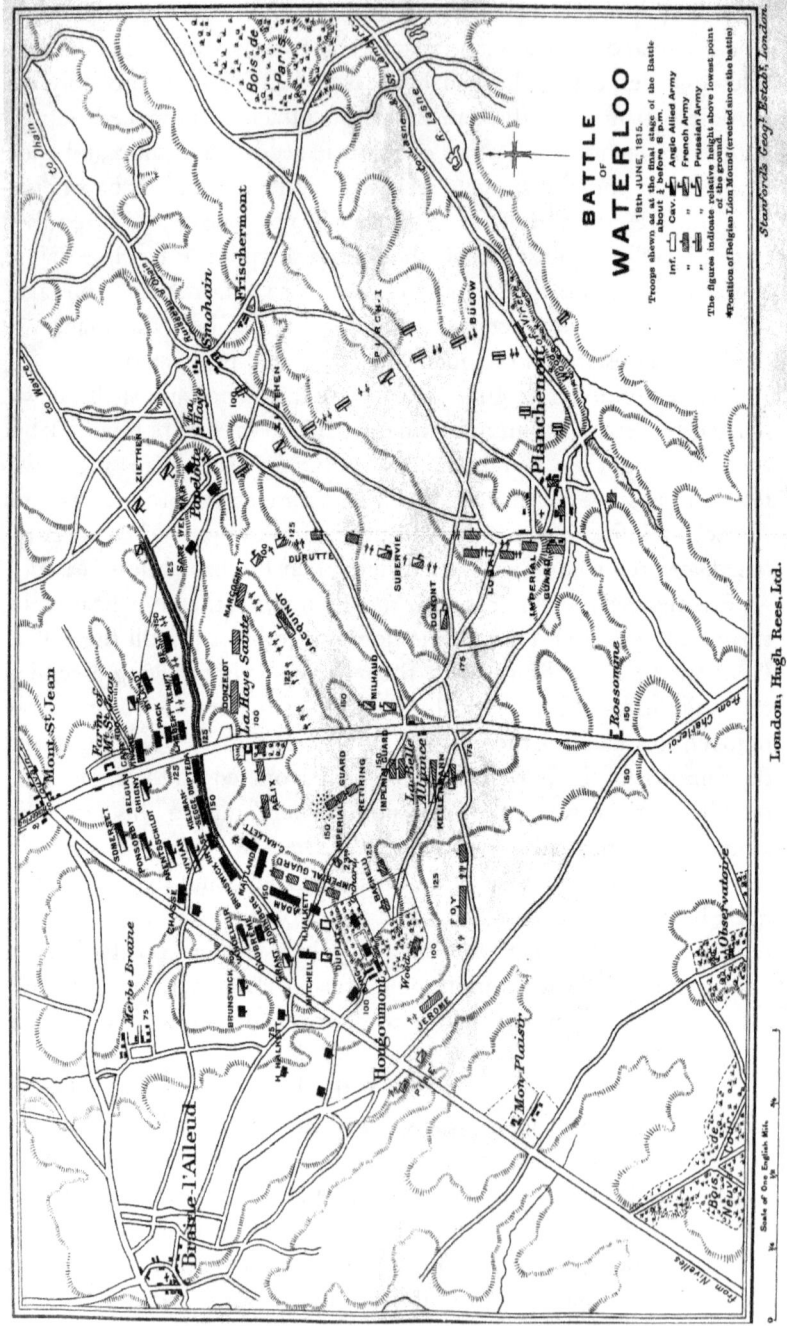

Hence, the French operations were confined to fierce and incessant onsets with masses of cavalry and infantry, generally supported by a numerous and destructive artillery. Knowing that to repel these desperate and sustained attacks a tremendous sacrifice of human life must occur, Napoleon, in defiance of their acknowledged bravery, calculated on wearying the British into defeat. But when he saw his columns driven back in confusion, when his cavalry receded from the squares they could not penetrate, when battalions were reduced to companies by the fire of his cannon, and still that "feeble few" shewed a perfect front, and held the ground they had originally taken—no wonder his admiration was expressed to Soult:

How beautifully these British fight! but they must give way!

And well did British bravery merit that proud encomium which their enduring courage elicited from Napoleon. For hours, with uniform and unflinching gallantry, they repulsed the attacks of troops who had already proved their superiority over the soldiers of every other nation in Europe.

When the artillery united its fire, and poured exterminating volleys on some devoted regiment, the square, prostrate on the earth, allowed the storm to pass over them. When the battery ceased—to permit their cavalry to charge and complete the work of destruction—the square was again upon their feet, no face unformed, no chasm to allow the horsemen entrance, but a serried line of impassable bayonets was before them, while the rear ranks threw in a reserved fire with murderous precision. The *cuirass* was too near the musket then to avert death from the wearer; men and horses went down in heaps; each attempt ended in defeat, and the cavalry at last retired, leaving their best and boldest before a square which, to them, had proved impenetrable.

When the close column of infantry came on, the square had deployed into line. The French were received with a destructive volley, and next moment the wild cheer which accompanies the bayonet charge, announced that Britain advanced with the weapon she had always found irresistible. The French never crossed bayonets fairly with the British, for when an attempt was made to stand, a terrible slaughter attested Britain's superiority.

CHAPTER 27

The Battle of Waterloo (continued), 1815

But the situation of Wellington momentarily became more critical. Masses of the enemy had fallen, but thousands came on anew. With desperate attachment, the French army passed forward at Napoleon's command, and although each advance terminated in defeat and slaughter, fresh battalions crossed the valley and mounting the ridge with cries of "*Vive l'Empereur!*" exhibited a devotion which never had been surpassed.

Wellington's reserves had been gradually brought into action—and the left, though but partially engaged, could not be weakened to send assistance to the right and centre. Many battalions were miserably reduced; and the fifth division, already cut up at Quatre Bras on the evening of the 16th, presented but a skeleton of what these beautiful brigades had been when they left Brussels two days before.

The loss of individual regiments was prodigious. The 27th had four hundred men mowed down in square without drawing a trigger; it lost all its superior officers; and a solitary subaltern who remained, commanded it for half the day. Another, the 92nd regiment, when not two hundred were left, rushed at a French column and routed it with the bayonet; and a third, the 33rd, when nearly annihilated, sent to require support—none could be given; and the commanding officer was told that he must "stand or fall where he was!"

Any other save Wellington would have despaired; but he calculated, and justly, that he had an army which would perish where it stood. But when he saw the devastation caused by the incessant attacks of an enemy who appeared determined to succeed, is it surprising that his watch was frequently consulted, and that he prayed for night or

Blucher?

When evening came on, no doubt Buonaparte began to question the accuracy of his "military arithmetic"—a phrase happily applied to this meting out death by the hour. Half the day had been consumed in a sanguinary and indecisive conflict; all his disposable troops but the Guard had been employed, and still his efforts were foiled; and the British, with diminished numbers, shewed the same bold front they had presented at the commencement of the battle.

He determined, therefore, on another desperate attempt upon the whole British line; and while issuing orders to effect it, a distant cannonade announced that a fresh force was approaching to share the action. Napoleon, concluding that Grouchy was corning up, conveyed the glad tidings to his disheartened columns. But an aide-de-camp quickly removed the mistake, and the emperor received the unwelcome intelligence that the strange force now distinctly observed debouching from the woods of Saint Lambert, was the advanced guard of a Prussian corps.

Buonaparte appeared, or affected to appear, incredulous; but the fatal truth was ascertained too soon.

While the delusive hope of immediate relief was industriously circulated among his troops, Napoleon despatched Count Lobau, with the sixth corps, to employ the Prussians, while in person he should direct a general attack upon the British line.

Meanwhile the Prussian advance had debouched from the wood of Frichermont, and the operations of the old marshal, in the rear of Napoleon's right flank became alarming. If Blucher established himself there in force, unless success against the British in his front was rapid and decisive, or that Grouchy came promptly to his relief, Buonaparte knew well that his situation must be hopeless. Accordingly, he directed the first and second corps and all his cavalry reserves against the duke; the French mounted the heights once more, and the British were attacked from right to left.

A dreadful and protracted encounter followed; for an hour, the contest was sustained, and, like the preceding ones, it was a sanguinary succession of determined attack and obstinate resistance. The impetuosity of the French onset at first obtained a temporary success. The British light cavalry were driven back, and for a time a number of the guns were in the enemy's possession; but the British rallied again—the French, forced across the ridge, retired to their original ground, without effecting any permanent impression.

It was now five o'clock; the Prussian reserve cavalry under Prince William was warmly engaged with Count Lobau; Bulow's corps, with the second, under Pirch, were approaching rapidly through the passes of Saint Lambert; and the first Prussian corps, advancing by Ohain, had already begun to operate on Napoleon's right. Bulow pushed forward towards Aywire, and, opening his fire on the French, succeeded in driving them from the opposite heights.

The Prussian left, acting separately, advanced upon the village of Planchenoit, and attacked Napoleon's rear. The French maintaining their position with great gallantry, and the Prussians, being equally obstinate in their attempts to force the village, produced a bloody and prolonged combat, Napoleon's right had begun to recede before the first Prussian corps, and his officers, generally, anticipated a disastrous issue, that nothing but immediate success against the British, or instant relief from Grouchy, could remedy.

The Imperial Guard, his last and best resource, were consequently ordered up. Formed in close column, Buonaparte in person advanced to lead them on; but dissuaded by his staff, he paused near the bottom of the hill, and to Ney, that "spoiled child of victory," the conduct of this redoubted body was intrusted.

In the interim, as the French right fell back, the British moved gradually forward; and converging from the extreme points of Merke Braine and Braine la Leud, compressed their extent of line, and nearly assumed the form of a crescent. The British Guards were considerably advanced, and having deployed behind the crest of the hill, lay down to avoid the cannonade with which Napoleon covered the onset of his best troops. Ney, with his proverbial gallantry, led on the Middle Guard; and Wellington, putting himself at the head of some wavering regiments, in person brought them forward, and restored their confidence.

As the Imperial Guard approached the crest where the household troops were couching, the British artillery, which had gradually converged upon the *chaussée*, opened with canister shot. The distance was so short, and the range so accurate, that each discharge fell with deadly precision into the column as it breasted the hill. Ney, with his customary heroism, directed the attack; and when his horse was killed, on foot, and sword in hand, he headed the veterans whom he had so often led to victory. Although the leading files of the Guard were swept off by the exterminating fire of the British batteries, still their undaunted intrepidity carried them forward, and they gallantly

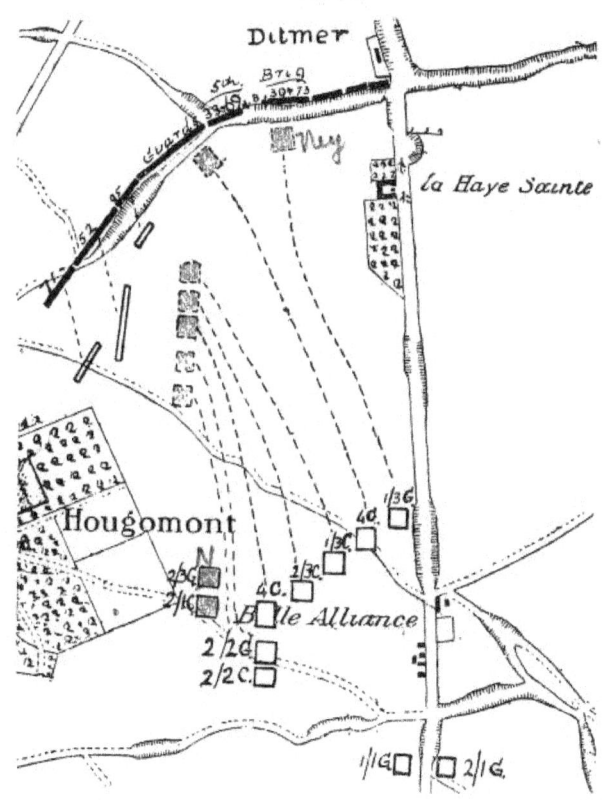

THE ATTACK OF THE FRENCH GUARD.

Scale 1/20000.

crossed the ridge.

Then came the hour of British triumph. The magic word was spoken—"Up, Guards, and at them!" In a moment, the household brigade were on their feet; then waiting till the French closed, they delivered a murderous volley, cheered, and rushed forward with the bayonet, Wellington in person directing the attack.

With the 42nd and 95th, the British leader threw himself on Ney's flank, and rout and destruction succeeded. In vain their gallant chief attempted to rally the recoiling Guard; but driven down the hill, the Middle were intermingled with the Old Guard, who had formed at the bottom in reserve.

In this unfortunate *mêlée*, the British cavalry seized on the moment of confusion, and plunging into the mass, cut down and disorganised the regiments which had hitherto been unbroken. The British artillery ceased firing, and those who had escaped the iron shower of the guns, fell beneath sabre and bayonet.

The unremediable disorder consequent on this decisive repulse, and the confusion in the French rear, where Bulow had fiercely attacked them, did not escape the eagle glance of Wellington.

"The hour is come!" he is said to have exclaimed, as, closing his telescope, he commanded the whole line to advance. The order was exultingly obeyed; and, forming four deep, on came the British. Wounds, and fatigue, and hunger, were all forgotten as with their customary steadiness they crossed the ridge; but when they saw the French, and began to move down the hill, a cheer that seemed to rend the heavens pealed from their proud array, as with levelled bayonets they pressed on to meet the enemy.

But, panic-struck and disorganised, the French resistance was short and feeble. The Prussian cannon thundered in their rear, the British bayonet was flashing in their front, and unable to stand the terror of the charge, they broke and fled. A dreadful and indiscriminate carnage ensued. The great road was choked with equipages, and cumbered with the dead and dying; while the fields, as far as the eye could reach, were covered with a host of helpless fugitives. Courage and discipline were forgotten; and Napoleon's army of yesterday was now a splendid wreck—a terror-stricken multitude! His own words best describe it—"It was a total rout!"

On a surface of two square miles, it was ascertained that fifty thousand men and horses were lying! The luxurious crop of ripe grain which had covered the field of battle was reduced to litter, and beaten into the earth; and the surface, trodden down by the cavalry, and furrowed deeply by the cannon wheels, strewn with many a relic of the fight. Helmets and *cuirasses*, shattered firearms and broken swords; all the variety of military ornaments; lancer caps and Highland bonnets; uniforms of every colour, plume and pennon; musical instruments, the apparatus of artillery, drums, bugles;—but good God! why dwell on the harrowing picture of "a foughten field"?—each and every ruinous display bore mute testimony to the misery of such a battle.

Could the melancholy appearance of this scene of death be heightened, it would be by witnessing the researches of the living, amid its desolation, for the objects of their love. Mothers and wives and children for days were occupied in that mournful duty; and the confusion of the corpses, friend and foe intermingled as they were, often rendered the attempt at recognising individuals difficult, and, in some cases, impossible.

In many places the dead lay four deep upon each other, marking the spot some British square had occupied, when exposed for hours to the murderous fire of a French battery. Outside, lancer and *cuirassier* were scattered thickly on the earth. Madly attempting to force the serried bayonets of the British, they had fallen in the bootless essay, by the musketry of the inner files. Farther on, you traced the spot where the cavalry of France and Britain had encountered.

Chasseur and hussar were intermingled; and the heavy Norman horse of the Imperial Guard were interspersed with the grey chargers which had carried Albion's chivalry. Here the Highlander and *tirailleur* lay, side by side together; and the heavy dragoon, with "green Erin's" badge upon his helmet, was grappling in death with the Polish lancer.

Never had France sent a finer army to the field—and never had any been so signally defeated. Complete as the *déroute* at Vittoria had appeared, it fell infinitely short of that sustained at Waterloo. Tired of slaughtering unresisting foes, the British, early in the night, abandoned the pursuit of the broken battalions and halted. But the Prussians, untamed by previous exertion, continued to follow the fugitives with increased activity, and nothing could surpass the unrelenting animosity of their pursuit. Plunder was sacrificed to revenge, and the memory of former defeat and past oppression produced a dreadful retaliation, and deadened every impulse of humanity. The *væ victis* was pronounced, and thousands besides those who perished in the field fell that night by Prussian lance and sabre.

What Napoleon's feelings were when he witnessed the overthrow of his guard, the failure of his last hope, the death-blow to his political existence, cannot be described, but may be easily imagined. Turning to an *aide-de-camp*, with a face livid with rage and despair, he muttered in a tremulous voice "*A present c'est fini! sauvous nous*"; and turning his horse, he rode hastily off towards Charleroi, attended by his guide and staff.

In whatever point of view Waterloo is considered, whether as a battle, a victory, or an event, in all these, every occurrence of the last century yields, and more particularly in the magnitude of results. No doubt the successes of Wellington in Spain were, in a great degree, primary causes of Napoleon's downfall; but still, the victory of Waterloo consummated efforts made for years before in vain to achieve the freedom of the Continent, and wrought the final ruin of him, through whose unhallowed ambition a world had been so long convulsed.

As a battle, the merits of the field of Waterloo have been freely examined, and very indifferently adjudicated. Those who were best competent to decide, have pronounced this battle as that upon which Wellington might securely rest his fame, while others, admitting the extent of the victory, ascribe the result rather to fortunate accident than, military skill.

Never was a falser statement hazarded. The success attendant on the day of Waterloo can be referred only to the admirable system of resistance in the general, and an enduring valour, rarely equalled and never surpassed, in the soldiers whom he commanded. Chance, at Waterloo, had no effect upon results; Wellington's surest game was to act only on the defensive; his arrangements with Blucher for mutual support being thoroughly matured, he knew that before night the Prussians must be upon the field.

Bad weather and bad roads, with the conflagration of a town in the line of march, which, to save the Prussian tumbrils from explosion, required a circuitous movement—all these, while they protracted the struggle for several hours beyond what might have been reasonably computed, only go to prove that Wellington, in accepting battle, under a well-founded belief that he should be supported in *four hours*, when single-handed he maintained the combat and resolutely held his ground during a space of *eight*, had left nothing dependent upon accident, but, providing for the worst contingencies, had formed his calculations with admirable skill.

The allied loss was enormous, (see list following), but it fell infinitely short of that sustained by Napoleon's army. Of the latter, nothing like an accurate return was ever made; but from the most correct estimates by French and British officers, upwards of five-and-twenty thousand men were rendered *hors de combat*, while multitudes were sabred in the flight, or perished on the roads from sheer fatigue, and in deserted villages for want of sustenance and surgical relief.

★★★★★★

Return of killed and wounded from the War-office, July, 1815.

Killed on the spot, non-commissioned and privates,	1715
Died of wounds,	856
Missing, supposed killed,	353
Total,	2924
Wounded,	6831
Total killed and wounded,	9755

French Artillery captured at Waterloo:—

12-pounder guns,	35	12-pounder waggons,		74
6-pounder guns,	57	6-pounder waggons,		71
8-inch howitzers,	13	Howitzer waggons,		50
24-pounder howitzers,	17			
Total cannons,	122	Total,		195

★★★★★★

On the evening of the 29th, Napoleon quitted the capital, never to enter it again. Hostilities ceased immediately, the Bourbons were recalled, and placed upon the throne, and Europe, after years of anarchy and bloodshed, at last obtained repose, while he, "alike its wonder and its scourge," was removed to a scene far distant from that which had witnessed his triumphs and his reverses, and within the narrow limits of a paltry island that haughty spirit, for whom half Europe was too small, dragged out a gloomy existence, until death loosened the chain and the grave closed upon the Captive of Saint Helena.

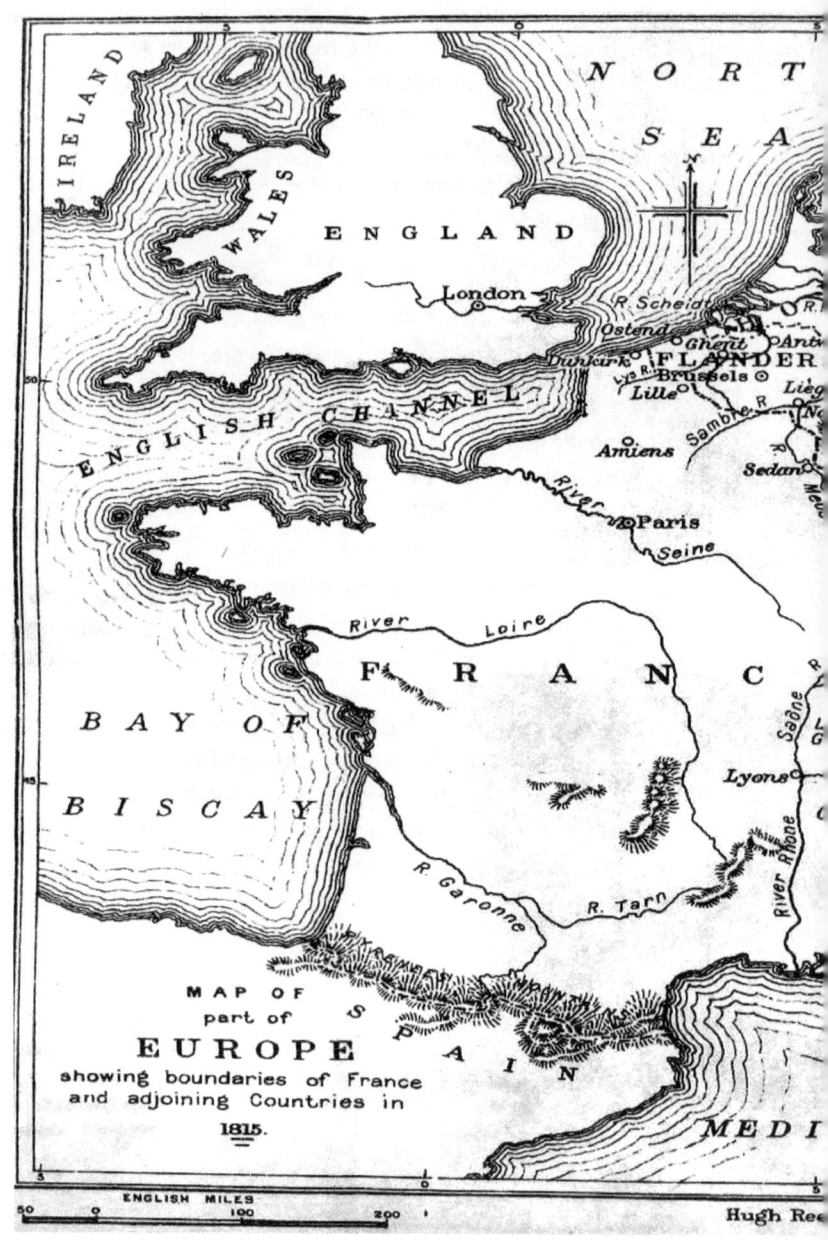

ALSO FROM LEONAUR
AVAILABLE IN SOFTCOVER OR HARDCOVER WITH DUST JACKET

OFFICERS & GENTLEMEN *by Peter Hawker & William Graham*—Two Accounts of British Officers During the Peninsula War: Officer of Light Dragoons by Peter Hawker & Campaign in Portugal and Spain by William Graham.

THE WALCHEREN EXPEDITION *by Anonymous*—The Experiences of a British Officer of the 81st Regt. During the Campaign in the Low Countries of 1809.

LADIES OF WATERLOO *by Charlotte A. Eaton, Magdalene de Lancey & Juana Smith*—The Experiences of Three Women During the Campaign of 1815: Waterloo Days by Charlotte A. Eaton, A Week at Waterloo by Magdalene de Lancey & Juana's Story by Juana Smith.

JOURNAL OF AN OFFICER IN THE KING'S GERMAN LEGION *by John Frederick Hering*—Recollections of Campaigning During the Napoleonic Wars.

JOURNAL OF AN ARMY SURGEON IN THE PENINSULAR WAR *by Charles Boutflower*—The Recollections of a British Army Medical Man on Campaign During the Napoleonic Wars.

ON CAMPAIGN WITH MOORE AND WELLINGTON *by Anthony Hamilton*—The Experiences of a Soldier of the 43rd Regiment During the Peninsular War.

THE ROAD TO AUSTERLITZ *by R. G. Burton*—Napoleon's Campaign of 1805.

SOLDIERS OF NAPOLEON *by A. J. Doisy De Villargennes & Arthur Chuquet*—The Experiences of the Men of the French First Empire: Under the Eagles by A. J. Doisy De Villargennes & Voices of 1812 by Arthur Chuquet.

INVASION OF FRANCE, 1814 *by F. W. O. Maycock*—The Final Battles of the Napoleonic First Empire.

LEIPZIG—A CONFLICT OF TITANS *by Frederic Shoberl*—A Personal Experience of the 'Battle of the Nations' During the Napoleonic Wars, October 14th-19th, 1813.

SLASHERS *by Charles Cadell*—The Campaigns of the 28th Regiment of Foot During the Napoleonic Wars by a Serving Officer.

BATTLE IMPERIAL *by Charles William Vane*—The Campaigns in Germany & France for the Defeat of Napoleon 1813-1814.

SWIFT & BOLD *by Gibbes Rigaud*—The 60th Rifles During the Peninsula War.

AVAILABLE ONLINE AT **www.leonaur.com**
AND FROM ALL GOOD BOOK STORES

www.ingramcontent.com/pod-product-compliance
Lightning Source LLC
Chambersburg PA
CBHW031619160426
43196CB00006B/198